An
for Labour

Salus populi suprema est lex – Cicero

The good of the people is the highest law – an inscription
which used to hang over the entrance to the Co-operative
College, Loughborough.

The Author

Before marrying, Rita Rhodes was the full-time Secretary/ Organiser of the Birkenhead and District Society Co-operative Party. She later became a Further Education Tutor and subsequently the Co-operative Union's Sectional Education Officer in Scotland. While there she also became involved with workers' co-operatives and the setting up of the Scottish Co-operative Development Committee. She later became the Education Officer of the Co-operative Development Agency in London from where she moved to become the Education Officer of the International Co-operative Alliance. More recently she was a Lecturer in Co-operative Studies at the University of Ulster and is currently Visiting Research Fellow at the Co-operative Research Unit at the Open University.

Dr Rhodes, who is author of *The International Co-operative Alliance During War and Peace 1910-1950*, began her adult education as a student at the Co-operative College, Stanford Hall, Loughborough. She has chosen the College motto "Salus populi suprema est lex" to be the inscription of this study.

An Arsenal
for Labour

The Royal Arsenal Co-operative Society and Politics 1896-1996

by Rita Rhodes

Holyoake Books

Holyoake Books is the imprint
of the Co-operative Union Limited,
Holyoake House, Hanover Street,
Manchester M60 0AS

First published 1998

British Library Cataloguing in Publication Data

A catalogue record for this book
is available from the British Library

ISBN 0 85195 253 4

Design by Paul Schofield

Printed in Great Britain by
MFP Design & Print
Manchester

CONTENTS

*Again, for Bernard, with
love and thanks*

Acknowledgements

Thanks are due to many friends and colleagues who have helped me in the preparation of this study. I have been particularly grateful to Ron Roffey, Honorary Archivist, CWS South East, for his ready assistance but most of all to the impressive archives of the Royal Arsenal Co-operative Society that he has assembled and maintained at Woolwich. Without the survival of those written sources this kind of history would not have been possible.

In addition to the primary sources in those archives I have been helped by the taped interviews given by Ron Roffey, Colin Shrive, Hilda Smith, Richard Balfe MEP, Shaun Spiers MEP, John Cartwright, the late Fred Styles, Glenys (now Lady) Thornton, Lord Graham of Edmonton, Peter Clarke, Richard Tomlinson, Marion Rilstone, Councillors Angela Cornforth and Kathryn Smith, Sylvia Fox, and John Tilley: I extend my warm thanks to them.

I acknowledge with further thanks Peter Collier's research and construction of the Financial Table at the end of this study; also for his preparation of the list of the members of the RACS Political Purposes Committee from 1922-1996. Thanks are also due to those who kindly read drafts of the book and offered comments. These were Ron Roffey, John Tilley, Parliamentary Secretary, Co-operative Union Ltd, Roger Spear, Co-operative Research Unit, Open University, and my husband, Bernard Rhodes, my sternest critic but my staunchest friend. I am grateful to Iain Williamson, Chief Information Officer of the Co-operative Union, for bringing order to the work through his editing and to Gillian Lonergan, Co-operative Union Librarian, for compiling its index.

Throughout the preparation of this work I have been grateful for the assistance and support given by colleagues in the

Co-operative Research Unit, Open University. I am also much indebted for the co-ordination and administration provided by the office of the Co-operative Party, particularly Peter Hunt, National Secretary, and Natasha Cendrowicz, Political Secretary. I should also like to give thanks to Marion Rilstone who, with her long service with the Co-operative Party, provided me with valuable insights, but also helped me greatly with her word processing skills.

The British consumer Co-operative Movement was a Movement of its time within which the Royal Arsenal Co-operative Society played a large and important part. This history of its Political Purposes Committee deserved to be written but it would not have got very far without the help of all the above, to whom I now extend my grateful thanks.

Rita Rhodes

CHAPTER ONE

The Beginnings of a Political Tradition

Introduction

This is a study of a British retail co-operative society and its involvement in politics over a one hundred year period. The society is the Royal Arsenal Co-operative Society in South East London. The area later widened to include other retail societies which merged with it. In 1985 the enlarged Society became part of the South East Region of the Co-operative Wholesale Society.

At the outset we should note that the relationship between co-operatives and politics has sometimes been a complicated one. On the one hand, the Principles of the Rochdale Pioneers, 1844, on which the modern Co-operative Movement has been based, included one of religious and political neutrality. On the other hand, co-operative ideas, coming as they did from the French Revolution's call for 'Liberty, Equality and Fraternity', had political overtones. Moreover, as co-operatives developed economic power they challenged other forms of economic enterprise and had implications for political parties and sometimes the state.

The idea that co-operatives should remain religiously and politically neutral stemmed from a number of influences. One was the belief of early co-operators that, although they owed much to the ideas of Robert Owen, 1771-1858, they should disassociate themselves from his anti-religious views. Early co-operators also recognised that if they excluded people because of their religious or political beliefs they undermined another Co-operative Principle, namely that of open and voluntary membership, and also weakened their collective capacity for self-help and mutual aid.

Another influence shaping ideas of religious and political

1

neutrality was that of Dr William King, 1786-1865. He had a profound influence on the Rochdale Pioneers. This included his view that 'Co-operation is a voluntary act and all the power in the world cannot make it compulsory, nor is it desirable that it should depend on any power but its own - the energies of government would only cramp its energies and misdirect them'.[1]

The British consumer co-operatives which developed from the mid-19th century onwards were based on the successful Rochdale formula. However, their underlying ideas, and inspiration, owed much to Owen and King. From King they took ideas of independence and self-sufficiency. As the power of governments increased in the 20th century, though, consumer co-operatives found it necessary to develop representational skills to lobby for taxation and legislation that was at least fair to co-operatives.

A number of other developments also made them less reluctant to take political action. One was the growing suspicion among British consumer co-operatives, and among some of their counterparts elsewhere in Western Europe, that private traders encouraged political action against them so as to counteract their growing economic strength. Such fears increased during times of crisis, as during the first world war.

Another reason why consumer co-operatives became less strict about maintaining political neutrality - religious neutrality hardly ever became an issue - was the growth of urbanised and industrialised work forces to whom the Co-op shop had strong appeal. It provided them with pure foods at prices that were lowered by the 'dividend', the periodic repayment of the 'surplus' or profit, after a society's trading costs had been met. People attracted into co-operative membership were often also members of trade unions or socialist parties and it was not surprising, therefore, that consumer co-operative movements tended to become identified with working class politics. Only in Britain, though, did this lead to the creation of a distinct Co-operative Party whose development will be traced later.

In the meantime we should note that the ideas of self-reliance and independence encouraged by King continued to hold sway in many parts of the British consumer movement. They remain to the present day, which means that the question of co-operatives' involvement in politics has never been clear cut. Moreover, it tends to be worked out with geographical variations. Even within London different co-operative political traditions developed. In studying that which emerged in the Royal Arsenal Co-operative Society we need to trace its development through different periods, and to place each within its own context. Let us, therefore, begin by noting the conditions in which the Royal Arsenal Co-operative Society first developed and also how these helped to shape its political attitudes.

Context of Royal Arsenal Co-operative Society
In the late 19th century the Royal Arsenal Co-operative Society (RACS) was part of a growing British Consumer Co-operative Movement. In 1881 the Co-operative Union, formed by primary retail societies in 1869, produced national co-operative statistics which showed that in that year there were 971 retail co-operatives with a membership of 547,000 and annual sales of almost £15 million. In 1881 also the Co-operative Wholesale Society (CWS), which had been established in 1863 and was owned by the retail societies, had net sales of over £3.5 million. Its counterpart in Scotland, the Scottish Co-operative Wholesale Society (SCWS), founded in 1868 and owned by Scottish consumer societies, had net sales of nearly £1 million. By 1881 the Royal Arsenal Co-operative Society had existed for 13 years and had 1,934 members, a share capital of £9,325 and annual sales of £36,874.[2]

At this point we should note the importance of the Woolwich Arsenal in the formation of the Society. It, and the Borough of Woolwich, became very much associated with RACS and, for many, the term 'Woolwich Society' became synonymous with the Royal Arsenal Co-operative Society. Originally known as the Royal Arsenal Supply Association, the Society had been formed in 1868. Encouraged by the success of a growing number of retail societies based on the Rochdale model, the RACS also set itself to work according to the Rochdale Principles. Knowledge of these had been spread by a growing number of co-operative journals which were joined in 1871 by the *Co-operative News*. This has had

3

an unbroken existence to the present day.

Besides this general co-operative knowledge RACS was also assisted by lessons learned from earlier local co-operative experiments. These included a corn mill set up by Woolwich shipwrights in 1760, a butcher's shop opened in 1805, a Woolwich Baking Society in 1842 and a Co-operative Coal Society in 1856. The Woolwich Co-operative Provident Society had also been set up among Woolwich Dockyard employees in May 1851 but had failed to survive the Dockyard's closure in 1869. It is interesting to note that in that connection, Alexander McLeod, who was to become prominent in the early years of the Royal Arsenal Co-operative Society, suggested that the Dockyard might be saved if its workers commenced 'Co-operative shipbuilding'.

Woolwich Arsenal, as distinct from the Dockyard, became prominent in the formation of the Royal Arsenal Society because a number of its engineers became the Society's founder members. Their conditions improved as the third quarter of the 19th century became one of economic expansion. Skilled workers, such as engineers, were among those who benefited most from the improving employment position. The Arsenal had added importance during the time of war and the threat of war. This was particularly the case during the Crimean and Boer wars and, of course, the first world war.

In passing we should note that the generally more favourable economic conditions helped other consumer co-operatives also to take stronger root. Those of their members who were skilled workers became less frequently out of work or in debt and were therefore better able to trade regularly with their co-operative societies. The growing strength of these and their increasing number led to the setting up of the English and Welsh Co-operative Wholesale Society in 1863 and the Scottish Co-operative Wholesale Society five years later. Both helped to create greater economies of scale for local retail societies by buying in bulk and later setting up factories and farms to supply local societies. To this infrastructure the Co-operative Union was added in 1869. Its members comprised both retail and wholesale societies, as well as a number of producer co-operatives.

Secondary or federal co-operative societies and organisations, such as the two Wholesales and the Co-operative Union Ltd, had become legally possible through the growing volume of Industrial and Provident Society legislation. Its successful passage through Parliament owed much to the work of the Christian Socialists. They also pioneered a number of early co-operative productive experiments.[3]

A number of those in London involved the Amalgamated Society of Engineers and its branch in Woolwich included many of the founder members of the Royal Arsenal Society. Besides this connection several Christian Socialists had personal links with south east London. Edward Vansittart Neale, who became General Secretary of the Co-operative Union, had a house there. Thomas Hughes, barrister and author of *Tom Brown's Schooldays*, became a Member of Parliament for Lambeth in the 1860s. A close co-operative colleague of Vassittart Neale, Edward Owen Greening, while not a Christian Socialist, strongly supported their ideas of co-operative production and later became a regular contributor to the Royal Arsenal Society's journal *Comradeship*. It can be argued, therefore, that when the RACS became a strong supporter of co-operative production, and introduced a profit sharing scheme among employees, it had been much influenced by the ideas of the Christian Socialists.

To return, however, to the actual setting up of the RACS, we should note that the proposal was first made by William Rose at a branch meeting of the Amalgamated Society of Engineers. As in the case of the Rochdale Society, prospective members each agreed to raise an initial share capital of £1 each. William Rose was elected the Society's first Secretary, Alexander McLeod its Chairman and George Bevan its Treasurer. T Coles, Henry Mee, Joseph Reed and John Veale became its first committee of management.[4]

Little is known about the committee members. However, we do know that William Rose was born in Woolwich in 1843. He served an apprenticeship in the Dockyard and, after moving around jobs in London, returned to Woolwich to work in the tool room of the Shell Foundry. Although Rose drafted the 'prospectus' for the fledgling society, and was a central figure in its establishment, he remained secretary for only three months. Then unemployment forced him to emigrate to Canada and later the USA and his close friend, Alexander McLeod, with whom he had attended evening classes in 'physical geography', succeeded him. Even by that time the Society's stocks had grown to the point where it had become necessary to rent a small shop. McLeod then married and an arrangement was reached that he and his bride would live over the shop and pay half its rent.

From that time on McLeod became a central figure in the Society. Unlike Rose he had not been born in Woolwich. Like other early RACS leaders, who were also skilled men, McLeod had been born elsewhere. In his case it was Fife in Scotland in 1832. He became a mechanical engineer and worked at Inverkeithing, Edinburgh and Greenock. From there he joined the Caledonian Railway Works at Glasgow, and it was while visiting an old friend at the Great Eastern Railway Works at Stratford in East London that he crossed the Thames and found work in the Royal Arsenal at Woolwich. As a consequence he joined the Woolwich Branch of the Amalgamated Society of Engineers and became a close friend of William Rose.

Until 1878 the Society's trade rested on the voluntary efforts of its committee. An early Society history records that they were assisted by Mrs McLeod who 'was also an enthusiast, and voluntarily worked hard by cleaning counters, scales etc., and scrubbing out the shop after each day's trading, and in other respects doing all she could to promote the growth of the Society'.[5] She died suddenly in 1878. This, coupled with the fact that the Society's growth had reached the point where it could now support a full-time worker, led to McLeod becoming its first paid member of staff and leaving the Arsenal. In 1878 when McLeod became Secretary the RACS had 1,234 members, share capital of £4,826, and a reserve fund of £234. Annual trade stood at £24,668 and the surplus this produced provided members with a dividend of 1s. 6d. in the £. Four years later in 1882 McLeod also became the Society's Manager and retained this dual position until his death in 1902.

At this point we should note that shortly before McLeod became full-time Secretary two important additions had been made to the Society's rules. One was that two and a half per cent of net surplus was to be allocated to an educational fund to be administered by a committee of eleven. The other made it possible for the Society to pay a bonus on labour to its future employees thus reflecting its belief in a 'just price' for labour, and its support for Christian Socialist ideas on co-operative production. It was not possible for these to be fully implemented in a consumer society, but it was feasible to introduce profit sharing to employees. Thus the new rule enabled future employees to receive a 'double dividend' comprising their dividend on purchases as members and another on their wages as employees. This profit-sharing scheme came to be one of a number of features which distinguished the RACS from other British retail societies. Whereas in the late 19th century a number of these also paid a dividend on wages, by the early years of this century most of them had phased out the practice. RACS, however, continued with it until 1985. To some degree the practice marked the Society's solidarity with labour and could be said to anticipate its subsequent political direction.

The provision in the Society's rules for a dividend on wages and an educational fund, both payable from profits, presupposed RACS's expansion. This, in fact, continued with the opening of a draper's shop in 1875 and a bakery a year later. Shortly afterwards grocery branches were opened at Plumstead, Charlton and Erith. The last of these had been urged by Arthur Sellicks, who had been a member of the RACS's Management Committee and was currently Chairman of the Woolwich ASE Branch.

Recognising that increased trade depended on a growing membership, one of the first jobs the Society's Education Committee was given was to spearhead RACS propaganda drives. These undoubtedly helped to increase the Society's membership and trade. They also brought in members who were active in radical Woolwich politics in organisations such as the Social Democratic Federation, the Socialist League and, from 1893, the Independent Labour Party. The radicalisation of Woolwich political and co-operative developments was also closely linked to the growing provision of adult education in the area. RACS itself had become a considerable provider of adult education. In line with many other co-operative societies of the period it established libraries for its members. The first, in Woolwich in 1879, was followed by others in Erith in 1887, Charlton in 1891, Belvedere in 1900, Abbey Wood in 1904 and Eltham Well Hall in 1906. In addition the RACS Education Committee arranged occasional joint lectures with the Working Men's College and Toynbee Hall. From 1897 it also published a monthly society magazine *Comradeship*. Such provisions were complemented by those made by others such as the Woolwich Polytechnic, founded in 1890, and the University Extension Movement.[6] Prominent among those in the University Extension Movement in Woolwich in the early 1890s was Charles Grinling. He also served on the RACS Education Committee from 1895 to 1898 and became the first editor of *Comradeship*. Grinling became a prominent figure in the setting up of the RACS Political Purposes Committee.

It is interesting to note that, like many other early RACS leaders, Grinling came from outside the area. He was, however, perhaps unusual in that he had previously been in Holy Orders. Before arriving in Woolwich in 1889, he had been a curate at St James's Church, Nottingham, but had drawn the censure of the church hierarchy when he criticised the low wages and bad working conditions of women lace makers. Grinling's attitudes were likely to have been shaped by his earlier training as a social worker at Toynbee Hall. On leaving Nottingham and eventually Holy Orders, Grinling became the secretary of the Woolwich Charity Organisation.[7]

Besides political and educational developments, the later years of the 19th century also saw significant trade union growth in the Woolwich area. Craft unionism remained important but the famous Dock Strike of 1889 prompted new growth among unskilled workers. Unions such as Ben Tillet's Dockers' Union grew alongside the Gas Workers and General Labourer's Union and the South Side Labour Protection League. These developments had the effect of encouraging an increase in the number of Independent Labour candidates in elections to boards and local authorities. One result was a weakening of working class electoral arrangements with the Liberals. A similar shift could be seen in RACS. Many of its early leaders, including Alexander McLeod, had been involved in Liberal politics after the Reform Act of 1867 had widened the franchise among working men. One consequence of this, and the fact that Woolwich Arsenal was expanding its skilled work force, was that the Greenwich constituency, including Woolwich, had as many as 57 per cent of voters who were identified as working class on its electoral register.[8]

During the 1860s and 70s the main political outlet for working class voters was the Liberal Party. It is therefore perhaps not surprising that RACS supported Gladstone, who was elected as Greenwich's MP in 1868. In recognition of this support Gladstone gave each member of the RACS management committee a copy of a portrait of himself and his wife taking tea. One of these survives to the present day in the RACS archives at Woolwich.

RACS's links with the Liberal Party weakened from the 1890s. From then on RACS figures became increasingly identified with working class organisations. This shift was a gradual one however and did not follow a direct course. For example, despite its links with the Liberal Party, the RACS also put forward its own municipal candidates in the 1890s.[9] This suggests that the Society had recognised that it sometimes had to make political choices, or to take political action to protect its economic and social position.

It also points to an emerging pro-active political tradition. John Attfield in his book *With Light of Knowledge*, commemorating a hundred years of co-operative education within the RACS, noted that in the last years of the 19th century, there was a growing view in the Society that trade unions, co-operatives and workers' political parties should work together. Attfield attributes this to a number of factors, including the 'geographical isolation of the RACS from the mainstream northern co-operative movement'. While there may be something in this argument, it cannot be taken too far because RACS developed different political traditions from those of other London co-operative societies, let alone those farther afield. Having said that we should note that a number of RACS leaders, including Arthur Sellicks mentioned previously subscribed to the views of Beatrice Webb about the inter-dependence of trade unions, co-operatives and socialists. Sellicks gave this practical expression. He had been a member of the

9

RACS Board of Management and later the Society's Education Committee and in the 1890s also became the national chairman of the Amalgamated Society of Engineers. Ben Jones was another example of someone spanning several branches of the working class movement. While manager of the London Branch of the Co-operative Wholesale Society in 1892 he became one of the first Labour candidates in Woolwich.

Another person receptive to Beatrice Webb's ideas on the inter-dependence of trade unions, co-operatives and socialists was Margaret Llewellyn Davies. She became General Secretary of the Co-operative Women's Guild, which had been founded in 1883. A prime mover in the establishment of the Guild had been Mary Lawrenson who was a leading member of RACS. It is interesting to note that although Lawrenson did much to lay the foundations of the Guild's strength in RACS she remained a Liberal. It was Margaret Llewellyn Davies's views, however, that came to be the more dominant among RACS Guild branches. As Arnold Bonner observed in his book *British Co-operation*, Margaret Llewellyn Davies had 'views of the place of the Co-operative Movement in the Labour Movement similar to those of the Webbs'.[10] She also argued for links between co-operatives and the 'new' trade unionism among unskilled workers.

Woolwich and the Wider Political Context
To end this chapter we should briefly trace wider political developments before the first world war. The period was one of shifting alliances. As we have seen in Woolwich, the alliance between trade unions and the Liberal Party weakened in the 1890s and did so for a number of reasons. One was the formation of the Independent Labour Party in 1893. Its leaders, including Keir Hardie, advocated a 'Labour alliance' under which socialists and trade unions would join to support candidates at local and parliamentary elections. However, this did not prove particularly successful. When the ILP, with a membership of just over 10,000, contested 28 constituencies in the 1895 General Election it won no seats. It did, however, have greater success in gaining increased support among trade union leaderships.

Another reason for the weakening of Liberal/Trade Union

links was that, in 1899, the TUC decided to set up a body to promote Labour representation. The TUC had recognised the need to try to standardise the label under which trade unionists fought elections. As in Woolwich, an increasing number of trade unionists were seeking election to councils, boards and other authorities because these bodies were becoming large employers as gas, water, roads, education and housing were municipalised. Allied to this was the fact that there was a rapidly rising trade union membership, which had grown from around 750,000 in 1888 to over 2 million in 1900. Much of this growth had occurred among the unskilled.

Yet another factor was growing working class consciousness which was being shaped by the spread of socialist propaganda. The late 19th century saw the birth of a number of socialist newspapers including the *Labour Leader* and the *Clarion*. Some were achieving large circulation. For example *Merrie England*, written by *Clarion* journalist, Robert Blatchford, sold over one million copies.[11] The RACS monthly journal *Comradeship*, under the editorship of Charles Grinling, should be included in this growing socialist propaganda as should be the Woolwich *Labour Journal*, a monthly paper which was first produced by the Woolwich Trades Council in 1901. It later became the *Woolwich Pioneer* and played a central role in Woolwich Labour politics.

We should return, though, to the TUC's 1899 decision to set up a Labour Representation Committee (LRC) and note that, although co-operatives were invited to join, they declined to do so. Other organisations also showed uncertainty about joining. The Social Democratic Federation disassociated itself after 1901 and the Fabian Society showed little interest.[12] This meant that the LRC's initial base was narrow and rested mainly on the trade unions. Its membership among these increased however as it achieved some success in the General Election which followed shortly its formation. Its 15 candidates averaged 4,000 votes and two of them were elected, one of them Keir Hardie.

There was further growth in trade union membership after the Taff Vale Case in 1901 and also as a result of the LRC's improving organisation and finances: Ramsay MacDonald, its first Secretary, was proving to be an effective organiser.

Consequently, when the 1906 General Election was held, the LRC was able to support 50 candidates. These averaged 7,500 votes and won 29 seats. In the same year the Labour Representation Committee became known as the Labour Party.

Back in Woolwich, Labour politics advanced through branches of the ILP and SDF and, from 1893, the Woolwich Trades Council. Up to the 1890s the RACS, as an organisation, had not been involved in independent working class political action. However, individual members were involved in campaigns to increase labour representation in Woolwich particularly in the Labour Representation League (LRL) formed in 1891. Initially set up by the London Trades Council, this quickly became a broad-based campaign comprising representatives from the ASE, unskilled unions, radical clubs and progressive clergymen. It had been the LRL which had sponsored Ben Jones's parliamentary candidature at Woolwich in 1892.

In 1894 the RACS, as an organisation and as distinct from individual members' initiatives, became active in local politics for the first time. It did so by agreeing to support its members who became candidates if they agreed to back the Society on specifically co-operative issues. A joint committee of the General and Educational Committees was appointed to select candidates and, to some extent, this can be looked on as a forerunner of the Political Purposes Committee that was to be created nearly 30 years later. A further step was taken when, at its September Half-yearly meeting in 1897, the Society passed the following resolution:

> That in the opinion of this meeting, the time has arrived when the RACS in conjunction with the various working men's organisations and the Trades Council of the district, should take a more active part in municipal affairs, and the Society hereby invites the co-operation of its members in supporting any action in this direction.

Until then RACS-supported candidates, like their trade union counterparts, had stood under a number of banners. This changed in 1897 when, however, John Arnold was elected as a joint RACS-Labour candidate in Woolwich. A year later the Society decided to make permanent the sub-committee it had set up three years earlier and gave it a general oversight for the Society's electoral policies. It was through this sub-committee that the Society worked with the ILP and the Trades Councils in supporting candidates for Local Boards and other authorities and, in 1900, for the new Woolwich Borough Council. The Society's political involvement was only at local level, however. It did not extend to Parliamentary elections. Consequently, while individual members were involved in Will Crook's campaign as the Labour Parliamentary candidate for Woolwich in 1902, the Society as such was not. Neither did it affiliate to the Woolwich Labour Representation Association when it was set up the following year, and which subsequently became the Woolwich Labour Party. In this the RACS was in line with the wider Co-operative Movement's decision not to affiliate to the Labour Representation Committee.[13]

From this time until the outbreak of the first world war, a struggle began in the RACS between left and right-wing members. While some RACS leaders had become active in the Labour Representation League and later the Labour Party, others had become 'anti-socialists'. Among the latter were Edward Owen Greening, still a staunch Liberal, and Mary Lawrenson, despite her close association with Margaret Llewellyn Davies and the Co-operative Women's Guild. Along with the Yorkshireman Arthur Hainsworth, who became the Society's Education Secretary in 1904, they believed that Co-operation was capable of helping the workers by replacing competitive capitalism but that it should remain non-political. In addition to these figures there were also Conservative members who, in 1908, formed a Royal Arsenal Vigilant Committee. This was intended to issue to local Conservative Ward Associations details of Conservatives who stood for the Society's committees but it had little success.

Even so, RACS leaders felt it prudent to try to bring the Society together on a non-political basis. Consequently, in their report to the Society's half-yearly meeting in March 1905, the General Committee reminded members that:

> ... the Co-operative Movement knows neither party nor creed, and the sympathetic and increased interest of all

13

members of whatever shade of opinion is earnestly solicited ... The higher moral attributes of the movement, including the humanising of employment and the recognition of individual identity and responsibility, should never be lost sight of.

The Society's Secretary, T G Arnold asserted:

The Co-operative Movement, composed as it was of all shades of political opinion, had no room for any partisanship so far as outside bodies was concerned ... The Society was not and never had been connected either directly or indirectly with any political party; political feeling or policy never entered into the consideration of any question dealt with by the Committee ...[14]

This was obviously intended to restore the RACS's political neutrality. Nevertheless, the working class nature of the Society's catchment area was reflected in the fact that the General Committee was now dominated by trade union and Labour Party members. Political restraint, however, survived until the outbreak of the first world war, but experiences during this were to lead to a change of policy both in the RACS and in the wider Co-operative Movement. In 1917 the Co-operative Union, at its Swansea Congress, decided to set up the Co-operative Party. This decision, and the RACS's political response to war-time situations, will be examined in the next chapter.

Conclusion

We conclude this Chapter by recalling the influences that shaped the Royal Arsenal Society. One was the skilled workers attracted into the area and employed in the Woolwich Dockyard and Woolwich Arsenal. Closely linked to this was their trade union, the Amalgamated Society of Engineers. Another influence was that of the Christian Socialists, whose views of co-operative production led the Society to introduce a system of profit-sharing among its employees. Other influences derived from personalities, particularly Alexander McLeod and Charles Grinling. Above all there was the influence of radical politics in the area. Before the first world war these were in their formative stages. It took the war and its aftermath to give them definite shape and elicit a response from the RACS.

Notes

1   Bonner, Arnold, *British Co-operation*, Co-operative Union Ltd, Manchester, 1961, p.26.

2   Cole, G D H, *A Century of Co-operation*, Co-operative Union Ltd, Manchester, 1944, p.179.

3   Rhodes, Rita, *The International Co-operative Alliance During War and Peace 1910-1950*, International Co-operative Alliance, Geneva, 1995, p.12.

4   McLeod, Alex and Arnold, T Geo, *Royal Arsenal Co-operative Society Limited - Origins and Progress*. A Short History compiled for the Society's Coming of Age Festival, June 25 1890, and rewritten for insertion in the Guide and Handbook of the 28th Annual Co-operative Congress held at Woolwich between May 23 to May 27 1896.

5   Davis, Walter T, *The History of the Royal Arsenal Co-operative Society Ltd, 1868-1918*, Royal Arsenal Co-operative Society Ltd, London, 1921, p.215.

6   Attfield, John, *With Light of Knowledge - A Hundred Years of Education in the Royal Arsenal Co-operative Society, 1877-1977*, London, 1981, p.11.

7   Snell, Lord, *Men, Movements and Myself*, J M Dent and Sons Ltd, London, 1936, pp.66-70.

8   Attfield, John, op. cit., p.18.

9   Ibid., pp.18-20.

10   Bonner, Arnold, op. cit., p.483.

11   Phillips, Gordon, *The Rise of the Labour Party 1893-1932*, Lancaster Pamphlets, Routledge, 1992, pp.5-10.

12   Ibid., p.12.

13   Attfield, John, op. cit., pp.21-26.

14   Ibid., pp.27-29.

CHAPTER TWO

The 1914-1918 War and Co-operative Politics

Introduction - The RACS in 1914

As we have seen from the previous Chapter, a radical political tradition had been developing in the Royal Arsenal Co-operative Society. The impact of the war was to help it to take more definite shape and direction. By the time the first world war broke out in August 1914, the Royal Arsenal Co-operative Society was only four years short of its half century. Its members numbered nearly 40,000 and its share capital stood at £431,355. Annual sales amounted to £909,607 and a dividend on purchases was declared at 1s. 2½d. or 6 pence in the £1. The employees' share of the surplus, amounted to £4,300. An education grant of £1,796 was paid.[1]

All this added up to the fact that the Society had become a mature organisation. It had established its credibility with its members and with the local population. The Society had also developed a considerable managerial capacity. Until 1914 it had been served by William Rose for three months and then by Alexander McLeod who had become the Society's full-time paid Secretary in 1878. He also became the Society's Manager four years later, and combined the two positions until his death in 1902. Thereafter, the positions were separated. T George Arnold became Secretary and James Hall, Manager. In passing it is interesting to note that both had been born in the Society's area: Arnold in Greenwich in 1866 and Hall in Woolwich eight years earlier. Both were still holding their positions when war broke out. By then RACS had spread geographically. During the previous ten years the Society's operations had extended rapidly, raising questions about boundaries with neighbouring societies. Consequently, boundary agreements were reached with the Bromley, Penge, West London and Dartford Co-operative

Societies. In early 1914 the Sutton Society had asked the RACS to take over three of its branches in Tooting, Wimbledon and Raynes Park. As a result the Society had spread into West London but leap-frogging part of the South Suburban Co-operative Society in Lambeth. Despite this expansion the RACS continued to be referred to then, and long after, as the 'Woolwich Society'.

Such boundary changes raised also the question of co-operation between the co-operative societies in London. There would later be repeated but abortive attempts to merge the two largest of these, the London and Royal Arsenal Co-operative Societies, as well as efforts to create joint trading interests. An example of the latter arose from a threatened bakers' strike throughout the Greater London area in 1913 and led to London co-operatives entering into a joint agreement with the Bakers' Union.

The Impact of War on RACS
From the above we can see that by the time war broke out the RACS had become well-established and was expanding. Nevertheless it was to be sorely tested by the war, and experiences during it helped to shape its later political actions.

One problem was severe disruption in the Woolwich area. The Arsenal, and factories producing munitions, quickly increased their production, thereby bringing thousands of new workers and their families into the area. Against that, many others faced the threat of unemployment as war disrupted existing industry and commerce and the Society set up a fund to relieve their anticipated distress. In addition, RACS faced changes in its work force as employees were called into the armed forces and replacements had to be found. Typical of its humanitarian traditions, the Society tried to help families of enlisted employees and assured workers that, as far as possible, they would be reinstated after the war.[2] By the end of the war the Society had spent over £27,000 in various forms of relief to its members and employees and to Belgian refugees who came into the area.

Other problems arose from the War Department commandeering many of the Society's horses and early motor vehicles. This caused problems in supplying branches as well as in making deliveries to members. Matters were complicated further by shortages which developed as German submarines dislocated imports. As a consequence prices rose although the Society soon suspected that some traders were making undue profits. It therefore joined with trade unions in calling on the government to prohibit profiteering and to introduce tighter food controls, possibly even rationing. In this the government was slow to act, and the position in Woolwich worsened still further with munition workers coming in by thousands'.[3] Particular difficulties arose over sugar supplies which led to the Society trying to ration it to members. In March, 1916 it introduced a scheme under which members could purchase no more that 2 lb of sugar with every 4 oz of tea or coffee they bought. There were soon problems however and so the scheme was changed to 1 lb of sugar with every 2 shillings of groceries bought, although no more than 2 lb could be taken with any one transaction. A further re-think became necessary when questions were raised in the House of Commons on the RACS scheme and the government's new Food Control Department objected. It did so on the grounds that the sale of sugar was conditional on the purchase of other commodities.

As a result RACS widened its rationing scheme. In early 1917, it issued cards to members that were based on their purchases in the previous half year. It had been possible to compute these from the 'checks' that members received when they made purchases and on which the payment of their dividend was based. Under the new system members who returned 'checks' from £2 to £10 from the previous half year could receive 1 lb of sugar per week. Those who returned checks for over £11 could receive 2 lb of sugar per week. Even so this method also ran into difficulties. Just at the time the Society was linking its supply of sugar to members' past purchases, so the government's recently appointed Food Controller decreed that retailers could obtain only a proportion of certain goods based on their purchases in 1915. The problem for the RACS in this 'datum' system was that the Woolwich population had grown massively with the influx of munitions workers. Consequently, demand for certain foods far outstripped supply and soaring prices led to the threat of unrest.

Elsewhere in Britain trade unions proved to be a safety valve against growing industrial unrest by gaining increased representation through shop stewards and Joint Industrial Councils. Similarly co-operative societies, such as RACS, provided another kind of safety valve through the rationing schemes they introduced which allowed some degree of internal fairness between members. Eventually the Government introduced a national scheme of rationing, but this was not until almost the end of the war.

In passing we should note that important in the administration of the RACS rationing scheme was the Society's new Secretary, William B Neville. It is interesting to note that his appointment came about because of RACS's growing standing in the British consumer Co-operative Movement. This had been acknowledged when the Movement's 1896 Congress was held at Woolwich. By 1900, in terms of membership, the RACS was the ninth largest society in the country. Increasingly RACS representatives were elected to the Movement's national bodies and, in 1916, T George Arnold, the Society's Secretary from 1902, was elected to the Co-operative Wholesale Society. Consequently he resigned the RACS's Secretaryship and was succeeded by William Neville, who was to become one of the Society's most notable figures. Many inter-war initiatives and developments would later become attributable to him. His first success, however, was the system of comprehensive rationing introduced in RACS.

In early 1917 the Society recognised that this had become necessary and, therefore, set up a special department under the control of the Society's Secretary. Neville prepared a scheme under which 33,000 member households in the Society's area, covering some 147,000 people, were registered with the Society's Food Registry Department. Each member was then supplied with a food registry certificate which gave particulars of the number of dependants and became the basis on which food cards were issued.

Thus, the Society's own system of rationing was introduced a year before a national system began in July 1918. It was intended to provide an equitable means of distributing scarce goods, but it could apply only to existing members. There was however still the problem of people moving into the area and applying for Society membership. In October 1917 the RACS General Committee passed a resolution declaring that 'the sale of goods from Grocery and Provision Departments be confined to members only'. While new members could still be admitted they were not immediately eligible for rationed foods. The continuing shortage of supplies led the RACS to join with the Woolwich Borough Council and the Arsenal Shop Stewards' Committee to renew pressure on Lord Rhondda, the government's Food Controller, to introduce a national system of rationing.

RACS was not alone in struggling with problems of food supply, which affected other co-operative societies as well and came to be a factor in moving them to take political action. This, therefore, seems to be the appropriate point to look at how the war affected the rest of the British Co-operative Movement, and then to trace the steps it took to set up the Co-operative Party in 1917. This event is important because it provides the background against which political developments in the Royal Arsenal Society should be seen.

The Co-operative Movement and Pre-War Politics
By the late 19th century the Co-operative Movement had recognised that, while it might wish to be politically neutral, governments could help and hinder it. An example of the former had been the Industrial and Provident Societies legislation which had given the Movement some protection and assisted its development. The latter was illustrated by recurring disputes over the taxation of co-operatives, particularly that part of their surplus representing dividend to their members.

By the late 1880s, and recognising that the Movement needed to be aware of what was happening in Parliament, the Co-operative Union asked the Southern Sectional Board to keep a general oversight of Parliamentary affairs. In 1900 representatives of the two Wholesales joined what had now become the Parliamentary Committee, and thereafter it became known as the Joint Parliamentary Committee. Its role was to keep a watch on Parliament and advise the Movement on how proposed legislation and changes in taxation might affect it. Gradually a two-way process developed as the Committee also began to channel the Movement's views on particular issues to government ministers and civil servants. In passing, it is interesting to note that among the Committee's members from the Southern Sectional Board was Henry May. He was from the Royal Arsenal Society and subsequently became Secretary to the Sectional Board. Later he combined this position with that of Secretary to the Joint Parliamentary Committee.

Despite its growing workload, some believed that the remit of the Joint Parliamentary Committee did not go far enough and that the Movement should be more pro-active in politics. Notable among the supporters of this view was William Maxwell, Secretary of the Edinburgh St Cuthbert's Society and Chairman of the Scottish Co-operative Wholesale Society. He presided over the Co-operative Union Congress in Perth in 1897 and Paisley in 1905, and two years later became the President of the International Co-operative Alliance. Ranged against such advocates were those who staunchly favoured the retention of political neutrality. Notable among these was Edward Owen Greening. He was active in the Royal Arsenal Society, but his main co-operative roots were among the producer co-operatives.

Others advocated the maintenance of political neutrality for a number of reasons. Some feared that to become overtly political could damage co-operative trade by antagonising members with different political views, while others objected to it on the grounds of its cost. The latter appeared to have the most telling argument because the decisions of two Congresses to engage in limited forms of political action were not implemented after societies subsequently failed to fund them. However, the question of whether to seek co-operative representation in Parliament and on local authorities soon became tied up with another issue: what should be the Movement's relations with the growing Labour Party?

By the 1890s the Movement's earlier links with Liberal MPs were proving increasingly inadequate which led to a growing view among a significant number of co-operative leaders in the Wholesales, Union and Joint Parliamentary Committee that the Movement needed to have a direct say in Parliament. In 1891 the

21

Co-operative Union decided to consult its Sectional Boards on whether the Movement should seek direct Parliamentary representation because reliance on the goodwill of existing MPs was no longer proving to be enough. Only two Sections, the Southern and Midland, were in favour, and the Central Board, therefore, had to drop the question. Nevertheless, in its Report to the next Congress it urged that co-operative societies, because they had become extensive property owners and large ratepayers, needed to secure representation on local governing bodies. To help them do so the Union issued a circular which gave the qualifications required for different boards; it also urged societies to look out for suitable candidates from among their members.[4] We have already noted similar developments in the Woolwich area when, in 1894, the RACS had set up a sub-committee to identify possible candidates from Society members and had widened its remit in 1897.

At national level a more definite step was proposed at the Co-operative Union's Congress at Perth in 1897. There the Congress President, William Maxwell, declared that, while he did not seek to introduce politics into Co-operation, he was 'most anxious to see Co-operation introduced more into politics'. Others supported this view and the Congress went on to pass a resolution which stated that the time had come for the 'direct representations of the Co-operative Movement in Parliament and other Councils of the United Kingdom ...'.[5] Again however, too few societies then proved willing to provide the necessary funds. The decision could, therefore, not be implemented, as the Cardiff Co-operative Congress of 1900 acknowledged.

The next national attempt was made at the Paisley Congress of 1905, which was again presided over by William Maxwell. T Tweddle, Chairman of the Joint Parliamentary Committee, and a CWS Director, presented a paper which observed that statesmen and politicians took note only of those 'who can voice their wants, who can effect a division by their votes, or influence the fate of governments'. Tweddle's paper concluded by proposing a motion which Congress again approved, this time by 654 votes to 271. It stated:

That this Congress is of ... (the) opinion that the time has arrived when it is necessary in the best interests of the Co-operative Movement that co-operators in and through their own organisation should take a larger share in the legislative and administrative government of the country.[6]

Possible relations with the Labour Representation Committee complicated the issue, however. Congress also discussed a motion proposed by the Manchester & Salford Co-operative Society which proposed that any political action by the Co-operative Movement should be taken after consultation with the Labour Representation Committee. This was decisively defeated by 807 votes to 135.[7] The original resolution suffered a slower death. As with the decision of the Perth Congress eight years earlier there proved to be little practical support when the matter was referred to member societies. Consequently, the next Congress in Birmingham decided that the Paisley decision could not be implemented.[8]

After this, the full frontal assault of a Congress resolution was replaced by more oblique approaches. With its growing maturity the Co-operative Movement was becoming adroit at internal politicking. There were now several examples of this. One was the decision of the Joint Parliamentary Committee in 1909 to issue a manifesto which advised co-operators on how to exercise their votes at the coming Parliamentary Election and thus 'safeguard their elementary rights of citizenship and freedom'. One hundred thousand copies of the manifesto were issued,[9] and when it was reported to the Plymouth Congress in 1910 adverse comments were raised. Critics included Edward Owen Greening who again attacked the idea of direct co-operative representation. The significant thing was, however, that the Congress did not censure the Joint Parliamentary Committee for issuing the manifesto,[10] and this could be interpreted as a slight step forward by those wanting more direct political action.

Another oblique approach emerged from the 1912 Congress in Portsmouth. This agreed that a Joint Committee should be set up comprising representatives from the Co-operative Union, the TUC and the Labour Party. Its remit was four-fold: how best to 'raise the economic status of the people'; to consider the possibility of 'investing the funds of the Unions in Co-operative undertakings'; joint education and propaganda; and possible assistance from co-operatives to trades unions during strikes and other industrial disputes. The ground had been well prepared. Prior to the Congress William Maxwell, who was to move the motion, had led a considerable correspondence on the question in the *Co-operative News*. During the actual Congress debate it was argued that the setting up of the Committee would represent only a change of degree. A Joint Committee already existed to deal with labour problems within the Co-operative Movement, so the proposed Committee would only have be an extension of that. Defenders of political neutrality were not convinced and began to mobilise opposition. However, an attempt was made to head this off at the next Congress by a motion from the Manchester & Salford and Cambridge Societies which endorsed efforts to 'secure closer union between the forces of organised labour and the Co-operative Movement ...'. By this time the opposition to the proposal for a Joint Committee had been well prepared and an amendment was tabled that had the effect of nullifying the motion. The amendment was overwhelmingly carried by 1,346 votes to 580.[11]

This defeat did not, however, lead to Co-operative withdrawal from the Joint Committee set up following the 1912 Congress. With the kind of constitutional delicacy that had become a feature of the Co-operative Union, the Report to the 1914 Congress noted that the Union had considered whether the next meeting of the Joint Committee could go ahead. It decided that it could because the amended motion had not rescinded the motion passed at the Portsmouth Congress agreeing to the setting up of the Joint Committee. The view was taken that the meeting could go ahead, provided that the Co-operative Movement did not seek 'union with the Labour Party'.[12] A further meeting of the Joint Committee had, therefore, followed which was reported to the 1914 Congress. It prompted another counter move in the form of another motion, seconded by Greening, instructing the Co-operative Union to maintain the political neutrality of the Movement, and not to join in conferences with political parties or to deploy co-operative personnel or money in support of the Labour Party. This motion was carried.

24

During the next year the Co-operative Union sounded out the views of local co-operatives which revealed continuing doubts about Co-operative Movement links with the Labour Party. As a result the Central Board of the Union recommended to the 1915 Congress in Leicester that no further action should be taken on the question. This was endorsed. Indeed, the debate was short. As the Congress President, quaintly named Bastard, pointed out, the issue had been discussed at the three previous Congresses. There the matter had to stand until wartime pressures led to the Co-operative Movement taking its own direct political action.

Before turning to this two points should be noted. One was that the political question had been kept before Co-operative Congresses from 1897 onwards The second was that the issue had become complicated by the related question of what should be the Co-operative Movement's relations with the Labour Party.

The Setting up of the Co-operative Party

The first world war created problems that tipped the balance in the Co-operative Movement in favour of political action. Difficulties experienced by the Royal Arsenal Society were felt in varying degrees by other British consumer co-operatives. At the start of the war these numbered 1,385 with a combined membership of 3,054,000.[13] They thus represented a significant part of the British population, and any mishandling of their political grievances could have repercussions.

Co-operatives had various wartime grievances but there were four common and major ones. The first was the shortage of supplies. All retailers were similarly affected, but an important difference for co-operatives was that they were membership organisations. This meant that member dissatisfactions could be expressed in quarterly and half-yearly meetings. Moreover societies' capital structures could be adversely affected if members lost confidence in their societies and withdrew their share capital. To avoid such risks co-operatives needed to safeguard their supplies.

The second problem was the datum system which applied to other co-operatives as well as to RACS. This meant their supplies were allocated on the basis of the volume of goods they had sold in an earlier period. While this might not seem unfair, it was, nevertheless, a crude measure of demand which failed to take into account movements of population or increases in co-operative membership. The latter increased by over a million during the war and, in 1919, stood at 4,131,000.[14] The problems of the datum system were compounded by the government appearing to take little account of the co-operative presence in retailing. Co-operatives complained that they were insufficiently being brought into consultations over how to distribute scarce goods, and that they were under-represented on bodies set up to advise government departments on basic commodity supplies. These appeared to be made up almost exclusively of private traders.

Co-operatives also believed that they were under-represented in appeals against compulsory military service, and this constituted their third major problem. At appellate tribunals the employees of private traders seemed to have greater success than those of co-operatives in appealing successfully against conscription. This was perhaps not surprising, given that the appellate tribunals largely comprised representatives of private traders and of existing political institutions and had very few co-operative representatives.

The fourth major area of co-operative protest concerned the imposition of a new Excess Profits Duty. Previously, various Chancellors had accepted the co-operative argument that societies' surpluses were mutual savings rather that profits. War, however, had increased the need to raise tax revenues and had caused the government to shift its position. As a result co-operatives feared that a dangerous precedent was being set. If it continued after the war, it could damage members' loyalty because their dividends would be subject to income tax. Making the problem worse was the fact that societies had to observe a cumbrous formula. The Excess Profits Duty on co-operatives was calculated on the excess of the profits per member in the year of assessment over the profits per members in the pre-war trade year, multiplied by the number of members in the year at the assessment. Not surprisingly, it was very unpopular among co-operatives!

Each of these grievances, compounded by the lack of response from the wartime Liberal government, eroded what remained of earlier Liberal sympathies in the Co-operative Movement. They also inclined the Movement towards independent political action. The mainspring for this was the Joint Parliamentary Committee which had earlier consistently argued for co-operative political representation. The difficulties the Committee experienced in representing the Movement with the government during the war had hardened its position. Consequently it made a robust and forthright report to the 1917 Co-operative Union Congress in Swansea:[15]

> It is no use blinking the fact that the co-operative movement carries but little weight, either with the legislators or the administration departments of State. By constant pressure of our case we are sometimes able to gain a little consideration, but in the things that matter most today our influence is practically nil. Those in authority do not even take the trouble to understand the general line of our organisation.

The Joint Parliamentary Committee Report went on to detail the action that it had taken on issues such as Income Tax, Excess Profits Duty, Military Service, Sugar and Other Food Regulations and for which it now sought Congress endorsement. Its Report ended with a significant resolution:

> That, in the opinion of this Joint Parliamentary Committee, the time has now arrived for the co-operative movement to take the necessary steps to secure direct representation in Parliament as the only way of effectively voicing its demands and safeguarding its interests.[16]

There was already support in Congress for the proposal in the shape of a composite motion from 104 societies. This urged co-operative representation on local authorities as well as in Parliament. In addition there were other resolutions along the same lines, but including proposals for changes that would be required to Co-operative Union Rules and for the setting up of appropriate machinery. We should note, however, that one went

27

further in proposing that there should also be negotiations between the Co-operative Union, the Labour Party and trade unions to take 'joint Parliamentary action'. Somehow this motion was overlooked in the major debate,[17] during which there were 34 speakers, but none from the Royal Arsenal. Although Edward Owen Greening spoke opposing the motions, he did so as a representative of a productive society, the London Co-operative Bookbinders, and not the RACS. He proposed that:

> Congress instructs the Central Board of the Co-operative Union to invite the assistance, impartially, of all friends of Co-operation in Parliament, members of all political parties, to resist attempts to levy taxation on our Societies for which there is clearly no equitable justification.[18]

The size of the vote against this motion, 1,883 votes to 199, showed the strength of feeling now running in favour of direct political action. The original motion, now composited with the motion of the 104 societies, when put to the vote was 1,979 for to 201 against. It demanded not only Parliamentary representation but also that on local bodies.

Thus a momentous decision had been taken. The Movement had changed direction and come down on the side of direct political action. Nevertheless there appeared a rear-guard action in the shape of a CWS amendment. This called on the Co-operative Union to issue a circular, asking whether societies were in favour of the Congress decision and, if so, whether they were prepared to contribute funds to implement it.[19] We may recall that it had been at this point on previous occasions that enthusiasm for political action had evaporated. Wartime problems and government insensitivity had created a decisive mood, however, and Congress rejected the CWS amendment by 'an overwhelming majority'.

Even with such a strong mandate for direct political action, it is possible to imagine that there might still have been some drawing back. At this point though Lloyd George, the Prime Minister, inflamed the situation further. The Joint Parliamentary Committee had sought a meeting with him after the Swansea

Congress but he declined to meet a Co-operative deputation. As a result a National Emergency Conference was called to prepare a draft scheme for 'securing Co-operative representation in Parliament and on local municipal and administrative bodies'. It was held in London in October 1917. Although this was almost five months after the Swansea Congress, enthusiasm for direct political representation was still running high, as was shown by the fact that the conference was attended by almost 1,000 delegates from over 500 societies.[20] It passed the following resolution unanimously:

> ... that this Conference desires to place on record its indignation at the contempt with which the present Prime Minister has treated British Co-operators, not only in refusing to receive the deputation appointed to place the grievances of the Movement before him, but also at his failure to take any steps, after repeated appeals, to recognise the existence or usefulness of the Co-operative Movement in the present national crisis.
>
> The Conference further pledges itself to organise to the fullest extent its political power, in order that co-operators may compel from this and other Governments that measure of common justice and recognition of their special economic position which the ordinary claims of loyal citizenship have so far failed to secure.[21]

The Conference was not only about protest. It also began to lay the foundations of policy and organisation. T W Allen, Chairman of the Joint Parliamentary Committee, presided and, in his opening address, asserted that 'Co-operation is a theory of society and, therefore, a legitimate basis for a political party'. An emergency programme was agreed which would seek to protect voluntary co-operation against unfriendly legislation and administration. Another aim was the 'eventual organisation on Co-operative lines of the processes of production, distribution and exchange', as well as the elimination of profiteering private speculators, a more equal education system and a national housing scheme.[22]

It can be seen that such a programme had much in common with what was then Labour Party policy. However, the question of Co-op/Labour relations was still a delicate one, although Arthur Henderson, Secretary to the Labour Party, attended the conference and spoke at it. In doing so he advocated a reduction of 'the number of sections into which democracy has been divided' rather than of joint parliamentary action:

> When I speak of lessening the sections I do not mean that I am here asking that the Co-operative Movement should at once affiliate with the Labour Party. I am treating the matter from a higher standpoint. I would be prepared to advise that the Labour Party as known should cease to exist if by so doing we could combine the whole of democracy.

Henderson continued:

> I would not insult the Co-operative Movement as a whole by suggesting that it should affiliate even with the Party whose secretary I have the honour to be. What we want is to have you properly organised; and until experience provides us with better means, to have you working with us for the same common cause... Under the terms of your proposed scheme it permits friendly relations between us. We of the Labour Party have begun to work with the Co-operative Movement.[23]

This points to sympathetic relations between co-operative and Labour leaders and to their hopes of closer working relations. Before examining early Co-operative/Labour relations, though, we should complete our description of the setting up of the Co-operative Party.

The new organisation did not take this name right away. Initially it was a sub-committee of the Joint Parliamentary Committee, but later became a separate department of the Co-operative Union. In the process it was renamed the National Co-operative Representation Committee and became a broad based organisation representing the Central Board of the Co-operative Union, the Joint

Parliamentary Committee and co-operative auxiliary organisations such as the Co-operative Women's Guild. The new Committee also included representatives of those societies which agreed to contribute to the special political representation fund set up as a result of the 1917 Congress decision. The initial rate of subscription was a halfpenny per member per year, although some societies added an additional and voluntary ¼d. (farthing) per £ of their sales. The new Committee's functions developed from those proposed at the National Emergency Conference in October 1917 and approved by the Liverpool Congress the following May. They were:

(1) To prepare and issue a statement of policy and a national programme on matters political in harmony with the decisions of the annual Co-operative Congress; to prepare for the approval of Congress such amendments of the statement of policy and programme as may be deemed desirable; and to work in co-operation with the sectional councils, hereinafter provided for, in carrying out the policy and programme as approved by Congress.
(2) To advise and help co-operative societies and co-operative political councils in their political work.
(3) To initiate and undertake, or co-operate with other committees of the Co-operative Union in initiating or undertaking schemes of propaganda and education for the furtherance of the objects for the attainment of which the committee is established.
(4) To administer the Co-operative Political Fund on lines hereinafter provided under the heading 'Finance'.
(5) To approve programmes of work and expenditure submitted by the sectional political councils, hereinafter described, and to make to them such grants from the Co-operative Political Fund as may be deemed desirable.
(6) To prepare a list of suitable candidates for Parliamentary elections and to receive nominations from the sectional councils for additions to the list.
(7) To approve or disapprove the Parliamentary

candidates proposed by the sectional councils, and to make such grants in support of the approved candidates as may be deemed desirable.

(8) To prepare, for issue through the Publications Committee of the Co-operative Union, such literature as may be deemed necessary for the success of the work of the committee.

(9) To secure the adhesion of such societies as have not yet given their support to the scheme for securing direct co-operative representation.

(10) To receive, quarterly, a report from each sectional council of the work done by the council, and to take such action thereon as may be deemed necessary.

(11) To submit, with its minutes, a report of its work to each quarterly meeting of the Central Board.

(12) To submit each year to the Central Board for inclusion in the report of the Central Board to Congress, a report of the work done by the committee and sectional councils during the Congress year.

(13) To arrange, annually, a combined meeting of the National Co-operative Representation Committee and the Sectional Councils for the purpose of taking counsel together in order to secure such a combination of united action and sectional freedom as shall be most conducive to successful working and to make such recommendations to the Central Board and Congress as may be deemed advisable.

(14) To undertake such other work as my be remitted to it by the Central Board or Congress.[24]

At the 1918 Liverpool Congress the funding of the Committee was also agreed under which staff of the Committee would be Co-operative Union employees. The Union also agreed to meet the costs of the Committee's other administrative expenses including its rent. The sum of these costs would be the Union's contribution to the Co-operative Representation Fund. Provision was made, however, for the Union's Central Board to pay additional sums if it thought them 'necessary or desirable'.

The above statement may have been drafted in language that now seems quaint and dated. It nonetheless laid down a framework that has proved remarkably durable. Its main features were that the new organisation - shortly to be renamed the Co-operative Party by the 1919 Co-operative Congress - would be answerable to the Co-operative Union and its annual Congress; it would have a sectional structure that was to be contiguous with the sections of the Co-operative Union; it was to establish a panel of Parliamentary candidates whose members would be financially supported by the Political Representation Fund, ie they would be sponsored. However, the main point that should be taken from the above was how closely the fledgling party was to be tied into the Co-operative Union and, through it, to the rest of the Co-operative Movement. Such organisational closeness, and the remnants of sentiments of political neutrality in parts of the Movement, became stumbling blocks to the Co-operative Party's closer relations with the Labour Party. Even so, and despite the fact that its constitution prevented alliances with other political parties, it agreed to sit on a Joint Committee with representatives of the Labour Party and trade unions. In the final stages of the war this Joint Committee issued a manifesto on war aims 'on behalf of working-class organisations in Great Britain'. It also agreed to try to prevent the 'overlapping' of candidates during elections.[25]

This last question had soon become an active issue because the new Party had moved quickly to compile a list of possible constituencies and candidates. As early as the 1918 General Election it fielded candidates in ten constituencies, mainly in the Midlands and the North. Only one, A R Waterson, was successful and, although designated 'Co-operative', he became a member of the Parliamentary Labour Party.

The options facing the Co-operative Movement of whether to join a new 'People's Party' advocated by Arthur Henderson, or settling for more limited joint arrangements with the trade unions and Labour Party, were raised at the 1919 Co-operative Congress in Carlisle. The Report on the work of the Joint Committee stated that:

> Mainly through (its) efforts ... conflict was prevented and co-ordination and combined effort were possible in

ten constituencies contested by Co-operative candidates. The development of this mutual confidence is essential to our ultimate success. The committee are of the opinion that the appointment of joint committees of the progressive forces should be encouraged for action in local elections; but it should be made clear that after it has been agreed that Co-operators should contest an election, the final election of the candidate must be left to the Co-operative Political Council, subject, of course, in Parliamentary contest to endorsement by the National Committee.[26]

The report also suggested that the 'vested interests' gathering in the political opposition were more likely to encourage 'the formation of a federation of democratic parties, whether in the shape of a Democratic or People's Party, or a working agreement between sympathetic organisations'.

That seemed to sum up the choice before the Co-operative Movement: either to join in a new 'People's Party' or to build on existing working relations with the trade unions and Labour Party. The same choice faced the Royal Arsenal Co-operative Society. The Co-operative Movement made one decision; the RACS another. Before considering the latter, we should end this chapter by briefly examining early Co-op/Labour Party relations which were to provide a backdrop to developments within RACS.

Early Co-operative/Labour Relations

Just as it had taken the Co-operative Movement a long time, and much heart-searching, to decide to take political action, a similar debate now began over what should be the relations between the Co-operative and Labour Parties. Initially, a two-stage process seemed to be favoured. It was reflected in the motion presented to the Carlisle Congress of 1919 by the National Co-operative Representation Committee which, later in that Congress, would be re-named the Co-operative Party. The motion read:

> ... Congress believes the time has arrived for the establishment of a closer relationship between all

democratic organisations in the common interest. It, therefore, instructs the National Co-operative Representation Committee to negotiate with the Labour Party and T.U.C. Parliamentary Committee with a view to a federation for electoral purposes and with the ultimate object of forming a United Democratic or People's Party ...[27]

In proposing this motion, the Committee's Secretary, S F Perry, emphasised that what was being proposed was not affiliation to the Labour Party. He believed that the Co-operative Party had a distinct message. Moreover, as one delegate claimed, the Co-operative Movement was large enough to stand on its own feet and create its own political organisation. In general, the thrust of the Carlisle Congress debate was towards finding a common meeting ground with the Labour Party. Indeed, some seemed to fear that affiliation to the Labour Party could lead to its domination of the Co-operative Party.[28] The motion was carried. Separate organisations would be retained, although it should be noted that there was already some convergence of policies: the 1919 Congress also passed resolutions supporting nationalisation of the land and of the coal mines.

Despite approval of the resolution there was some uncertainty about how to give it practical expression, and also what kind of alliance should be formed with the Labour Party. A complicating factor was that there was also some fluidity in the situation. Between 1918 and 1921 while the Co-operative Party was in its formative stages the Labour Party was relatively weak. It was, therefore, not unreasonable to think, as Arthur Henderson had done, in terms of a new 'People's Party'. As the 1920s progressed, however, the position changed. Whereas the Labour Party became stronger, the Co-operative Movement remained undecided and in some disarray on the question of its relations with the Labour Party.

This was graphically shown at the 1920 Congress in Bristol, where the Co-operative Party reported on discussions with the Labour Party and Trades Union Congress. These had resulted in the recommendation 'that a Labour and Co-operative political alliance should be formed'.[29] However, the Congress President, G A Ramsay BA, ruled the resolution out of order on the grounds that the 1919 Congress resolution had directed the Co-operative Union's Central Board 'to take the necessary steps to ensure adequate discussion by the movement of any proposals ...' Ramsay ruled that because there had been insufficient consultation on the proposals contained in the resolution it was, therefore, out of order. This ruling caused uproar. One delegate, Neil McLean, Labour MP for Govan, asked how the resolution could be out of order if the Central Board of the Union had considered it only six weeks earlier and had not been advised by its officials that it was out of order. A member of that Central Board, J Millington, confirmed that indeed there had been no such advice and that Standing Orders Committee had also not suggested that the resolution could be out of order. In spite of this the President repeated his ruling and then asked those in favour of proceeding to the next business to say 'aye'. Apparently there was a loud chorus of 'ayes' and the Chairman quickly moved to next business.

In view of the lack of previous warnings that the resolution might be out of order, the Congress President's ruling must be suspect. However, the loud chorus of 'ayes' for next business suggests that there was undoubtedly uncertainty about the proposal on the floor of Congress. The delay caused by Ramsay's ruling meant that something of the momentum towards alliance with the Labour Party had been lost.

Neither was the situation retrieved by a further inconclusive result at the next Congress when the Party's resolution was resubmitted.[30] Between the two Congresses there had been numerous district and sectional conferences to discuss the proposed alliance with Labour. Even so, Congress now revealed an almost even split. Votes for the re-submitted resolution numbered 1,682, while those against were 1,686.[31] Professor Tom Carbery observes in his book, *Consumers in Politics - A History and General Review of the Co-operative Party*:

> In retrospect one can see that 1921 was the last chance the Co-operative Party had of securing an electoral agreement with the Labour Party based on the equality

36

of the two sides. There were to be future 'agreements' but henceforth the bargaining position of the Co-operative Party was to be weaker and that of the Labour Party considerably stronger than in 1921.[32]

Conclusion

In this chapter we have traced the impact of the 1914-18 war on the Royal Arsenal Co-operative Society and on wider politics in the Co-operative Movement. We have seen how the Co-operative Party came into being and its early relations with the Labour Party. Early on it faced questions of whether it should join a new 'People's Party', or form an alliance with the Labour Party. Political uncertainties in the wider Co-operative Movement meant that it would be 1927 before it would conclude its first electoral agreement with the Labour Party. In the meantime, however, the inconclusive situation was unsatisfactory to many.

This, then, was the background against which, in 1921, the Royal Arsenal Co-operative Society decided to establish its Political Purposes Committee and to affiliate directly to the Labour Party. Athough these decisions were shaped by conditions internal to the Society, the protracted debate in the wider Co-operative Movement on direct political action and relations with the Labour Party undoubtedly helped to colour them.

Notes

1 Davis, Walter T, *History of the Royal Arsenal Co-operative Society Ltd. 1868-1918*, RACS Ltd, London, 1921, pp.264-265.

2 Ibid., p.133.

3 Ibid., p.142.

4 Co-operative Union Ltd, *Report of 1892 Congress, Rochdale*, p.166.

5 Co-operative Union Ltd, *Report of 1897 Congress, Perth*, p.30.

6 Co-operative Union Ltd, *Report of 1905 Congress, Paisley*, pp.431-432.

7 Ibid., p.451.

8 Co-operative Union Ltd, *Report of 1906 Congress, Birmingham*, p.135.

9 Co-operative Union Ltd, *Report of 1910 Congress, Plymouth*, p.92.

10 Ibid., pp.452-453.

11 Co-operative Union Ltd, *Report of 1913 Congress, Aberdeen*, p.489.

12 Co-operative Union Ltd, *Report of 1914 Congress, Dublin,* p.125.

13 Cole, G D H, *A Century of Co-operation,* Co-operative Union Ltd, Manchester, 1944, p.371.

14 Ibid., p.371.

15 Co-operative Union Ltd, *Report of 1917 Congress, Swansea,* pp.137-152.

16 Ibid., p.150.

17 Ibid., p.151.

18 Ibid., p.552.

19 Ibid., pp.563-567.

20 Co-operative Union Ltd, *Report of 1918 Congress, Liverpool,* p.154.

21 Co-operative Union Ltd, *Report of National Emergency Conference, London,* October, 1917, p.15.

22 Ibid., pp.95-98.

23 Ibid., p.99

24 Co-operative Union Ltd, *Report of 1918 Congress, Liverpool,* pp.164-165.

25 Ibid., p.159.

26 Co-operative Union Ltd, *Report of 1919 Congress, Carlisle,* p.187.

27 Ibid., p.527.

28 Co-operative Union Ltd, *Report of 1920 Congress, Bristol,* p.127.

29 Ibid., p.137.

30 Co-operative Union Ltd, *Report of 1921 Congress, Scarborough,* p.31.

31 Ibid., p.496.

32 Carbery, Thomas F, *Consumers in Politics - A History and General Review of the Co-operative Party,* Manchester University Press, 1969, p.28.

CHAPTER THREE

RACS Decides a Political Course

Introduction

What was the RACS's response to the decision of the British Co-operative Movement to take direct political action? We have seen that the Society's representatives had contributed little to the 20-year debate leading to that decision. The most notable RACS member to speak in it had been Edward Owen Greening, but he had attended Congresses as a delegate from other co-operative organisations rather than the RACS. Moreover, he proved to be out of line with RACS thinking in that he opposed any political action, other than that of trying to influence friends of the Co-operative Movement in Parliament. Above all, he was anxious for the Movement to retain its political neutrality.

Before we trace the RACS's response to the setting up of the Co-operative Party, two factors should be noted. The first is that contemporary consumer co-operatives were strongly geographically based which enhanced their sense of autonomy and independence. They might feel part of a wider movement and elect representatives to its national federal organisations; they might also join with other societies in taking decisions at the Movement's annual Congresses; but they remained sovereign and could choose to implement, or not, such decisions. Moreover, if their members approved, they could take a quite different course of action, as RACS was shortly to to do. Independent action was all the more likely if a society was successful and if it was developing its own distinctive practices, as RACS certainly was. It had already developed the practice of paying a double dividend to employees, but in the 1920s it developed other distinctive features. One was the introduction of a system of proportional representation in elections for Society committees. Another was the creation of a full-time Board of Management, while a third was direct affiliation to the Labour Party. Generally speaking, other co-operatives did not adopt these practices, which thus tended to set RACS apart, even from its London neighbours. Having said that, however, we should note that, in 1979, the London Co-operative Society also affiliated directly to the Labour Party.[1]

The second factor to be kept in mind is that a co-operative society is a people's organisation. Shifts of opinion can occur among its members which lead to changes in its policies and practices. One such shift occurred among RACS members during the first world war. In Chapter 1 we noted how the 1867 Reform Act had helped to make the Greenwich Constituency, including Woolwich, a predominantly working-class constituency. Over 57 per cent of voters were then identified as being working-class. That position continued and was accentuated by the first world war, which also encouraged a shift of working class support from the Liberals to the growing Labour Party. Even so, by the end of the war, the Labour Party was in some state of flux with Arthur Henderson still talking in terms of a broad-based 'People's Party' in 1917 rather than the Labour Party.

Events were in train however that would strengthen the Party. When Arthur Henderson resigned from the War Cabinet in 1917, he headed moves to strengthen the Labour Party's organisation and policy. This led, in 1918, to the presentation and approval of a new constitution, together with endorsement of a policy that was distinctly more socialist.[2] The latter undoubtedly found support among RACS members, but it was the Labour Party's new constitution that had a more immediate effect on them. It created an enlarged executive which would be nominated by, and represent, different sections of the Party. However, it would be elected by, and answerable to, the Party Conference. Such a system of sectional nomination helped to pave the way for RACS to gain a seat on the Labour Party Executive and to hold it for many years. The new constitution also helped to improve local party organisation. It laid down rates of subscriptions which made more extensive machinery possible, and also established constituency structures better able to fight elections. Although a few Labour Party organisations had previously allowed individual members, including the Woolwich Labour Party, it was the 1918 constitution that provided for all constituency parties to do so. This move helped to bring the Party in line to benefit from the 1918 Representation of the People Act which had extended the vote to all men over the age of 21 and to all women over the age of 30. More significant, from the point of view of RACS, was the fact that the new constituency organisations were open to the affiliation of organisations such as trade union branches, the ILP and co-operatives. As we shall see, the RACS directed its initial affiliation to the Labour Party through new constituency organisations in its area.

As far as policy was concerned the Labour Party and the new Co-operative Party were in step. In Chapter 2 we saw how the Co-operative Union's Congress at Carlisle in 1919 had passed resolutions in favour of the nationalisation of the coal mines and of the land. In its new policy, *Labour and the New Social Order*, the Labour Party also advocated the nationalisation of industries such as coal mining and the railways, which had come under state direction during the war. It also proposed the public ownership of electricity generation, insurance and the land.

Personalities
In view of increased working class consciousness among RACS members it was always likely that changes in the Labour Party would impact on the Society. Linked to this was the influence of a number of people active in it. Among them was Herbert Morrison, who had contributed much to the Labour Party's growing strength by the successful establishment of the London Labour Party. While he was later seen mainly as a Labour Party leader, he was also an important background figure in the Royal Arsenal Society. His influence was indirect and arose mainly from what became the shared interests of the London Labour Party and RACS. Moreover, it was channelled through others in the Society rather than through any actual positions Morrison held in RACS. Nevertheless he became strongly identified with the Society, speaking frequently at its public meetings and attending many of its events, such as the annual International Co-operative Day celebrations. In 1923 Morrison moved to Eltham,

within the Society's area, and remained there until his death in 1965. During those 42 years he lived at only three addresses, the first of which he leased from the RACS.[3] When Morrison died in 1965 the RACS's Funeral Department conducted his funeral. While early Minutes of the RACS's Political Purposes Committee show that Herbert Morrison urged the Society to affiliate to the London Labour Party, none point to his being active in the actual setting up of the Committee.

Another figure we should note was the RACS Secretary, William B Neville. He was the Secretary of the Society between 1916 and 1937 and, therefore, a central figure in the Society during the time when the lines of its political action were being laid down. Neville's reputation as an effective and successful co-operative official survives to the present day, and much of RACS's considerable financial strength was attributed to his leadership. He epitomised many co-operative managers and secretaries of the period in that he was born into, and educated by, the Labour Movement. Neville was born in Eastwood in Nottinghamshire in 1884. His father was a councillor and a miner, and for many years a member of the Council of Notts Miners' Association. However, William Neville himself did not go into the mines but began work at fourteen in the office of the Langley Mill & Aldercar Co-operative Society. He studied for Co-operative Union examinations through evening classes, and in one year became the top student in exams for the Co-operative Secretaries' Certificate.[4]

A brief note about the historical role of Co-operative Secretaries would perhaps be appropriate at this point. Since the 1960s their functions have tended to become subsumed in those of societies' Chief Executive Officers. Before that these functions were specialist and derived from responsibilities laid down under Industrial and Provident Societies legislation. They included calling a co-operative society's meetings, preparing its accounts, balance sheets and reports to members, conducting its elections, making returns to the Registrar of Friendly Societies, and heading the society's administration. In the case of RACS the Society's Secretary was elected by the members and was always considered to be their representative. He was charged with acting in their best interests and on their behalf. This meant that the Manager could make no financial undertakings without the prior agreement of the Society Secretary.

It can be seen from the above that, on becoming Secretary of the Royal Arsenal Co-operative Society, William Neville was placed at the heart of its organisation. His move from Nottinghamshire had come in 1912, when he became the RACS's Chief Clerk. Two years later he was promoted to the position of an Assistant Secretary, and two years after that he was elected the Society's Secretary. His advancement in the Society was thus rapid and indicative of ability. He remained Society Secretary until he moved to take the same position in the London Co-operative Society in 1937. This was after a failed attempt to persuade the LCS and RACS to amalgamate of which Neville had been a strong advocate.

While Morrison and Neville, who were believed to be close personal friends, had indirect influence on the question of RACS's future political course, someone who played a major and more immediate part was Joseph Reeves. His period in the Royal Arsenal Society largely coincided with that of William Neville's. He was appointed Education Secretary in 1918 and left in 1938 to become the first Secretary of the Workers' Film Association, a joint body formed by the Labour Party and the TUC to promote the greater use of film in the Labour Movement. In the 1945 General Election Joe Reeves was elected Labour MP for Greenwich.[5] It can thus be seen that he was both an educationist and a politician. Like Neville, the regard in which he was held has far outlived him. In the context of this study, however, we are mostly concerned with his influence on RACS politics.

The form on which Reeves applied for the position of RACS Education Secretary still survives and included a job description. From this we can gather that, even in an organisation as enlightened as the Royal Arsenal Society, it was unlikely that a woman would be appointed. The job description stated unequivocally that, 'He will be required to ... perform the usual duties of Secretary and Chief Librarian at the Central and Branch Libraries; to organise the work of the Education Department; and to edit *Comradeship*'. Reeves's neatly handwritten application reveals that he was then 30 years of age, married, living in Peckham, and was a 'first-class Book Keeper in charge of Principal Foreman's Office, Woolwich Arsenal'. He had been a member of the RACS only five years and held no educational qualifications 'except a Diploma for Art which includes designing, type display and advertising'. His experience included three years as Secretary to the Christian Socialist Fellowship, lecturing for the Independent Labour Party, and being the editor of a Christian Socialist publication. Reeves acknowledged that 'My experience in teaching has not been extensive'. The wages he sought were £240 a year.[6]

Despite obvious gaps in his qualifications Reeves was appointed. Controversy surrounds the appointment. It is believed that his predecessor, Arthur Hainsworth, had left because of the leftward swing of RACS. He had moved to take the position of Metropolitan District Organiser for the Co-operative Union in London after 14 years as RACS Education Secretary. RACS's move to the left was particularly marked in the Education Committee, which he served and to which Joe Reeves had been elected in 1917. Hainsworth came from an earlier and more liberal co-operative tradition which was now being superseded in South East London. He had been born in Queensbury, just outside Bradford, in Yorkshire, in 1863.[7] and was more in the Rochdale tradition including adherence to a belief in political neutrality. Hainsworth had placed on record his opposition to the Co-operative Movement becoming too closely allied to the Labour Party.[8] On his departure the position of Education Secretary was advertised and applicants interviewed. For reasons that are not clear, no appointment was made and the position was readvertised.

About this time a dispute arose between the RACS Education and General Committees. It was over the latter's attempt to veto an article by Joe Reeves advocating Labour Party affiliation which would have appeared in the December 1918 issue of *Comradeship*. The actions of the General Committee suggests that either it was less keen on Labour Party affiliation, or was being more sensitive to possible criticisms from Society members who were not Labour Party supporters. There were two reactions to the General Committee's intervention. The first was that the RACS Education

Committee unanimously resolved to cease publishing *Comradeship*. The second was that Joe Reeves decided to apply for, and was appointed to, the position of Education Secretary.[9] On his appointment, which included the editorship of *Comradeship*, the Education Committee rescinded its decision not to continue publishing the journal. For its part the General Committee limited itself to requesting to see the file containing all the applications for the position of Education Secretary. After doing so it proceeded to admonish the Committee for taking 'insufficient care' in making the appointment[10] and left it at that.

Joe Reeves's appointment, and events surrounding it, point to shifts in opinion in the Society. These were bound to have a bearing on RACS's response to the setting up of the Co-operative Party. We should now move to examine what happened.

RACS's Response to the Co-operative Party

Following the National Emergency Conference in London in October 1917 the RACS General Committee had talks with representatives of the embryonic Co-operative Party. These resulted in proposals which the General Committee published in *Comradeship* in February 1918.[11] They outlined a local scheme of organisation but also underlined difficulties that would apply peculiarly to the RACS:

> The society's position is greatly different from that of the majority of societies, probably all other societies, by reason of the area covered and the many constituencies touched in the several counties in which our operations extend. Our problem is in this respect a very complex one, and, therefore, any scheme of local work to be affective would have to be supported by substantial grants from the members.

The General Committee's statement went on to propose a scheme of Constituency Organisation Committees throughout the Society's area to be co-ordinated by a Central Advisory Committee. Each of these Committees would include representatives of the General and Education Committees, the

Women's Guilds and directly elected members. The Central Advisory Committee would be responsible for organising work in elections, but the determination of policy would remain with society members at their quarterly meetings.

The point to emphasise is that these proposals would have meant that the proposed structures would have been part of the new Co-operative Party. In the debates in the Society that followed the question of relations with the Labour Party soon came to dominate. This was not necessarily unreasonable during a period of flux when many expected that the Co-operative Party would become part of the Labour Party. During the rest of 1918 and 1919, a groundswell of opinion grew in RACS that any new political structure should include links with the Labour Party on the grounds that the Co-operative Movement was part of the wider Labour Movement.

This view came to be expressed in a variety of ways. One was through a series of meetings held throughout the Society to discuss the General Committee's proposals. Another was through occasional Co-operative and Labour Weeks, details of which were advertised in *Comradeship*. Typical of these was one held in Woolwich in December 1918. Heralded as a 'Great Co-operative and Labour Week', it was organised 'Under the Joint Auspices of the Educational Committee of the Royal Arsenal Co-operative Society Ltd, and the Woolwich Trades and Labour Council', with the slogan 'Another Advance towards working-class solidarity'.[12] The week included various meetings, propaganda and social events. Joe Reeves spoke at a number of these, always advocating labour unity in order to better represent the proletariat; Reeves did not believe that co-operative candidates by themselves would be able to do this adequately.[13]

It soon became clear that within RACS there was a lack of enthusiasm for a separate co-operative political organisation. As a result the General Committee shifted its position. It withdrew its original proposals and, instead, paid a grant of £120 to the Co-operative Party. Secondly, the General Committee proposed to the Society's quarterly meeting in June 1918 that RACS Rules should be amended to provide for the creation of a political fund to support the Society's future political work. This was defeated because it made no provision for direct affiliation to the Labour Party, a further indication of the strength of feeling in the Society that there should be links with the Labour Party.

It can be seen from its organisation of the 'Co-operative and Labour Weeks' as well as other events during 1919 and 1920, that the RACS Education Committee led moves for the Society's affiliation to the Labour Party. While Joe Reeves was undoubtedly in the forefront of these moves, it would be wrong to attribute them to him alone. His appointment was symptomatic of a shift in a major committee of the Society whereby its members were also members or supporters of the Labour Party. An insight into their composition is provided from the research that John Attfield did for his book *With Light of Knowledge*. In that he stated:

> The men and women with whom Reeves worked in the RACS Education Committee in the inter-war years were almost without exception members of the Labour Party, in many cases the veterans of local struggles to build the Party before and during the 1914-18 War. Fifty-six members served on the Education Committee between 1919 and 1940, including twenty-four men and thirty-two women. They were overwhelmingly working-class. The majority of the male members were manual workers - engineers or shop employees - and only five had what could be regarded as white-collar or professional jobs. All were trade unionists. The women on the committee were the wives of working men, who came mainly into co-operative work through the Women's Guild; they included many who were active in the Labour Party as local councillors or guardians, and members of voluntary or municipal committees - care committees, school meals committees, public assistance committees, hospital visitors - activities typical of the committed local political workers of the period.[14]

Reeves's significance lay in his leadership skills and his ability to articulate arguments and to propagate ideas. He was to become an eminent propagandist whose reported speeches, extensive articles and surviving pamphlets point to his being hard-hitting, eloquent and persuasive. Above all, he was prolific. The General Committee of the Society followed the Education Committee in that its members were also soon drawn mainly from Labour Party supporters. Even so, in the immediate post-war period the General Committee was more cautious in trying to avoid offending non-Labour Society members. As we have seen, it attempted to veto Reeves's article on Labour Party affiliation in *Comradeship*.

A head of steam now developed in the Society for affiliation to the Labour Party. It reflected, among other things, a belief that there should be unity between the various sections of the Labour Movement. That view was shared by parts of the wider Co-operative Movement but, as we saw in Chapter 2, it proved insufficiently strong to be able to be translated into a national policy. Co-operative Congresses had reservations about joining in any arrangement that went beyond that provided by the Joint Co-operatives and Labour Committee. At the beginning of this Chapter we also noted that because co-operative societies were autonomous and, therefore, independent of national federal organisations, they could take independent action. RACS now proceeded to do so on the issue of Labour Party affiliation. Nevertheless, it took time for a distinct RACS policy to emerge; moreover, this did not develop without reference to the rest of the Co-operative Movement. Congress had called on the embryonic Co-operative Party to consult with local societies, and the discussions it had begun with RACS continued despite the rejection of early proposals because they did not provide for local affiliation to the Labour Party. Even so Co-operative Party/RACS discussions continued and, in 1919, the RACS General Committee gave a platform to the Party when it organised a conference of Society members to discuss co-operative political representation. Its main speaker was S F Perry, who had been appointed the first Secretary of the Co-operative Party, and who also had the distinction of being father to Fred Perry, the leading British tennis player in the 1930s. The outcome of the meeting illustrated the duality of the RACS position and also the growing success of the Education Committee in its campaign for local

Labour Party affiliation. A resolution was passed which stated:

> That the Society proceed to put into operation the decisions of Congress respecting political representation and that the Society come to a working arrangement with the local Labour Parties for electoral purposes.[15]

At the Society's Half-Yearly meetings the following March a further resolution was passed by 1,500 votes to 47, which paved the way for the Society's Rules to be revised so as to allow political representation.[16] At the Society's Half-Yearly Meetings in September 1920 a Special Political Committee was elected to draft the proposals that would become the basis of rules changes. In passing we should mention that the RACS had now become too large to hold only one members' meeting, and a series of meetings was held in its main centres with their votes being aggregated. The Special Political Committee comprised eight representatives elected by the September Half-Yearly Meetings plus two each appointed by the General and Education Committees.

While the Committee began to frame its proposals, the arguments in favour of Co-operative/Labour links continued to be made by Reeves in *Comradeship*. For example he wrote in the February 1921 edition:

> Ethically, co-operation is a method of living which is totally and fundamentally at variance with the present economic arrangements of society. Co-operation is the economic articulation of that urge which is within the conscious co-operator to organise society on the principles of equity and justice. Therefore, the co-operator finds himself "up agin" the present system of capitalist exploitation and definitely opposed to the orthodox political parties, for the reason that they are both out to preserve the present system of the private ownership of the means of life. Again, the co-operator accepts the principle of democracy, or community rule and applies it to all functional operations, thus doing away with privilege and class rule politically, socially and industrially.

Understanding, therefore, the source from which the co-operative urge springs, the co-operator distinguishes between friends and enemies, and turns to the Labour Party - his natural political affinity - for help. The Labour Party in turn having received inspiration from the ethical outlook of the co-operator, joins him in his effort to usher in the co-operative commonwealth. The Labour Party becomes inevitably co-operative ...[17]

While Reeves was writing in such terms a variety of meetings within the Society provided platforms for Co-operative/Labour unity. In the same month the above article appeared a Unity meeting was held at Bermondsey at which the speakers included Dr A Salter JP, the Parliamentary Labour Candidate for West Bermondsey. At a Co-operative Guild Council Demonstration held at the Co-operative Institute, Woolwich, also in February 1921, the speakers included Ramsay MacDonald and Margaret Llewellyn Davies who, as we noted in Chapter 1, had consistently argued in favour of the Co-operative Movement being part of the wider Labour Movement, and Margaret Bondfield, who was to become the first woman Labour Cabinet Minister. In the same month Ramsay MacDonald addressed another meeting, this time at the Co-operative Institute, Parsons Hill, at which he appealed 'to co-operators to support the Labour Party and so unify the working class forces'.[18]

To the Labour Party

The question of the Society's future political role was decided by a Special General Meeting, 'held in sections' at Belvedere, Catford, Peckham, Upper Tooting and Plumstead, in May 1921. Its sole business was to receive the Majority and Minority Reports of the Special Political Committee. The two reports did not represent a major split; rather they reflected a difference in degree with both favouring Labour Party affiliation.

Before looking at their proposals we could perhaps note the composition of the Special Committee. Two women served on it. One was appointed from the General Committee, Mrs Real. The other, Mrs Munson, came from the Education Committee. The contemporary practice in some official RACS documents seems to have been to give the initials of men but not of women.[19] The men on the Special Committee included Charles Grinling, previously mentioned in connection with early adult education in Woolwich. He had joined the RACS Education Committee and, as we have noted, become the first editor of *Comradeship* in 1897. Twenty-four years later he thus represented some degree of continuity in the Society and in the meantime had become a Councillor on the Woolwich Borough Council. Another Councillor on the Special Political Committee was H E Sykes, who had moved the resolution at the Members' Meeting in December 1919 urging implementation of the 1919 Congress decision and a 'working relationship with the local Labour Parties for electoral purposes'.[20] An indication of the importance attached to the Committee was the fact that the Chairman of the General Committee, R Wale, also became its Chairman and served as an ex officio member. William B Neville, Secretary of the Society, also became the Special Committee's Secretary. Altogether the Committee held eight meetings and, as has been noted, produced both majority and minority reports.

The Committee had been thorough in its work. It had inquired of other consumer co-operatives what they were doing about the 1919 Congress decision and the Co-operative Party. The Majority Report stated that the replies received disclosed a variety of practices:

> Whilst in some cases the societies had allied themselves with the Co-operative Party, developing their own political machinery, others had been content merely to pay the annual subscription to the party. Several societies stated that they had affiliated to the local Labour Parties; in other cases they were paying dual subscriptions to the Co-operative Party and the Labour Party. A large number of societies appear not to have taken up the question of political action in any form whatever.[21]

The report then briefly recalled the arguments for political action, after which it listed the Parliamentary Divisions, both metropolitan and county, within the RACS area, and the numbers of Borough, County, Urban and District Councils plus the Boards of Guardians that also existed within it. Such a multiplicity of electoral areas led to the conclusion that:

> because of the urgent necessity for consolidation, the Committee recommend affiliation to the Labour Party in preference to Co-operation with the separate and distinct co-operative machinery, viz. the Co-operative Party.[22]

Proposals were then made to give practical expression to this aim. These can be summarised as follows:

1 Out of each half year's surplus 3d. per member would be allocated to a political fund. One penny per member was to be set aside to pay affiliation fees to local Labour Parties pro rata to the Society's membership in the area of each. Another penny per member would be devoted to the expenses of a Parliamentary candidate who would be put forward by the Society as its Parliamentary nominee. The last penny per member would be put to form a general political purposes fund to pay administrative expenses and to support the candidates for local governing bodies not otherwise covered.

2 Administration of these funds would be placed under the control of a Special Committee, the Political Purposes Committee, which would derive its authority under a new Rule in the Society's Rules. In other words, its position would be directly analogous with that of the Society's Education Committee. Its membership would be made up of directly elected representatives of Society members, and members appointed by the General and Education Committees.

3 Where affiliation fees were paid to local Labour Parties the Society, through the Political Purposes Committee, would seek 'fair representation'.

4 Priority was to be given to seeking Parliamentary representation on the grounds that it was in Parliament that laws were made and where Co-operation was under attack. There was to be one Society nominee who would be put forward to the Labour Party which the Political Purposes

Committee selected. The costs of the candidature would be met by the Political Purposes Committee in addition to £200 per year to be paid to the MP because MP's salaries were insufficient.

5   As far as local elections were concerned Society candidates would be selected by joint meetings of the General, Educational and Political Purposes Committee.

6   There would also be joint conferences of the three Society Committees so as to co-ordinate action and provide exchanges of views and information.

7   A new Standing Order would be introduced to ensure that all Society nominees were 'bona-fide Co-operators' by requiring that they observe the same qualifications as those others seeking election in the Society in terms of membership and purchases.[23]

The Minority Report was made in the names of Charles Grinling and A Dashwood. Their disagreement with the Majority Report concerned only one area, namely that of Parliamentary candidates. Whereas the Majority Report proposed that there should be only one Society candidate the Minority Report urged that 'proportional aid should be given to all constituencies within our area with a view to making the best possible fight for a Labour candidate within each'. It went on to say that whereas 'The majority propose a subsidised candidate ... We claim that all candidates should be free'. Moreover, the Minority Report members argued that Parliamentary Candidates should not be restricted only to members of the RACS but that it was 'enough for a man or woman to be a member of any Co-operative Society and that we need the best discoverable candidates'. The position of the members of the Minority Report can perhaps best be summed up by their later statement that 'Principles, methods, and men come before money'. That view won the day. By a comfortable majority in each of the Society's sectional meetings, and therefore overall, the Minority Report was accepted.[24]

The major point to keep in mind is that a decision had been taken to affiliate to the Labour Party rather than to the Co-operative Party; moreover, that this decision was to become enshrined in the Society's Rules and Standing Orders.

Conclusion

It had taken a long process over some four years to achieve this result. To reverse it and take it out of the Society Rules would probably be a similarly long process. It can be concluded, therefore, that a definite course of action had been entered upon. This outcome had been reached during a time of fluidity in the Labour Movement. As we saw earlier, the Labour Party itself was becoming organisationally stronger, with clearer local structures; it was also developing a more distinct and socialist policy.

The period during which these developments occurred was also the one in which the Co-operative Party was formed. That had resulted from a wave of outrage at the way the Co-operative Movement had been treated by the wartime government, both by ignoring Co-operative contributions to the war effort and by changing the basis of taxation on co-operatives. While the resulting indignation had helped the Movement to overcome its earlier ambivalence to political action, it had not been strong enough to give it a clear idea of what should be its relations with the Labour Party. Moreover, concerted action was unlikely while individual co-operative societies remained independent and autonomous.

This meant they could take local action that was not always fully in line with national co-operative policy. Although this is what RACS appeared to do, we should remember that the fluidity of Labour politics in the immediate post-war period included the expectation of some that the Co-operative Party would become part of the Labour Party. Indeed, Joe Reeves had publicly expressed the hope that it would be 'absorbed' in it. Such expectations could mean that, in its decision to affiliate locally to the Labour Party, the Royal Arsenal Society was wanting to be in advance of events rather than behind them.

Notes

References to Minutes are to RACS Minutes held by the CWS SE Archive. *Comradeship* was published by RACS Education Department.

1   Newens, Stan, *Working Together - a Short History of the London Co-op*

Society Political Committee, CRS (London) Political Committee 1988, p.50.

2   Phillips, Gordon, *The Rise of the Labour Party 1893-1931,* Lancaster Pamphlets, London, 1992 pp.27-30.

3   Donoughue, Bernard and Jones, G W, *Herbert Morrison - Portrait of a Politician,* Weidenfeld & Nicholson, London, 1973, pp.85, 171, & 553.

4   Davis, Walter T, *The History of the Royal Arsenal Co-operative Society, Ltd 1868-1918,* RACS, London, 1921, pp.217-218.

5   Attfield, John, *With Light of Knowledge - A Hundred Years of Education in the Royal Arsenal Co-operative Society, 1877-1977,* London, 1981, pp.33, 55 & 65.

6   CWS SE Archive, Joe Reeves's application form for position of Education Secretary, Royal Arsenal Co-operative Society Ltd, dated 4 December 1918.

7   *Comradeship,* September 1922, p.iv.

8   Attfield, John, op. cit., p.32.

9   Ibid., p.32.

10 Ibid., p.33 & 41.

11 *Comradeship,* February 1918, p.11.

12 *Comradeship,* November 1918, p.14.

13 Attfield, John, op. cit., p.32.

14 Ibid., p.44.

15 *Comradeship,* January 1920, p.9.

16 *Comradeship,* April 1920, pp.77 & 78.

17 *Comradeship,* February 1921, p.51.

18 *Comradeship,* March 1921, p.77.

19 CWS SE Archive, Notice of Special General Meeting to be held May, 1921.

20 Attfield, John, op. cit., p.34.

21 CWS SE Archive, Report of Special Political Committee, Majority Report, p.5.

22 Ibid., p.6.

23 Ibid., pp.6-9.

24 *Comradeship,* June 1921, p.129.

CHAPTER FOUR

RACS Political Purposes Committee is Set Up

Background to the Founding of the
RACS Political Purposes Committee

It might be reasonable to suppose that, from this point, the newly-created Political Purposes Committee would become the main focus of the political activities of the Royal Arsenal Co-operative Society. This however was not immediately the case, and for two main reasons. One arose from the nature of the recommendations of the Special Political Committee whose Report had led to the setting up of the Political Purposes Committee. The other was inherent in the nature of the Royal Arsenal Society itself, particularly during the 1920s and 1930s when much of the Society could have been said to have been political.

In connection with the first of these two reasons we should note that two main consequences flowed from the acceptance of the Report of the Special Political Committee. One was that, because the proposed Political Purposes Committee would be a committee of the Society, in the same way as the General and Education Committees were committees of the Society, any RACS member would be eligible for nomination to it. This universal right of nomination had existed in the Society from its earliest days and stemmed from its acceptance of the important Rochdale Principles of equality between members and of open and voluntary Society membership. Accepted also was the corollary of the latter that nominees to Society committees could not be excluded because of their religious and political beliefs.

We shall later see that this observance had strange consequences as far as the Political Purposes Committee was concerned. Subsequently supporters of the Communist and Labour Parties were elected to it and, in the 1980s, even members of the short-lived Social Democratic Party. While the situation was undoubtedly strange, it worked. It did, however, set RACS apart from other co-operatives that were also setting up new political machinery but doing so under the aegis of the Co-operative Party. These societies usually had a rule that membership of the Co-operative Party was a qualification that those seeking election to their Political Committees were required to hold. Eventually, this distinction between RACS and other societies had ramifications for the Parliamentary candidates they nominated. Those sponsored by the RACS did not have to be members of the Co-operative Party, whereas those nominated by other societies to join the Co-operative Party's Parliamentary Panel were required to be members of the Party. In later years the existence of two Parliamentary Panels sometimes led to friction between the RACS Political Purposes Committee and the national Co-operative Party.

The second main consequence of the acceptance of the Report of the Special Political Committee was that the Royal Arsenal Society would affiliate to Constituency Labour Parties in its area. Such a close alliance with a specific political party seems to be at variance with the practice that Society members of any political persuasion could seek election to the Society's Political Purposes Committee. Nevertheless the arrangement worked and lasted for almost 70 years. Linked to its payment of affiliation fees to local Labour Parties, the committee also became responsible for appointing delegates to Constituency Labour Parties, and later making nominations for local authority and Parliamentary candidatures. It can thus be seen that the RACS Political Purposes Committee had a limited remit which meant that it was to be a largely functional body. Unlike its counterparts in other co-operatives that were linked to the Co-operative Party, it was not required to organise Party branches. It therefore never became a membership body: the parent organisation, the Royal Arsenal Co-operative Society, remained that.

Moreover, the Political Purposes Committee was not in its early days an organiser of political events or propaganda; the RACS Education Committee tended to be the prime mover in these areas. We have already noted how it had been responsible for organising the Unity, or Joint Labour and Co-operative Weeks, that had played such a part in achieving the Society's Labour Party affiliation. After the setting up of the Political Purposes Committee this propaganda role tended to remain with the Education Committee and continued in two important ways. One was through the Education Committee's educational work. Although the traditional forms of staff training and member education continued and, indeed, expanded considerably in the late 1920s, stronger emphasis came to be placed in the latter on political education. In his book *With Light of Knowledge*, John Attfield observed:

> With the establishment of the Political Purposes Committee in 1923 the direct conduct of political activity by the RACS became the responsibility of that committee e.g. selection of local and parliamentary candidates, representation of the Society on local Labour Parties, electoral work and campaigning. In this narrow sense the political affairs of the Society were separate from educational work. But in the context of the inter-war period it is clear that no real separation took place. This was because, for Reeves and other workers in RACS education, politics was seen as having a far wider meaning than the simple mechanics of party campaigning. All the day by day activities of the Education Department - classes, drama groups, travel - were imbued with a deep sense of social purpose, a purpose aptly summed up in the title of one of Reeves's pamphlets, *Education for Social Change*. This outlook expressed widely-shared assumptions about the role of education for the advancement of the working classes.[1]

The other important way in which the Society's Education Committee boosted RACS's political work came through its Journal, *Comradeship*. This became an important means of political propaganda in the Society, not only because of its content but also because of its extensive circulation. This was assisted by the fact that the Education Committee had contact with great numbers of RACS members. For example, in the session 1926/7 it enrolled almost 3,000 students in the 100 or so classes it organised for RACS members.[2] Three years later a census showed that 250 auxiliary organisations, with which the Education Committee worked closely, existed within RACS. Mainly they were Co-operative Women's Guilds, which became quite a political force in the Society during the inter-war years, but there were also the Men's and Mixed Co-operative Guilds. The combined membership of the RACS auxiliary organisations came to around 7,500.[3] With such mass participation it is not surprising that the Society's journal achieved its wide circulation. By 1916 this was already over 10,000 per month.[4] By the late 1930s it had doubled to over 20,000 per month.[5]

During the inter-war years *Comradeship* maintained a strongly left-wing political tone. The point to make, however, is that although it was a Society journal, it was edited by Joe Reeves and published by the Education Committee. It was not a paper of the Political Purposes Committee which, indeed, had no need to publish one.

The Setting Up of the Political Purposes Committee

In February 1922 nominations for election to the new Political Purposes Committee were sought for the first time; the election would be held at the Society's Half-Yearly Meeting the following month. There was usually considerable competition for elections to the General and Education Committees. For example, in the election for members of the General Committee in 1923, 39 candidates stood for seven places. For some reason there was no competition in the first election for members of the Political Purposes Committee. Under its constitution Society members could elect eight representatives. The General and Education Committee would each then appoint a further two. As far as the election of members' representatives was concerned, only eight nominations were received and there was thus no need for an election.

Since it had first been published in 1897, *Comradeship* had always given the names and biographical details of candidates for Society elections. It is from this source[6] that we are able to learn about the original members of the Political Purposes Committee who were nominated from Society members. Interestingly two were women. Whereas the men standing in Society elections invariably had trade union, Labour Party or local authority membership, the women did not. Often they had only co-operative experience in the Society, and this proved to be the case in this election. The fact that women were coming forward to contest such elections, and that there was no bar to their doing so, suggests that the RACS was proving to be a valuable training ground for women. One of the women nominated was Emily Real, who had previously served on the Special Political Committee that had drawn up the Report leading to the setting up of the Political Purposes Committee. Married, aged 46 and from Nunhead, she had been a member of RACS for eight years. In that time she had been a member of the Education Committee two and a half years and a member of the General Committee for six months. The other woman nominated was Annie Alexander from Catford, who was also married and aged 49. She had been a member of the Society for nine years and had also served on the Education Committee for two and a half years. She held the Co-operative Union's Certificate in Co-operation.

Among the men nominated were the two authors of the Minority Report of the Special Political Committee, Charles Grinling and Alfred Dashwood. We have already noted Grinling's past work in the Society, having been *Comradeship's* first editor in 1897. Now aged 61 he had been a member of RACS for 31 years. Living in Woolwich, he had served on the Woolwich Borough Council for six years and other public bodies including the Board of the Woolwich Polytechnic. Professionally, Grinling was still a social worker. Alfred Dashwood had been a member of RACS for some 27 years. Aged 56 and from Abbey Wood, he was an engineer. He had already served six years on the Society's General Committee and, like Annie Alexander, had taken various Co-operative Union examinations including those for the Certificates in Co-operative Book-Keeping and Co-operation.

The four other nominees, while all long-time members of the Society, had stronger political and trade union experience rather than co-operative experience. They had not been elected to any

RACS committees although that is not to say that they had not stood in any elections; as we have seen, competition for places could be strong. However, their co-operative enthusiasm could be judged from the fact that like Annie Alexander and Alfred Dashwood, several had gained Co-operative Union Certificates.

The four included James Butts, who had also served on the Special Political Committee. From Peckham, he was aged 51 and a trade union official of the Amalgamated Engineering Union, as the Amalgamated Society of Engineers had now become. Although he had been a member of the Society for 17 years, his public work had been primarily as a Poor Law Guardian and as a Borough Councillor. Another of the four was James Newman, who lived in RACS property in Rochdale Road, Plumstead, and was a school teacher. Now aged 43, he had been a member of the Society for 18 years and had gained the Co-operative Union's Certificate in Industrial History. His main experience had been political in that he had been a member of the Woolwich Borough Council, also for 18 years, and was currently Chairman of its Finance Committee. Perhaps we can move forward to note that Newman would serve on the RACS Political Purposes Committee for some 24 years and hold the Chair for 11 of those years. He continued to serve on the Woolwich Borough Council and was Mayor for 12 years. In the Labour Party he served on the Executive Committee of the London Labour Party. By the time of his death in 1955 he had become sufficiently renowned for one of the Woolwich ferry boats to be named after him.[7]

Returning though to 1922 we should note that the two remaining nominees were both named Reynolds. Charles, of Raynes Park, had previously been a member of the Special Political Committee. He was 53 and a publisher's representative. A member of RACS for seven years, he also held various Co-operative Union Certificates. Apart from his previous election to the Special Political Committee, he had not been elected to any position in the Society, although he had acted as a stocktaker: this was a position held by members' representatives to assist in the periodic checking of the Society's stocks. Charles Reynolds was also Secretary to a branch of the Mixed Co-operative Guild in the Society. Perhaps more significant was the fact that he had a strong trade union and Labour Party background, being a branch chairman of the Typographical Association and an Executive member of the Trades and Labour Council, and Labour Party. His namesake, Frederick Reynolds, was 36 years of age. An engineer, he lived in Erith and, although he had been a member of the Society for eight years, he had had no committee experience in it. His voluntary work had included the Secretaryship of a branch of the AEU and of the Erith branch of the British Socialist Party.[8]

In observing the number of the above who had previously served on the Special Political Committee, it seems reasonable to suppose that their uncontested election to the permanent Committee represented a further endorsement of the recommendations of the Special Political Committee, Minority Report and all. All the above became the first members of the RACS Political Purposes Committee. They were joined by two members of the General Committee, J Farrell and Councillor H Sykes. The latter had also served on the Special Political Committee and had moved the resolution at the Society's Half-yearly Meeting in March 1920 paving the way for Rules changes to allow political representation.

The Committee in Action

The Political Purposes Committee of the Royal Arsenal Co-operative Society first met on Thursday 18th March 1922. Charles Grinling was elected its Chair, a position he held for the next three years. The question of the Secretary to the Committee could not be so easily settled. For the time being, the Committee asked the General Committee if they would allow 'a clerk from the General Office to carry out the Secretarial work of the Political Committee'.[9] A Mr F R Cooper was provided and the Committee accepted him for 12 months.[10] Besides setting up the operational side of the Committee, the main business of its first meetings was to agree which Labour Parties to affiliate to, and on what numbers of Society members affiliation fees should be paid. At its second meeting the Committee considered suggested membership figures and eventually agreed the following[11] formulation:

Woolwich	29,516	members
Southwark	3,485	"
Bermondsey	1,644	"
Greenwich	5,015	"
Deptford	6,213	"
Wimbledon	5,003	"
Mitcham	1,157	"

However, figures in other parts of the Society would not necessarily be agreed so easily. For example, the same meeting also resolved:

> That the question of affiliation to Lewisham, Camberwell, Lambeth, Wandsworth, Dartford and Malden Labour Party be adjourned and that in the meantime the Secretary write to the Secretaries of the Local and Borough Parties stating the difficulties of the Committee, and asking for their observations.[12]

At the same meeting the Committee agreed a further resolution:

> That we accept the following basis of representation on the local Labour Parties:
> 1 Representative for 100 members with a minimum of 2 representatives, and a maximum of 5 representatives with the exception of Woolwich, which shall be 7 representatives.[13]

By the June Quarterly Meeting of the Society the Committee was able to report that it had been able to agree affiliations to the Labour Parties in Bermondsey and Rotherhithe, Deptford, Greenwich, Mitcham, Southwark, Wimbledon, Woolwich, Camberwell and Lewisham.[14] At this stage RACS members were invited to nominate Society representatives to those Labour Parties where affiliation had taken place:

> Notice is hereby given that the Political Purposes Committee invite nominations from members of the Society, in accordance with Standing Order No 41(1) to serve as the Society's representatives on the Councils of

the undermentioned Local and Divisional Labour Parties to which the Society in affiliated.

There followed a list of Labour Parties and the notice continued:

The representatives appointed will be required to serve for a period of two years, and the selection of nominees will be made is due course in accordance with Standing Order No 41(1).

Nominations must be made on the prescribed form, which may be obtained from the Secretary of the Society, or from any of the branches, and must be received by the Secretary at the Registered Office not later than May 20th, 1922.

William B Neville, Secretary.

April 22nd, 1922

NB - Attention is directed to Standing Order No 44, which provides, inter alia, that nominations for the aforementioned representatives shall be received from those members of the Society only who would be eligible under the Rules and Standing Orders of the Society to be nominated for and to serve upon the General Committee, subject to the regulation that no candidate shall be disqualified for the reason that the candidate is an employee of the Society or had a relative employed by the Society.[15]

Periodically this statement, or variations of it, was repeated as further affiliations were made, more society representatives were required, or reappointments became due.

It has been quoted at length for several reasons. The first is that it illustrates the involvement of the whole Society in affiliation to local Labour Parties. Second, as with election to the Political Purposes Committee, nomination was open to all members of the Society irrespective of a nominee's views. It would, however, be reasonable to assume that those most keen to gain nomination would already be Labour Party supporters. Third, it shows that those nominated nevertheless had to be eligible to stand for the

Society's General Committee. That meant that they qualified in terms of their trading with the Society and the share capital they held in it. Fourth, it illustrated the fact that the Political Purposes Committee negotiated, rather than administered, the affiliations to local Labour Parties which was the responsibility of the Society's General Office. It can be gathered that some considerable work was involved in the administration of affiliation, as well as in the appointment of Society representatives. Finally, we might also note the almost civil service tone of Neville's notice calling for nominations. It was typical of that applying in large consumer co-operatives of the period, and also of their national federal organisations such as the Co-operative Union. In the case of RACS it reflects the fact that, in the year its Political Purposes Committee was established, it was a large democratic trading organisation with a membership of 95,818 and sales of £2,864,526.[16] The conduct of its affairs had to be open and irreproachable. Hence the legalistic observance of formalities in areas such as accounting, elections and nominations.

At the Society's Half-Yearly Meeting the following September a report was made on the Political Purposes Fund to date. It showed that the initial grant of £1,136 had been paid. Of that £296 had gone in Labour Party affiliation fees. The 'balance in hand' was £735, and, with there being no secretarial expenses, the rest had been designated for the promotion of Parliamentary and other candidates.

As far as 'other' candidates are concerned, we should note that calls for nominations soon widened to include those for Local Governing Bodies.[17] However, concern with Parliamentary candidates was further indicated when, at the meeting of the Political Purposes Committee on 6th May 1922, James Newman moved the following resolution:

> That in view of the desirability of local Labour Parties immediately doing preparatory work, especially registration work and ward organisation, in preparation for the elections in November, and the next Parliamentary Election, a grant equivalent to the amount paid for affiliation fees for half a year be paid to local Labour

Parties to which affiliation fees are paid for the current half year.[18]

It was seconded by E Salmons, a member of the Political Purposes Committee nominated by the Education Committee. However, it was opposed by A Dashwood, one of the two authors of the Minority Report of the Special Political Committee and, when put to the vote, was lost. The resolution does show, however, the concern that was being felt for the coming General Election. In the next Chapter we will look at the part played by RACS in that election, and the subsequent formation of the first Labour Government in 1924, albeit a minority government. Having covered the early work for the Committee, which quickly became typical of what followed, we should end this Chapter by looking at RACS's political developments from the Labour Party's point of view.

The Labour Party and RACS

So far we have looked at developments mainly from the RACS point of view. However, the Labour Party was an equal partner and the main financial beneficiary of RACS political activity. This outcome should be seen as the culmination of a process that had lasted some 25 years and which had contained a number of elements. These included the traditionally close ties between the RACS and first of all the craft unions, and later the unskilled or general unions, in its area. Another factor was the swing of working class support from the Liberals to the Labour Party in the RACS's area which was shown to have a high number of voters on electoral registers that could be classified as 'working class. During the 25 years Party and trade union supporters were increasingly elected to RACS committees. There was thus strong mutual identification between the various elements in the Labour Movement in South London during the period. Another factor was undoubtedly Labour Party lobbying which now continued in different ways. Labour Movement solidarity had also been assisted by the role that RACS, and the wider Co-operative Movement, had played in looking after co-operative members' interests during the 1914-18 war. The war had shown more clearly that consumer co-operatives were on the side of the workers and thus identified them more closely with the wider Labour Movement.

Woolwich provided fertile ground for co-operation between the various elements of the Labour Movement. We have already noted that in 1885 in the Greenwich Parliamentary Constituency, which included Woolwich, over 57 per cent of votes were identified as being working class. Noted also was the swing of working class voters from the Liberals to Labour, typified by Will Crook's famous election victory at Woolwich in 1903. At that stage, however, RACS's political action was limited only to municipal elections. The resolution passed at its Half-Yearly Meeting in September 1897 had made no mention of Parliamentary activities.[19] It nevertheless recognised that 'the time has arrived when the RACS in conjunction with the various working men's organisations and the Trades Council of the district, should take a more active part in municipal affairs ...' and represented an important stepping stone to RACS's future political activities. It also reflected its affinity with 'working men's organisations'.

At this stage co-operation with early Labour lay mainly with individual co-operative members rather than with the Society itself. As in the wider Co-operative Movement there was concern not to offend Liberal or Conservative co-operative members. Prominent co-operators such as Edward Owen Greening and Mary Lawrenson, who were also members of the Society, argued passionately against political involvement and certainly identification with one party. Such opposition undoubtedly played a part in the Society's decision not to become part of the Woolwich Labour Representation Association which was set up in 1903 and later became the Woolwich Labour Party. This became famous for the many Labour Party developments it pioneered, including individual membership long before the Party's 1918 Constitution provided for it. It is likely that many co-operative members joined the Woolwich Labour Party including members of the Co-operative Women's Guild. These eventually became a significant force in RACS elections but they were also strongly pro-Labour. They are likely to have been influenced not only by developments within Woolwich itself but also by the views of Margaret Llewellyn Davies, General Secretary of the national Co-operative Women's Guild, who was advocating closer Labour/Co-operative relations.

The Woolwich Labour Party soon had growing success in elections to local Councils, the London County Council and Local Boards of Guardians. New traditions were developing which are well described below:

> A ... feature of Woolwich was ... its self-contained isolation from the rest of London. The majority of the population were employed within Woolwich, and there was little commuting into the centre, eight to nine miles away. Woolwich was very much a separate community with its own civic life, very untypical of London, and similar to isolated mining communities in Welsh valleys. A commitment to Labour was part of belonging to the community. At elections in Woolwich, as in other distinct communities, turn-out was high; indeed for years the polls at Woolwich were the highest in London. Voting, and voting for Labour, was a declaration of membership of the Woolwich community.[20]

It was never likely that RACS, with its very strong roots in Woolwich, would remain detached from such developments. We have already noted how, for many years, the Royal Arsenal Co-operative Society was affectionately known as the 'Woolwich Society' in the wider Co-operative Movement. The importance of Woolwich in RACS membership was illustrated when, in 1922, it became necessary to work out a basis for local Labour Party affiliation. We then saw that the figure for Woolwich was 29,516 while the next largest was Deptford with 6,211. The figures speak for themselves. Against such a background it can be said that the RACS's decision to affiliate to local Labour Parties was the formalisation of a relationship that had developed over the previous quarter of a century. While there was some opposition in the Society it proved not to be numerically strong. As we saw in Chapter 3[21] the resolution that paved the way for Labour Party affiliation was passed at the RACS

Half-Yearly Meeting in March 1920 by 1,500 votes to only 47 against.

Affiliation to local Labour Parties was to be only part of the process, however. Later would come affiliation to the London Labour Party and, in 1928, affiliation to the national Labour Party. The decision to affiliate to the London Labour Party was influenced by two factors. The first was that, by the 1920s, the London County Council had become the top tier of local government in London. It was therefore important for Labour to gain control of it and while Woolwich played its part in returning Labour candidates, other parts of the capital were finding it more difficult. There was thus a need for an effective electoral vehicle which the London Labour Party eventually became. Much of its success was attributable to Herbert Morrison who became its Secretary in 1918. Through the London Labour Party, and by virtue of the fact that he successfully contested Woolwich East in the LCC elections in 1922, Herbert Morrison became the second influencing factor. His election in Woolwich East and his moving to Eltham from Hackney in 1923 brought him into close contact with RACS. Indeed, as we have seen, between 1923 and 1929 he lived in a house in Well Hall Road, leased from the Society. Before that, however, he had attended a meeting of the Political Purposes Committee on 17th June 1922 with the specific purpose of obtaining the RACS affiliation to the London Labour Party.[22] He was successful and the Society paid £50 for the remainder of that year. In the next full year its affiliation fee rose to £150. Thereafter it increased and reached the figure of £400 by the end of the decade and remained at that level until 1941.[23]

According to Bernard Donoughue and G W Jones in their biography of Herbert Morrison, the RACS affiliation played a significant part in his subsequent rise in the Labour Party:

> The three most important forces which built up the LLP and enabled Morrison to gain fame were the national Labour Party, the trade unions, especially the Transport and General Workers' Union of Ernest Bevin, and the Royal Arsenal Co-operative Society.[24]

However, the benefit was not all one way. As Donoughue and Jones point out, after its affiliation the RACS 'always had at least one representative on the Executive' of the London Labour Party, and Herbert Morrison became 'a superb propagandist for the RACS'.[25]

Besides such formal links, Morrison had close personal friendships in RACS. Two in particular should be mentioned. That with the Society's Secretary, William B Neville, has already been noted. The other was with William Barefoot. A member of the RACS General Committee, Barefoot was a notable Woolwich Labour Party leader who was said to have 'guided Herbert when he was raw and young' and had also 'arranged for (him) to be adopted as the Party's LCC candidate at Woolwich East'.[26] For us Barefoot provides yet another example of the link between RACS and the wider Labour Movement in Woolwich. Born in Woolwich in 1872, he began work as an office boy in the Arsenal but later moved to the engineering room of the gun shop where he became an active member of the Amalgamated Society of Engineers, the union from which so many early RACS leaders came. Although he became a member of the RACS Board, Barefoot was more closely identified with Woolwich Labour Party politics having been election agent to Will Crooks, full-time Secretary and Agent to the Woolwich Labour Party and, eventually, Leader of the Woolwich Council.[27]

Conclusion

In concluding this Chapter we can see that there were many factors in the RACS decision to affiliate to the Labour Party. These included the distinct circumstances of Woolwich, figures who were active in both the Labour and Co-operative Movements, effective proselytising by people such as Joe Reeves, and personal friendships. The decision to affiliate should be seen as the culmination of a gradual process. Once made, however, it became long-lasting. Mutually beneficial relations were forged with local Labour Parties and the London Labour Party. Later, in 1928, there would also be affiliation to the National Labour Party.[28]

This Chapter has also seen how the RACS, through its Political Purposes Committee, set up the mechanics for its links with the Labour Party. While there was growing success in elections to local councils and Boards of Guardians, there was less success in Parliamentary elections. There had not yet been a Labour Government. In the next Chapter we will trace how, in 1924,

RACS played a part in helping to elect the first Labour Government, albeit a minority government.

Notes

References to Minutes are to RACS Minutes held by the CWS SE Archive. *Comradeship* was published by RACS Education Department.

1   Attfield, John, *With Light of Knowledge - A Hundred Years of Education in the Royal Arsenal Co-operative Society, 1877-1977*, London, 1981, p.50.

2   Ibid., p.45.

3   Ibid., p.49.

4   Davis, Walter T, *The History of the Royal Arsenal Co-operative Society, Ltd 1868-1918*, RACS Ltd, London, 1921, p.169.

5   Attfield, John, op. cit., p.53.

6   *Comradeship*, February 1922, p.ix.

7   CWS SE Archive, Details in connection with Long Service Medal.

8   *Comradeship*, July 1922, p.xv.

9   Minutes, Political Purposes Committee, 18 March 1922.

10 Minutes, Political Purposes Committee, 19 April 1922.

11 Minutes, Political Purposes Committee, 25 March 1922.

12 Ibid.

13 Ibid.

14 *Comradeship*, July 1922, p.xv.

15 *Comradeship*, May 1922, p.iii.

16 See Table at end of study.

17 *Comradeship*, July 1922, p.xii.

18 Minutes, Political Purposes Committee, 6 May 1922.

19 See Chapter 1, p.12.

20 Donoughue, Bernard and Jones, G W, *Herbert Morrison - Portrait of a Politician*, p.85.

21 See Chapter 3, p.49.

22 Minutes, Political Purposes Committee, 17 June 1922.

23 See Table at end of study.

24 Donoughue, Bernard and Jones G W, op. cit., p.64.

25 Ibid., p.65.

26 Ibid., p.84.

27 Ibid., p.84.

28 See Table at end of study.

CHAPTER FIVE

The Inter-War Years

Introduction

The inter-war years from 1918 to 1939 form a distinct period and for that reason this Chapter will deal with them as a whole. We have previously noted RACS's affiliation to local Labour Parties and, later, to the London Labour Party. In this Chapter we will see that it also affiliated to the national Labour Party in 1928 and also to the Co-operative Party in 1930. Both affiliations occurred after the Co-operative Movement had concluded its first National Agreement with the Labour Party, the Cheltenham Agreement, in 1927. Despite its affiliation to the Co-operative Party, the RACS's first loyalty remained to the Labour Party.

Besides examining the 1927 Cheltenham Agreement this Chapter will also look at the RACS's involvement in the General Elections of 1923 and 1929 which led to the first two minority Labour Governments. The inscription for this study is Cicero's maxim, 'Salus populi suprema est lex' - 'The good of the people is the highest law'. That reflected RACS's underlying ethos. It also underlay its political concerns which were that, locally and nationally, legislators should pass laws for the 'good of the people', rather than for the benefit of a few privileged by class or wealth. Because Parliament was the chief law-maker elections to it were particularly important.

A fact underlying this study has been that co-operative politics were always closely linked to co-operative trade, not only in respect of its funding but also in the way it was organised. For example, the RACS Political Purposes Committee was specific to the Royal Arsenal Co-operative Society. Elsewhere, other sovereign co-operative societies formed the basis of affiliation to the national Co-operative Party. The pattern of co-operative trade, therefore, always had ramifications for co-operative politics. The nature and patterns of retail trade have always been changing, however, sometimes more obviously than others. Co-operative organisation has been forced to respond to them. While such shifts have become more marked in the post-war years, they were nevertheless apparent in the inter-war years. They led some in the Co-operative Movement to believe that there was need for rationalisation and, in London, there was an ambitious scheme to merge the four London societies; RACS, South Suburban, Enfield Highway and London. While this could have helped to strengthen co-operative trade in the capital, it was also likely to have changed the way in which co-operative political activities of the four societies were organised. We shall, therefore, look briefly at this attempted merger.

The Labour Government

The main part of this chapter, though, is concerned with the first two minority Labour Governments. In moving to consider that of 1924 we should note that Labour's position in Woolwich had, somewhat surprisingly, become uncertain. In the 'Khaki' election of 1918 the Labour leader, Ramsay MacDonald, failed to hold the Woolwich East seat. While we have been concentrating on the working class nature of Woolwich, we have perhaps tended to overlook the fact that it was also a military town that housed a garrison and an arsenal employing some ten thousand people. During the 1914-18 war that number had risen to 80,000. The end of the war, therefore, brought the threat of unemployment as well as a surge of patriotic fervour in the town. While Ramsay MacDonald was popular in the Labour Party, and identified with its growing success, he had taken a semi-pacifist position during the war. He had, in fact, become a leading opponent of the Government's war policy. MacDonald was, therefore, unpopular in Woolwich East, as a number of accounts of the 1918 General Election campaign testify. At one meeting his opponents issued ex-servicemen with nailed sticks and bottles in order to cause disruption.[1] Harry Snell, who was later to regain the seat, also observed that:

The Tory Party in the borough were delighted (at

MacDonald's selection) and the constituency went patriotically mad and dirty. Labour women were assaulted, MacDonald was stoned, execrated, and defeated; England's honour was saved - by Horatio Bottomley.[2]

MacDonald failed to hold the seat but subsequently returned to Parliament as the Labour MP for Aberavon in 1922. In that election, Harry Snell defeated Horatio Bottomley and regained the Woolwich East seat for Labour. It was on returning to the House, where he had previously sat as the MP for Leicester, that MacDonald became Leader of the Parliamentary Labour Party. This had grown from 59 in the 1918 Election to 142 in 1922. In the General Election, held in December 1923, that figure went up to 191. The Parliamentary Labour Party had thus become the second largest party in Parliament.

It was in these circumstances that Stanley Baldwin made a tactical move when he proposed that Labour should take office. Equally tactically, the Parliamentary Labour Party accepted, despite lacking real power to govern and having little scope to introduce radical measures. While some argued that it should, therefore, not have formed the Government, MacDonald and other Labour Leaders feared that the Party could lose support if it were thought that it was afraid to form a government. They also believed that by taking power the Liberals could be prevented from regaining their earlier public support. Above all, they hoped to be able to take some measures, even if limited, that could help their working class supporters.

As far as the Co-operative Party was concerned the 1923 Election had increased the number of Co-operative MPs from four to six. A V Alexander, Alf Barnes, R C Morrison and T Henderson were re-elected and were now joined by the Party's Secretary, S F Perry, and A Young. All took the Labour Whip and became members of the Parliamentary Labour Party.[3]

The Royal Arsenal Society's main contribution to the 1923 General Election was financial. Until now the Political Purposes Committee, which had been established for less than two years, had been more concerned with local and LCC elections. It had still to develop a Panel of Parliamentary Candidates, although it had begun to organise the Society's financial support in Parliamentary elections. At its meeting in November 1923, the Committee approved a scheme under which grants of £500 would be allocated each half year to divisional labour parties. These grants were to be distributed in three proportions; £250 in proportion to co-operative membership in each divisional labour party area; a further £125 was to be allocated to each party, but paid only if they appointed a full-time officer; a further £125 could be paid if a Divisional Labour Party was increasing its membership. In addition the Committee agreed to pay a special election grant to those parties which have built up an election fund ...'[4] In other words, the RACS Political Purposes Committee was targeting those Labour Parties that were already reasonably well organised and thus likely to make productive use of the Society's money. We should also note that the money was not linked to specific candidates, and this remained the case even when the RACS developed its own Panel of Parliamentary Candidates, although from time to time the formula changed.

The first minority Labour Government survived only ten months and, during this period, the RACS Political Purposes Committee appeared to be more concerned with local politics. However, one of its members, G J Anstey, became the Parliamentary Labour Candidate at Norwood;[5] and by posters in the Society's stores, the Committee sought the names of members who were prepared to be nominated to Labour Parties as Parliamentary and LCC candidates.[6]

It is interesting to note that, during the period of the first Labour Government, the RACS and its Political Purposes Committee still hoped that the Co-operative Party would become part of the Labour Party. This was reflected in Joe Reeves's comments in *Comradeship* in July 1924, when he was referring to the recently held Co-operative Congress:

> The resolution welcoming the formation of the first Labour Government in the history of this country

identified the movement with its counterpart on the political plane, and the full degree of support accorded to the resolution indicates the tendency of the movement to merge itself in the wider political movement rather than continuing its political exclusiveness by promoting an independently political party for co-operators. Ramsay MacDonald, by including some of our best men in his Government, makes the continued existence of the Co-operative Party unnecessary, and although it may take some time to merge this sectional party into the larger labour movement, this tendency will grow as the Labour Party becomes the greatest political party in the State.[7]

By 'some of our best men', Joe Reeves was referring to the fact that A V Alexander had become Parliamentary Secretary to the Board of Trade and Alf Barnes, R C Morrison and S F Perry had each become Parliamentary Private Secretaries to Labour Ministers.[8] However, Reeves was wrong in his belief that the Labour Party was about to become 'the greatest political party in the State'. In the General Election in October 1924 that followed its fall, the number of Labour MPs was reduced to 151. Although the core of Co-operative MPs - Alexander, Barnes, Morrison and Henderson - survived, Perry and Young, were defeated.

Again the RACS supported no specific candidates in the 1924 Election. It did, however, adhere to its earlier policy of giving grants where they would do the most good. At its meeting in October 1924, the Committee decided that grants of £25 be made to each of the 22 constituency Labour Parties in the Society's area, but that an additional grant of £25 be made to only eight constituency parties which already had an election fund of £100 or over.[9]

Before moving on to the 1929 General Election we should note two developments in the wider Labour Movement which had a bearing on RACS politics. The first concerned the Labour Party's decision to proscribe Communists from membership and the second was the 1927 Cheltenham Agreement between the Co-operative Union and the Labour Party which created an electoral alliance.

The Labour Party, Communists and RACS

A study of the political actions of the Royal Arsenal Co-operative Society must necessarily be placed in the context of what was happening during the same period in the Labour and Co-operative Movements. In 1920 the Communist Party was formed and absorbed the British Socialist Party and the Socialist Labour Party.[10] The new Party, although small with an estimated membership of around 3,000, made repeated requests to affiliate to the Labour Party, but these were rejected because of the Communist Party's loyalty to Moscow and the nature of its organisation. Labour Party attitudes hardened and, in 1924, it decided that members of the Communist Party could no longer be individual members of the Labour Party. Easier said than done and, two years later, it was thought that a quarter of the Communist Party were still members of the Labour Party.[11] Herbert Morrison gained notoriety in trying to expel them, becoming known as 'our chief witchfinder'.[12] Others, such as Ernie Bevin in the Transport and General Workers' Union, were equally zealous in trying to block communist entryism.

Despite its close association with the Labour Party and with Herbert Morrison, the RACS made no moves to follow these examples. The reason was its continued observance of the Rochdale Principle of Open and Voluntary Membership. This meant that RACS membership was open to people from a variety of religious and political persuasions, or none. All, including communists, were equally eligible for nomination and election to the Society's Committees, and could be elected to the Political Purposes Committee or nominated as the Society's representatives to local Labour Parties. Thus, for communists, the RACS offered a potential back door to the Labour Party. A period of some confusion ensued in relations between local Labour Parties and RACS in the mid-1920s.

The Minutes of meetings of the Political Purposes Committee in the mid-1920s reveal that a number of queries were received from representatives of the Society acting as delegates to local Labour Parties in areas such as Walworth, Deptford, Greenwich, Wimbledon, Dartford and Erith. That from Wimbledon drew attention 'to a situation which had arisen within the Wimbledon

Labour Party owing to the action of the Communists, and asking that the Society's delegates be instructed how to act'. The Political Purposes Committee decided to pass the query 'to the whip of the group'.[13] By this time the RACS had developed a system of 'whips' to provide a means of communication and a method of helping its representatives keep to agreed lines. Towards these ends quarterly meetings were, therefore, held with whips and representatives of the General, Education and Political Purposes Committees.

The communist question rumbled on mainly because some Labour Parties failed to abide by Labour Party Conference decisions to proscribe communists. As far as RACS was concerned, although under its Rules registered with the Registrar of Friendly Societies it could not ban communists from its membership, or prevent them from seeking election to Society Committees or other representative positions, it could maintain a party line. It had the authority to do this under its Rules passed in 1921, which allowed the Society to undertake political action. Now, in support of the party line, the Political Purposes Committee decided to withhold the Society's affiliation fees and grants to Labour Parties that did not implement Labour Conference decisions on Communists. In its Half-Yearly Report to the Society in October 1926, the Political Purposes Committee stated:

> It is with regret that the committee records that the action of certain Labour Parties has made it imperative to withhold for the time being the usual affiliation fees and grants. Members will remember that in 1925, at the Liverpool Party conference and later this year at the Margate conference, certain decisions were reached which affected very vitally the relationship of the Labour Party with certain phases of political thought. The majority of the parties in the Society's area have locally abided by these decisions, but disruptive forces have in some districts been predominant, and the organisation has been split. Until such time as the committee is satisfied that a constitutional party has been established and is carrying out loyally the Party decisions, no payments will be

handed over to these parties. Indeed, were the committee otherwise minded, it would have no option, under the standing orders under which it works, but to take this course.[14]

In line with this decision the convention developed that the Society would not nominate communists to local Labour Parties. Thus the back door was closed. However, it threw into sharp relief the fact that a similar 'condition was not imposed on the members of the Political Purposes Committee'.[15] Communists were eventually elected to this, although never in such numbers that they formed the majority. Moreover, the convention developed that they, and members from parties other than the Labour Party, abstained from voting on Labour issues. It is interesting to note that a number of voting blocs eventually emerged in the Society. Linked to its system of proportional representation, and the resulting trade off in single transferable votes, they helped to encourage a high turn out in Society elections. Among the voting blocs that developed was a small but active communist one. At the Society's Half-Yearly Meetings in December 1927 the supporters of this moved the following motion:

> That in view of the declaration of the Communist Party that it is prepared to accept the constitution of the Labour Party and affiliate on the same terms as other organisations, it be a general instruction to delegates of RACS on their various Divisional and Local Labour Parties to support by vote and otherwise any resolution having for its object the rescission of the Liverpool Conference decisions respecting the Communist Party affiliation to the Labour Party.[16]

Although the resolution 'caused animated discussion at all the meetings' of the Society, it was 'finally lost'. Undoubtedly, one reason was the strength of another voting bloc that had emerged, namely that of Labour supporters. This had become the largest in the Society and, as we have seen, had come to dominate

Society affairs. Closely linked to it was the bloc comprising those Co-operative Women's Guilds whose branches also contained many active Labour supporters.

A less visible but quite distinct bloc was that of Catholic voters. Irish Catholic communities in many British cities had become an important element of the Labour vote. Until 1918 they had supported the Liberals because of their advocacy of Irish Home Rule. This support gradually shifted to Labour after the Irish uprising of 1916 and the setting up of the Irish Free State in 1921. Labour had supported the Irish cause in the military struggle which had preceded the 1921 treaty. It had also supported issues, such as education, in which Irish Catholic communities were interested, and later made deliberate efforts to enlist Irish community leaders.[17] The Catholic vote in RACS should, therefore, not be seen as being purely anti-communist, but also as a token of growing Irish identification with Labour.

There were many aspects of the communist question, including the right of communist RACS members to be nominated for local and Parliamentary elections. The latter question came before the Political Purposes Committee in November 1924 when a Mr J G Clancy was nominated to the RACS Parliamentary Panel. The Political Purposes Committee decided to enquire whether he remained a member of the Communist Party. When he replied that he did, it resolved:

> That in view of the recent decisions of the Labour Party Mr Clancy's nomination be not recommended to the joint meeting with the General and Educational Committees for endorsement. [18]

The Society's mechanism for approving local and parliamentary nominations remained a joint meeting of the General, Education and Political Purposes Committees.

Despite its paradoxical position the RACS had largely settled the communist question by the late 1920s. It did not arise again until the communists changed tactics in the late 1930s and began to advocate a popular front of left-wing organisations. Even then the RACS position did not change, although communists remained active in the Society until its transfer to the South East Retail Group of the Co-operative Wholesale Society in 1985.

The RACS's handling of the communist question reflected the importance that the Society attached to its relations with the Labour Party. Its relations with the wider Co-operative Movement were no less important. Consequently the Society, and its Political Purposes Committee, followed very closely the question of whether the Co-operative Party would also eventually affiliate to the Labour Party, or whether it would restrict itself to an electoral agreement with it.

Co-op/Labour Agreement 1927

Shortly after its formation the Co-operative Party began the practice of organising a meeting or demonstration at annual Co-operative Congresses. Following that held in Edinburgh in 1923, the co-operative journal *Wheatsheaf* commented:

> Someone has said with comic disgust that the worst of the co-operative movement is that you can't name anything they haven't got! They've got everything, from matches to MPs.[19]

The advent of Co-operative MPs, even though they joined the Parliamentary Labour Party, put pressure on the need for there to be some kind of agreement between the Labour and Co-operative Movements. However, the delay in achieving this was due mainly to the difficulties on the co-operative side.

Geoffrey Rhodes, in his study *Co-operative-Labour Relations 1900-1962*, suggests that in the Co-operative Movement at this time there were three main schools of thought on the question.[20] The first held that the Co-operative Party, because it largely shared aims and membership with the Labour Party, should affiliate to it both nationally and locally. Supporters of this view, including the Royal Arsenal Co-operative Society, also argued that there was no room for another left-wing political party, an opinion shared by a number of later commentators. A J Davies in his book *To Build a New Jerusalem* observed of the 1920s that 'The tragedy was ... that no space remained on the British left for any organisations other than the huge and dominant Labour Party and a small Communist Party'. G D H Cole wrote similarly in his centenary history of the British Co-operative Movement in 1944 that 'there was no possible room for a second entirely independent working-class party on a really national scale side by side with the new Labour Party of 1918'.[21]

Some co-operators challenged the view that because 'Co-operators and trade unionists had acted in unison in the industrial field, then why not in the political field?' Instead, they suggested, this view overlooked the fact that the Labour Party often protected the producer interests of trade unions whereas the Co-operative Party was 'pre-eminently a party of consumers'. It should, therefore, be allowed to remain 'perfectly free to act independently in politics'.[22]

The second school of thought, which included the Executive of the Co-operative Party, advocated an alliance with the Labour Party rather than direct affiliation which it feared would effectually merge the two parties. Advocates of an alliance, rather than affiliation, also believed that it could bring the advantages of affiliation while still permitting political relations for electoral purposes.

Supporters of the third school of thought argued against both affiliation and an alliance. They feared that either would damage co-operative independence and unity. Moreover, they suggested that there were fundamental differences between a Labour Party which was becoming increasingly concerned with state forms of socialism, and a Co-operative Movement which had developed from, and was still based on, voluntary action. They, therefore, supported the maintenance of an independent Co-operative Party as a way of pre-empting those co-operative societies, such as Royal Arsenal, that were tempted to affiliate directly to the Labour Party. In addition, they argued that, after ten years of life, the Co-operative Party was functioning well and that it was, therefore, unwise to risk co-operative unity for the small advantages that a more formal alliance might bring.

All these arguments can be traced in the debates at Co-operative Congresses and at Co-operative Party Conferences in the run up to the 1927 Agreement and reflect the complexity of the question. There were also related issues. For example, some co-operative societies had far more uncertain relations with their local Labour Parties than those which applied in RACS. These sometimes made it difficult to achieve local agreements, as one speaker at the 1925 Co-operative Congress at Southport indicated:

> ... the Labour Party realised its duty to the worker as producer long before the Co-operative Movement had realised the necessity of the consumer being recognised in Parliament, and that time did not arrive until we as a Movement had received a shock! When we came along and decided to seek direct representation in Parliament we found that the Labour Party had in many constituencies not only organised the workers, but had secured for them representation in Parliament ... we want to get an arrangement with the Labour Party ... whereby we shall have the freedom in local action without infringing on each other.[23]

The question was also bedeviled by the intervention of Conservative and Liberal co-operative members who objected to closer Co-operative and Labour relations. For example, Mrs E Barton of the Co-operative Women's Guild stated at the 1925 Co-operative Party Conference:

> ... you have prominent Conservatives as Chairmen of political councils in particular towns ... We in Sheffield can prove that other political parties are trying to get into the Co-operative Party to capture the position ... That is why we have this difficulty between ourselves and the Labour people, for they do not know where we are.[24]

Accounts of other attempts at infiltration by Liberals and Conservatives were reminiscent of communist attempts in Royal Arsenal. Even in Woolwich, however, Liberals and Conservatives protested at a possible Co-operative Labour Agreement. In October 1926 a Mr L Lovegrove wrote to *Comradeship* and said that he feared the RACS was more concerned with 'the political and trade union side of things than about co-operation'. He also believed that the motto 'All for each, and each for all' was a sham because RACS's political business was 'preventing a great number of people from joining the movement'.[25] His letter prompted a stronger one two months later from an Emily Rollason who signed herself 'Co-operator since 1880'. She said:

> I wish to endorse every word of the letter signed by L Lovegrove in the October issue ... Co-operation was built up on trading, not on politics which should never have been allowed to creep in and cause dissension. Your meetings are frauds; anyone differing from a Labour point of view has no chance of speaking at your meetings. Where does the motto, 'Each for all, and all for each', come in?
>
> In your educational programme for this month you have Dr Hugh Dalton MP and Dr Haden Guest MP as speakers. Are there no Liberal or Conservative speakers? Do you suppose for one moment that if you had a proper ballot of your members you would get a Labour majority? You get your members by dividends, not by your political views. Half of your members do not know that they are levied for political purposes. I make it my business to tell all I know and get them to object.[26]

There were other letters from non-Labour RACS members in other editions of *Comradeship*. In December, 1927 a John W W Simpson wrote:

> The Socialist policy is dictation, and that is why I say most emphatically that co-operation is not a plank in the Socialist platform. Co-operation is working for one end - mutual understanding with the absence of mistrust and suspicion, and has been a plank in the Liberal platform for years ... Co-operation is here flourishing, thanks largely to the principles of the Liberal Party, which has Liberty as its watchword. We do not want politics in the

co-operative movement, but if politics are necessary let that be the business of a Co-operative Party.[27]

Such letters reflect that, even in RACS, there was a range of opinions about the proposed Co-operative/Labour Agreement.

In the years leading up to the Agreement, the debate ranged at a number of different levels at Co-operative Congresses. One concerned organisation. Problems at local levels obviously influenced the framing of the resolution passed at the 1925 Southport Co-operative Congress by 2,368 votes to 854. This deplored 'the lack of co-ordination among the progressive forces' and urged that there be a 'definite arrangement or agreement with the National Labour Party regarding constituencies etc, and that this would be binding both nationally and locally on the Co-operative and Labour Parties'.[28]

Another level apparent in Congress debates was that concerning future relations between the state and co-operative sectors. We have already noted concern that the Labour Party was increasingly favouring state intervention rather than the traditional voluntaryism and members' democratic control practised in the Co-operative Movement. Throughout the 1920s and 1930s concern about the potential competition between co-operative and state and municipal enterprises was voiced in a number of co-operative debates and pamphlets.[29] For example, Alf Barnes, Chairman of the Co-operative Party, touched upon the question in a speech to a fringe meeting at the 1925 Southport Congress:

> Most of the industries that are ripe for State action are not those that the Co-operative Movement is primarily interested in ... we have only to dwell for a moment on this great range of problems to realise that it will be many years before Socialists bring these industries under common ownership, therefore, the Labour Party will have plenty to occupy itself with, without overlapping the Co-operative Movement ... The more services and industries which Co-operation can be encouraged to bring under common ownership without the principle of

purchase and the capital liability which purchase means, then the more immediate and beneficial the results will be ... One important aspect of Co-operative political representation is to bring this fact home to the Labour Party, and if the Co-operative Movement does not help with its political power we shall find that the workers of this country will move irresistibly more and more along the lines of national and municipal purchase without the knowledge of what contribution the Co-operative Movement can give.[30]

In passing we should note that, in their commitment to the Labour Party, spokespersons for RACS were much further along the road towards accepting state socialism, than many of their contemporaries in the Co-operative Movement. This was particularly true of Joe Reeves and members of the Political Purposes Committee. The point to note is that in the debates leading up to the first Co-op/Labour Agreement there was concern not only about organisational issues, but also about the future boundaries between state and co-operative enterprises.

Moves towards an agreement were hastened by the decision of the 1925 Southport Co-operative Congress to instruct the National Executive of the Co-operative Party to negotiate a 'definite arrangement or agreement with the National Labour Party ...'

At the next year's Congress in Belfast the Co-operative Party reported that, 'Matters have so far developed that your National Committee have submitted draft proposals to the Labour Party for agreement, and several joint meetings with a strong committee of the Labour Party have been held'.[31] These eventually led to a draft agreement which, by the time of the Cheltenham Congress in 1927, had been ratified by the Co-operative and Labour Parties, and also by the Central Board of the Co-operative Union.

The debate at the 1927 was not a mere formality, however. While there were speakers in favour of the draft agreement, there were others who argued the case of political neutrality, and also others who supported various positions in between. The proposed Agreement was set out in the Report of the Central Board to

Congress.[32] At national level it proposed a joint committee to discuss and agree matters of mutual political concern. At local level it proposed that Co-operative Parties and Councils should be eligible to affiliate to Divisional Labour Parties, their representation and voting powers proportionate to the affiliation fees they paid. The Agreement was to be optional upon both local Labour and Co-operative Parties, and was not intended to 'interfere with existing arrangements where Co-operative Societies are already affiliated to the Labour Party, or where an agreement has been established'. The debate revealed that a number of societies, other than Royal Arsenal, were also affiliated to the Labour Party. However, these were not listed and the only one named in the debate was Bristol.[33]

It is interesting to note that although 39 delegates and officials spoke in the debate - six of them women - none came from RACS. Neither had the Society's Political Purposes Committee taken any position on the proposed agreement; its Minutes show that its main preoccupation continued to be the Society's relations with local and Divisional Labour Parties and the London Labour Party. However, *Comradeship* made a number of passing references to Co-operative/Labour relations in the run up to the Cheltenham Congress. In its February 1927 edition Joe Reeves referred to adverse comments in *The Times*. He commented:

> The proposals which the Co-operative Party propose placing before the Cheltenham Congress merely regularise what has been in operation between the two parties for some time ...

He went on to say:

> The proposed arrangement between the two parties makes the Co-operative Party auxiliary to the Labour Party. Although, nationally, an independent party, in actual work it becomes part of the labour movement. Thus, in local affairs, the societies are recommended to affiliate to the Labour Party, and our own Society becomes officially endorsed by the co-operative

87

movement when once the scheme is accepted. By our own method we enter politics without becoming a political party. We use those who have specialised in politics for the advancement of our ideas. Our next move should be to see that they become well-informed in things relating to our general requirements.[34]

Despite the long debates leading up to the Agreement, the Cheltenham Congress endorsed it by the barest of majorities. On a card vote those in favour were 1,960 to 1,843 against, a majority of only 117. This led Reeves to observe in *Comradeship* in July 1927:

> The history of the steps taken by the co-operative movement towards political action is interesting on account of the extreme caution which the political leaders of the movement have had to employ in carrying the movement with them on their journey. Timid to the very last, the movement, by just a bare majority, discards its neutrality in politics and definitely identifies itself with the great Labour Movement.[35]

Apart from such comments RACS seemed to hold aloof from the debate. However, the outcome of it is likely to have influenced its decision to affiliate to the national Labour Party only two months after the Agreement was endorsed at Cheltenham. At its meeting in July 1927 the Committee resolved that 'application be made for affiliation to the Labour Party on the basis of an annual payment of £50'.[36]

The 'bare majority' for the Agreement at the Cheltenham Congress reflects the considerable reservations that large parts of the Co-operative Movement still had about working with the Labour Party. These contrast sharply with RACS's certitude in its relations with the Labour Party. It could be thought that the RACS showed some degree of arrogance at Cheltenham. The fact that not one of its delegates spoke suggests that it felt no need to justify its position or to urge other societies to support the Agreement. The impression thus given is that, on this question,

RACS was prepared to hold to its own course and was not too much concerned whether other societies followed. On the other hand, Joe Reeves's comment about the 'extreme caution which the leaders of the movement have had to employ in carrying the movement with them' on the question, could suggest that RACS delegates felt it wiser to restrain themselves.

Besides what it suggests about the RACS position, the debate on the Cheltenham Agreement reflects current co-operative political preoccupations. Alf Barnes, Chairman of the Co-operative Party, spoke of:

> ... the natural development of the economic power of the Co-operative Movement in the country at large. In other words you cannot have £180,000,000 worth of capital, and you cannot do a trade of £300,000,000 a year in every industry in the country without it causing some trouble somewhere. As private enterprise does not welcome this enormous development of co-operative trade its representatives seek, through their political power in Parliament and through local government, to hamper Co-operation wherever they possibly can.[37]

Barnes also spoke of the coming role of women in politics. The 1927 Representation of the People's Act had just given the vote to all women over the age of 21. He said:

> ... if you had had experience in Parliament you would realise that the work of our Parliamentary Committee depends upon the co-operative voting strength in the country, and if we want to change the constitution in future no movement and no section of democracy has the potential political power that the Co-operative Movement holds. The bulk of our members are women and the purpose of all political organisations is to find out how that fluid women's vote is going to crystallise within the next ten or twenty years. According to the way that crystallises, so the political destiny of this country will be determined and the co-operative

machinery is in daily contact with the best women's movement in the country. Why should we not harmonise in relating co-operative principles to public affairs so that the co-operative vote of the housewife and the trade union vote of the husband combine ten million votes which will produce a Co-operative and Labour Government that is bound to legislate in the interests of the whole people?[38]

Co-operative Congresses have always been the place for serious business. However, their debates occasionally reveal touches of unintentional humour. One occurred in that on the Cheltenham Agreement which took place during a morning and afternoon session. The Congress Report reveals that:

> Immediately he had taken the chair of the afternoon session the PRESIDENT said: It has been suggested to me that delegates, particularly at the back of the hall, cannot hear me. Can you?
> DELEGATES: Yes.
> THE PRESIDENT: Good. Then I must ask you to stop smoking.[39]

The Cheltenham Agreement between the Co-operative Movement and the Labour Party represented the culmination of a long debate in the former. It set the pattern for subsequent Agreements between the two. The Co-operative Movement retained its own political machinery and did not affiliate to the Labour Party. Its constituent co-operative societies, except for a very few such as RACS, similarly did not affiliate nationally to the Labour Party. Instead, their Society Parties joined divisional and later constituency Labour Parties on a similar basis to trade unions. Nationally, the Co-operative Party has remained responsible for the political views of the Co-operative Movement and has reported to its annual Congresses. It administers the Movement's Panel of Parliamentary Candidates whose members are sponsored by Co-operative funds in much the same way that trade union nominees are funded by trade union monies.

Subsequent Agreements have been primarily concerned with electoral arrangements. The basic principles of the 1927 Agreement have provided the framework for these Agreements.

One of the major aims of 1927 and later Agreements has been to secure Labour and Co-operative representation in local government and in Parliament. The first General Election in which the new Agreement became operative was that of 1929. Before examining this it would be helpful to take a brief look at the RACS in the latter years of the 1920s and, in particular, at its relations with the Labour and Co-operative Parties.

Society Affairs and Relations with Labour and Co-operative Parties

The size, success and local impact of the Royal Arsenal Co-operative Society were celebrated in 1927 by a 'Great Co-operative Exhibition'. Organised by the Society, it was held over two weeks and was dubbed 'A Woolwich Wembley'. The actual Wembley had been opened only three years previously, and the use of the name suggests the sheer scale of the Exhibition. Buildings previously used as government stores covering some 15 acres, and purchased by RACS in 1925 and re-named Commonwealth Buildings, were converted into a series of exhibition halls. They included a Hall of Industry in which CWS goods figured; a Handicraft Hall displaying goods from the RACS drapery, tailoring, footwear, mantle and millinery departments; a Homeland Hall illustrating a model bungalow containing CWS and RACS furnishings and paints as well as stands displaying RACS fruit, vegetable, coal and bakery goods. Alongside the last mentioned was the claim that RACS now sold 400,000 2lb loaves weekly. The Exhibition also included a 'Memorial Hospital Pavilion' which housed a small hospital ward and a crèche where visitors could leave their children. Besides these physical exhibits there was also a programme of concerts and lectures, as well as a celebration tea. Greetings were received from various parts of the British Co-operative Movement. A Civic Day included lectures by Harry Snell and Herbert Morrison. There was a mile-long procession of RACS vehicles, brass bands and tableaux arranged by branches of the Co-operative Women's Guild and the Society's

Education Department. Over 100,000 visitors came to the Exhibition, the most notable being HRH the Prince of Wales. In the first six days 13,092 new members joined the Society.[40]

The Great Co-operative Exhibition undoubtedly had lasting impact. In the year that followed 60,216 new members joined the Society which also saw trade increase by £1,894,033.[41] In the next year also the Society celebrated its Diamond Jubilee. The climax of this was a vast gathering of Society members in the Royal Albert Hall on 22nd November 1928. Ramsay MacDonald, Leader of the Labour Party, was one of the main speakers. Another was William Rose, one of the founding members of the Society and its first Secretary. Now 85 years of age he had travelled from the USA to be present and was given a rapturous reception.[42]

Whereas these two events reflected the might of RACS, its spirit was reflected in a far more sombre event a few years later. In 1931 one of the Society's two Assistant Secretaries, F W Scolding, was killed in a railway accident. Writing in *Comradeship* the Society's Secretary, W B Neville, said: 'No other event of recent times in connection with the Society has produced such a spontaneous manifestation of regret ...' That was reflected in Scolding's funeral:

> The cortège left the private chapel at Commonwealth Buildings, Woolwich, where the body of Mr Scolding had been lying, and a great crowd there collected, while equally large crowds lined the streets. Between sixty and seventy cars followed the hearse and the wreaths and other floral tributes numbered upwards of 250.[43]

Such events provide a background against which the Society's political developments were taking place. Until now the Society had provided the Political Purposes Committee with its Secretary and office accommodation. However, in October 1927 the Society's Secretary, W B Neville, wrote to the Political Purposes Committee 'intimating that the services of Mr Cooper and the present office accommodation would not be available after the close of the present half-year'.[44] Writing later in *Comradeship*, F R Cooper, the Committee's first Secretary, said that the change 'had been precipitated by the remarkable growth of the Society during the last year' - namely that of the Great Exhibition. He also said that 'there must come at some stage in the development of the political side when a permanent and full-time secretary would be necessary'.[45] After thanking Mr Cooper for his work the Committee decided to advertise 'for a full-time secretary at a salary not less than the scale laid down for labour party agents'.[46] It also accepted the Society's offer of office accommodation over its 'new Pharmacy Department at 132/134 Powis Street at an inclusive rental'.[47]

One hundred and seventy-one people applied for the position of Political Secretary. On 21st December 1927 the Committee met to short-list six candidates. Of these three were local and three were from other parts of the country.[48] However, only the three local ones were interviewed on 31st December 1927 when the successful candidate was Walter Green. He was appointed at an annual salary of £340.[49] Green had a strong background in local government, having been the first Labour Mayor of Deptford for two years in the early 1920s, and also Leader of that Council's Labour Group for ten years. Green was also a member of RACS and had been a founder member of the Men's Guild in Deptford.

Walter Green was the first of a line of notable Political Secretaries at Royal Arsenal. He was later followed by Edwin Furness, John Cartwright, Richard Balfe, Paul Rossi, Glenys Thornton and Shaun Spiers. He began a tradition that the RACS Political Secretary was also an active politician. Sometimes this was in local and/or national government and, more recently, the European Parliament while sometimes senior positions were also held within the Labour Party.

Besides such internal developments, two external ones occurred during this period which have a considerable bearing on this study. The first, in 1927, was the Committee's recommendation that the Society should affiliate to the national Labour Party. The second was its affiliation to the Co-operative Party in 1930. Together they completed the framework in which the Political Purposes Committee operated for almost the next 70 years.

To varying degrees both were contingent on the Cheltenham

Co-operative Congress of 1927 and its ratification of the Agreement with the Labour Party. As early as July 1927 the Political Purposes Committee received a letter from the Labour Party indicating that it 'would be prepared to receive a definite application from the Society for affiliation and suggesting that the Society should submit its proposals'. The Committee, therefore, resolved 'That application be made for affiliation to the Labour Party on the basis of an annual payment of £50'. This was subsequently reported to the Society's Half-Yearly meeting in October 1927:

> After mature deliberation the committee has taken steps to affiliate to the National Labour Party. The decision of the last Co-operative Congress to ratify an agreement with the Labour Party proved that the movement as a whole was ripe for a step forward, and that it was generally recognised that if political action were to be effective, it could not be undertaken without association with the official Labour organisation. The members of the Society took that view when the present political machinery was set up some years ago, and the committee is confident that the members will endorse its latest action in carrying the sequence of affiliations to its logical conclusion. It is gratifying to know that in accepting the affiliation of the Society, the Labour Party has granted it the status of a national organisation. The committee's delegation to the recent conference at Blackpool was, it is believed, the first time the co-operative movement has been officially represented at a Labour Party Conference.[50]

Several observations should be made about this statement. The first is that the Society's affiliation to the national Labour Party was always likely because it carried forward 'the sequence of affiliations to its logical conclusion'. Second, it had been delayed until the ratification of the national Co-op/Labour Agreement. Third, the affiliation to the Labour Party had brought the Royal Arsenal Society the status of a national organisation within the Labour Party. This had two consequences. The first was that

RACS believed itself to be the representative of the Co-operative Movement within the Labour Party. As the report to the Society's members stated, the Blackpool Conference was the 'first time the co-operative movement has been officially represented at a Labour Party conference'. The second consequence was that a Society candidate could now be nominated for election to the Labour Party's Executive Committee. This right was soon taken up. At the Labour Party Conference in Birmingham in 1928, the Society nominated C H New who became the highest loser with 1,540,000 votes, only 100,000 fewer than the lowest successful nominee.[51]

Relations with the Co-operative Party had also not taken a definite form before the Cheltenham Agreement. Until then RACS had been uncertain whether the Co-operative Party would be absorbed in the Labour Party or relegated in importance in some way. Before the conclusion of the Agreement Joe Reeves had written:

> The Co-operative Party has a special work to do in backward districts, and it has a special point of view to bear upon the deliberations of the Labour Party, but it could never hope to build a party large enough to warrant independent existence. The effect of this decision when ratified by Congress, will be to merge the local Co-operative Councils into the local Labour Parties.[52]

However, the Co-operative Party was not absorbed into the Labour Party. There is some debate about whether it was relegated in importance. Both Carbery[53] and Rhodes shared doubts about its efficacy in the years after the Agreement. Carbery described the period 1930-45 as 'The Wasted Years', characterised by a 'dreadful lack of clarity as to the political philosophy of the Party'. Rhodes agreed, believing that the Co-operative Party had 'developed a programme, but it was a piecemeal one, not ... based on any systematic theory'. Believing that the Co-operative Movement had gone into the Agreement for practical electoral convenience, Rhodes found it surprising that the Co-operative Party had not yet decided its attitude to fundamental issues such as collective and state forms of socialism.

Perhaps one reason for the lack of a coherent co-operative policy was that the Party was finding it necessary to give much of its attention to securing itself organisationally within the Co-operative Movement. The problems it faced in this direction are well outlined by G D H Cole in his *Century of Co-operation*.[54] In this connection it is reasonable to suppose, as G D H Cole does, that the RACS's affiliation to the Labour Party was an embarrassment to the Co-operative Party. While not seeking to change that, the Co-operative Party did, however, begin to campaign to secure the Society's affiliation to itself. The main route it used was through branches of the Co-operative Women's Guild to whom it sent a number of speakers. In early 1926, the Guild's Council passed a resolution urging the affiliation of RACS to the Co-operative Party.

Commenting on these moves in *Comradeship*, Joe Reeves stated that there was 'no reason under the sun why we should not also make a grant to the Co-operative Party'. But, he continued, it would not:

> ... impair our loyal support of the Labour Party. Ultimately there can be only one party for the workers, the Labour Party, and no party can ever hope to build up an electoral machine comparable with the one built up by the Labour Party; but if the co-operative movement is to enter politics seriously the efforts it is now making should be encouraged.[55]

The 'efforts' that Joe Reeves was referring to were those that led up to the Co-op/Labour Agreement the following year. In the meantime, the Co-operative Party's moves through the Guilds in RACS appeared to bear no fruit. In 1928 it therefore made a direct approach to the RACS Political Purposes Committee when it asked it to receive a deputation to discuss affiliation.[56] The Committee agreed and received a high powered deputation at a Special Meeting on 7th November. The deputation included two MPs, A V Alexander, who retained his position of Parliamentary Secretary to the Co-operative Movement's Joint Parliamentary

Committee, and Alf Barnes, together with Mr Riddle, a CWS Director, and S F Perry, the Party Secretary.

Even so there was no immediate outcome to this approach. The Political Purposes Committee merely promised to give 'every consideration ... to the various points raised by the deputation'.[57] However it later decided that its Secretary, Walter Green, should attend the next Annual Conference of the Co-operative Party but only 'as a visitor'.[58] The Committee seemed hesitant to commit itself further until it had sought the views of the Labour Party Executive, although these subsequently proved inconclusive. Declared 'Private and Confidential', the Minutes of the Committee's meeting in April 1929 included the following statement:

> In further considering the application of the deputation from the Co-operative Party that the Society should affiliate to the Party, a letter was received from the National Executive of the Labour Party stating that they were not prepared to advise the Committee on the matter. After careful and prolonged consideration of the matter, and the expression of opinion of every member of the Committee present, the following resolution was carried, and the Secretary instructed to forward a copy to the Secretary of the Co-operative Party.
>
> > We are of the opinion that the decision of the members of this Society to take political action through the method of direct affiliation to the Labour Party was and still is the right course, in the interests of Co-operation, both in National and Local spheres.
> >
> > While recognising the good work which has been done by the Co-operative Party, we believe that such work is only preparatory to political action similar to that taken by the Royal Arsenal Co-operative Society, being adopted by the Co-operative Movement generally.
> >
> > In view of all the circumstances we feel that no useful purpose would be served by any alteration of

our present methods, in the direction of dual affiliation. At the same time we recognise that joint action can be taken where desirable under our present methods, between the Co-operative Party and ourselves.[59]

This position was subsequently endorsed by the Society's Political Council which had evolved from the quarterly meetings of the Society's 'whips' to local Labour Parties. At a meeting of the Council in June 1929 the Political Purposes Committee's position was reported. At the end of a long discussion:

The opinion expressed was unanimously in favour of the course adopted by the committee in deciding that affiliation was not desirable, and that the present method of political activity, in direct association with the Labour Party was preferable'.[60]

As if to underline its loyalty to the Labour Party the following October the Committee voted to increase the Society's annual affiliation fee to the National Labour Party from £250 to £400.[61] At the same time the Political Purposes Committee declined to appoint representatives to the next Annual Conference of the Co-operative Party.[62]

Signs began to appear that unanimity was fraying, however. The decision to send no-one to the Co-operative Party Conference was later rescinded, and two representatives were appointed.[63] There was also a decision to send two further members to the Co-operative Party's Annual Summer School.[64] These were mere straws in the wind. How they coalesced into positive support for Co-operative Party affiliation is not clear. The mechanism through which the RACS position was changed was a sub-committee of the Political Purposes Committee charged with looking into the question of grants and matters such as staff and accommodation.[65] At a meeting of the Political Purposes Committee in July 1930, and under the heading of grants, the sub-committee unanimously proposed affiliation to the Co-operative Party:

That the committee affiliate to the Co-operative Party,

the affiliation fee to commence on a basis of 168,000 members. This having the effect of bringing the amount paid to the Co-operative Party (£350) somewhat near an equality to that paid in affiliation fees to the National and London Labour Parties (£400).

That the decision to affiliate to the Co-operative Party be subject to an undertaking that no attempt be made to secure the establishment of local political councils, or in any other way to seek to alter the present methods of affiliation, and representation on local labour parties, adopted by the Society.[66]

This was agreed and the meaning of the decision was explicit. The Society was to affiliate to the Co-operative Party rather than make a grant as had been previously suggested. However, there was to be no local Co-operative Party organisation in the Society's area: the 'present method of affiliation and representation on local labour parties' was to remain paramount.

By 1930 the framework in which the Committee would operate was clear. It comprised the Society, the Labour Party and the Co-operative Party. The major partners were RACS and the Labour Party. The Co-operative Party was only a minor partner.

The 1929-31 Labour Government

The General Election of May 1929 resulted in a second minority Labour Government with 288 seats, almost 100 more than that with which it had formed the first Labour Government. It was the first General Election the Co-operative Party had contested within the framework of the Cheltenham Agreement. With the agreement of the Labour Party it fielded twelve candidates, nine of whom were elected. In constituencies where there was not a Co-operative candidate, Co-operative members were urged to support Labour candidates.

The resulting minority Labour Government brought leading Co-operative politicians into Government. For the first time one of these, A V Alexander, who became First Lord of the Admiralty, entered the Cabinet. Two others joined the Government: Alf Barnes as a Lord Commissioner of the Treasury and T Henderson as Comptroller of the King's Household; both were Government Whips. R C Morrison and S F Perry became unpaid Parliamentary Private Secretaries to the Prime Minister and the President of the Board of Trade respectively.[67]

RACS's celebration of the victory focused mainly on the success of the Labour Party in its area. The Labour vote in the Society's area had risen by 30 per cent from 279,191 in 1924 to 365,605 five years later. The number of Labour seats held had increased from 10 to 15. *Comradeship* proudly listed the 'Members of the RACS holding responsible positions in the Government': Herbert Morrison, Minister of Transport, Robert Young, Deputy Chairman of the House of Commons, C G Ammon, Civil Lord of the Admiralty and Hugh Dalton, Parliamentary Under-Secretary of State for Foreign Affairs.[68]

It was during the period of the second Labour Government, and after its affiliation to the Co-operative Party, that some ambiguity arose over whether the RACS would retain its own Parliamentary Panel or whether it would move to that of the Co-operative Party. The Society, in fact, began moves to do away with its Panel of Parliamentary Candidates in favour of that of the Co-operative Party in November 1930. The Political Purposes Committee then proposed to the Society's Joint Committee, comprising the Management, Education and Political Committee, that the RACS's existing Parliamentary Panel 'be regarded as ended'.[69] At a later meeting it recommended that 'in future the only Parliamentary Panel to be recognised be that of the Co-operative Party', and that 'a complete list of nominations be submitted to the Joint Committee, not more than three of whom shall be recommended by the PPC as suitable for the Co-operative Party Panel'.[70]

For reasons that are not clear this proposal was not accepted although the Political Purposes Committee was given permission to 'display posters in branches inviting nominations to a Parliamentary Panel'[71] (author's underlining). Despite this apparent setback, the Political Purposes Committee sought advice from the Co-operative Party on the procedures and financial assistance that would be available if candidates from its panel were adopted.[72]

The matter became further confused when, in March 1931, the Political Purposes Committee proposed that T E Williams, one of its members, and a full-time member of the Board of Management, be nominated as a candidate for a by-election in East Woolwich. This had arisen from the elevation of Harry Snell to the House of Lords. Williams's name was submitted 'to the National Committee of Co-operative Party, for their endorsement for submission to East Woolwich and for placing on the Parliamentary Panel of the Co-operative Party'. At the same time RACS nominated Williams directly to the East Woolwich Labour Party, 'in association with Co-operative Party'.[73] However, the East Woolwich Labour Party failed to accept Williams's nomination.[74]

Uncertainty about the status of RACS parliamentary candidates continued. At a meeting of the Society's Joint Committee in March 1931 the names of T E Williams, W H Green, the RACS Political Secretary, and Joe Reeves, the Society's Education Secretary, were approved as members of the Society's 'Panel of members willing to be adopted as Labour Party candidates for Parliament ...'[75] Three weeks later the Political Purposes Committee resolved to submit only the names of Reeves and Green to the Co-operative Party's Parliamentary Panel. After his failure to become adopted at East Woolwich, T E Williams appears to have settled for the Committee's nomination to the National Executive of the Labour Party.[76]

Despite nominating Reeves and Green to the Co-operative Party's Panel, the Political Purposes Committee still seemed to feel some uncertainty on the question. It, therefore, decided to seek an 'interview with the National Executive of the Labour Party to discuss the question of Parliamentary representation, and questions arising from affiliation to the Co-operative Party'. In the meantime, though, Reeves and Green were accepted on to the Co-operative Party's Panel.[77] The outcome of the deputation to the Labour Party Executive is not known. Correspondence and other papers relating to this period no longer survive; it is believed that they were destroyed in the late 1940s. Minutes record that the report of the deputation was merely 'received'. However, it can be deduced from the Political Purposes Committee's later reports and Minutes that some kind of dual arrangement emerged under which the RACS retained its Parliamentary Panel, but in association with the Co-operative Party. In July 1931 *Comradeship* published a report headed 'Our Parliamentary Representatives'. The sub-heading was 'Three RACS Representatives nominated for Parliamentary Panels. An acquisition of strength to the Co-operative Party'. The three were T E Williams, Joe Reeves and Walter Green.[78]

This report suggests that Williams's Parliamentary ambitions had returned, and points also to the existence of two panels. That view is confirmed by a decision of the Political Purposes Committee in September 1931 when it resolved:

> That power be given to sub-committee in case of emergency to carry on the necessary negotiations in connection with the possible adoption of a candidate from our Parliamentary Panel subject to a full report to committee at the earliest moment. That in the event of the committee sanctioning the adoption of one of our candidates the necessary expenses prior to election be paid from the political fund.[79] (author's underlining)

The need to move quickly arose from the collapse of the Labour Government, followed by the formation of a National Government, and the likelihood of an imminent General Election.

In the summer of 1931 the Labour Government had faced problems of rising unemployment caused by a major economic slump. Consequences included a rise in public expenditure and a fall in tax receipts. There was also a rapid fall in Britain's reserves of gold and foreign currency as foreign bankers and financiers sold sterling. The Labour Government was divided on how to overcome the crisis. Unable to reach agreement it resigned in August 1931.

Joe Reeves saw this as a crisis of capitalism. Writing in *Comradeship* he said:

> We are experiencing the greatest, the most unprecedented crisis in the history of capitalism. Because countries are

102

no longer self-contained units, and because we are active members of a world economic system, a crisis in one country has its repercussions throughout the world. The financial difficulties of Germany and the Central European countries are difficulties for all the capitalist world. Anyone who understands the trend of international events of the last decade is suffering from no illusions as to the portents.

We are moving rapidly from crisis to worse crisis. The first crisis was the World War, the second the thieves' treaty of Versailles, the third the slump in 1921, the fourth the price slump of 1929 and now, worst of all, the money crisis of 1931.[80]

Reeves's perception of events was widely shared in the Labour and Co-operative Movements. In attempting to set straight the record of the Labour Government, Walter Green produced a list in *Comradeship* of *Thirty Things the Labour Government has done*. In particular this showed how the Government had attempted to help the workers and the poor.[81]

Within the Co-operative Party the crisis led to fevered activity. A V Alexander, the most senior member of the Co-operative MPs, was one of nine Cabinet Ministers to resign from the Cabinet, declaring that he would not accept the 'dictation' of foreign bankers.[82] Other Co-operative MPs also refused to accept the conditions being imposed on the Government by foreign bankers. S F Perry, the Co-operative Party Secretary, described the political situation during the period between the break up of the Labour Government in August, and the General Election in October, as one of 'unprecedented confusion'. He called an emergency meeting of the Party's National Executive, together with Co-operative MPs, which was held at the Party's summer school at Bangor. At this the Party's National Executive approved the above resignations. It also agreed that the 'Co-operative Members of Parliament should associate themselves with the official Opposition to the Government'.

In the election that followed, A V Alexander lost his seat and returned to his position as Secretary to the Joint Parliamentary

Committee. All but one of the other Co-operative MPs, William Leonard of St. Rollox in Glasgow, also lost their seats.[83] In the landslide against Labour only 52 of the previous 288 Labour MPs were returned. It was not surprising, therefore, that two of the aspiring RACS candidates were also not successful. At the last minute the Cardiff Central Labour Party invited T E Williams to stand for a Cardiff seat. While the RACS Political Purposes Committee agreed to nominate him, and to meet his necessary expenses, the Co-operative Party failed to endorse him.[84] Nevertheless, Williams secured a last minute nomination from the Political Committee of the London Co-operative Society for the Finsbury seat. There he was unsuccessful, as was Joe Reeves who stood at the last moment for the West Woolwich seat. Reeves had been nominated by the RACS Political Purposes Committee[85] which had agreed to meet a third of his election expenses.[86]

Commenting on the result of the election Walter Green observed that while there had been a 'landslide' of lost Labour seats, Labour votes had declined far less from only 8,306,477 to 6,612,230. Other commentators have also observed this point.[87] They have gone on to link it to the fact that, organisationally, the Labour Party was still largely intact. Despite recriminations the Party did not disintegrate.

While looking at the 1929-31 Labour Government we have noted fluidity in the procedures for nominating Co-operative candidates, at least those from RACS. After the election a kind of duality emerged in the Society. Many Labour Parties began adopting their Prospective Parliamentary Candidates and three RACS figures received nominations. These were T E Williams who was re-selected for Finsbury, Joe Reeves who was chosen for Greenwich, and Walter Green who was selected for his home division of Deptford.[88] The RACS Political Purposes Committee was concerned only with the last two, both of whom were endorsed by the Co-operative Party.[89] At a meeting of the Political Purposes Committee in December 1931 the Committee spelt out the financial support that it would give:

> ... when a candidate from the Parliamentary Panel, for whom the committee has undertaken financial

104

responsibility, is adopted by a constituency the following provision shall be made. In place of the grant at present paid in respect of agent and co-operative membership a sum of £150 per year shall be paid to the Labour Party concerned, as a contribution towards agents salary and general propaganda expenses. This grant to be in addition to affiliation fees at present paid ...[90]

Although RACS had retained its Parliamentary Panel it sought Co-operative Party endorsement for the candidates it nominated and supported financially. As *Comradeship* observed with the nominations of Williams, Reeves and Green:

... the committee is pleased to report that each of the three candidates on the Society's Parliamentary Panel, who are also on the Panel of the Co-operative Party, have been adopted.[91]

As well as being renominated for Finsbury, Williams gained election to the Labour Party National Executive at the 1931 Party Conference. He was nominated by the RACS and secured 994,000 votes. The following year his vote increased when he was re-elected with 1,897,000.[92] Thus began a long period when an RACS nominee sat on the Executive Committee of the National Labour Party.

To conclude our study of the impact of the 1931 General Election on RACS we could, perhaps, note the fate of two Parliamentarians who were always closely linked to the Society. One was Herbert Morrison. Although he had moved to Eltham, and had held on to the Woolwich East seat on the London County Council, it had been for Hackney South that he had become MP in 1928. He lost it in 1931 and, for the rest of the 1930s, concentrated on the LCC and the London Labour Party.[93] The other figure was Harry Snell, who had won East Woolwich in 1922 and held it thereafter with increasing majorities. He avoided the fate of many Labour MPs by consequence of having been moved to the House of Lords in March 1931, where he became Parliamentary Under-Secretary of State for India. In his autobiography he gives an insight into the depth of ill-feeling that such moves could prompt, and thus some idea of the opprobrium in which Ramsay MacDonald and Philip Snowdon and others would later be held:

> Attendance at Labour meetings became for the first time an unpleasant experience, and on more than one occasion I was cut, or snubbed, by old associates, regardless of the fact that I had gone to the Lords, not for personal reasons, but to satisfy party as well as constitutional requirements.[94]

Snell remained in the Labour Party. MacDonald and Snowden were expelled.

Moving on from 1931, we should close this Chapter by looking at what was happening in RACS itself and, in particular, at proposals for it to join a Greater London Co-operative Society.

Changing Patterns in Co-operative Trade

By the 1920s a number of people, including Joe Reeves, were becoming concerned about the democratic structures of co-operative societies. There were two main reasons for this concern. The first was that as societies became larger there was a risk that they could become remote from their members thus adversely affecting member loyalty, participation and identification. By the 1930s the democratic structures that had been created almost a century earlier, in quite different conditions, needed to be overhauled. Joe Reeves recognised this to be a problem for RACS but also saw that it had ramifications where co-operatives amalgamated.

In connection with RACS Reeves drew up proposals in a pamphlet published by the RACS Education Committee in 1936. Entitled *New Forms of Government in the Co-operative Movement*, Reeves proposed in this that member sovereignty could be maintained by the creation of Members' Councils to which all the members of a co-operative would belong. The Members' Council in each society would then become the governing body which would formulate policy and elect sub-committees for specific functions such as management, education and politics etc.[95]

Even in RACS Reeves's ideas made little progress. A motion to create a Members' Council in the Society was defeated at quarterly meetings in June 1936. Attempts were then made to introduce the idea through a different route, namely a Rules Revision Committee which reported in 1938. Its proposals, which were adopted at a series of Special General Meetings later that year, were far less radical than Reeves's original ideas. Although they provided for a Members' Council, it was empowered to make only representations or submissions. It was not to become a governing body.[96]

Proposals for new democratic structures, therefore, made little progress. Consequently, they played little part in attempts to create co-operative mergers. The most notable during this period was the attempted amalgamation of the four London co-operative societies - RACS, South Suburban, Enfield Highway and London. Had this succeeded the Greater London Co-operative Society would have been formed.

There was strong support for the proposed merger in important sections of RACS. As early as September 1929 the RACS Education Committee had begun to promote the idea of such a merger. In conjunction with the Society's Guild Council it organised a series of conferences under the heading of 'The Government of Co-operative Societies', the first of which looked at the possible amalgamation of the four London societies. Its main speaker was Alf Barnes, then an MP and Chairman of the Co-operative Party. Until recently he had been the President of the London Co-operative Society, which had resulted from the merger of the Stratford and Edmonton Co-operative Societies in 1920 and joined by the West London Society a year later.[97] At the RACS conference Barnes suggested that the Co-operative Movement needed to develop the 'mobility and rapidity' which were current characteristics of private trade. To achieve them, though, it was necessary for co-operatives to centralise; the greater the number of competing or overlapping groups, the more difficult it was to make quick and vigorous decisions of the kind demanded by modern commerce and production. Barnes also pointed to London's importance as a national centre for business organisations, as well as huge department stores that attracted customers from inside and outside the capital. London co-operatives had so far made little impact on central London's trading. Amalgamation would make them better able to do this. It would also bring other advantages such as a common price policy for basic commodities like bread and milk, an improved dividend policy arising from greater uniformity, and the provision of better services for the consumer. Barnes argued that an improved capital position would make it possible to extend co-operative services to new parts of London:

> The long looked for invasion of the West End and the development on a bigger scale of the catering business would also come within the bounds of practical possibility. A far stronger front could also be presented to any attempts to restrict supplies or boycott the co-operative movement.[98]

Barnes optimistically suggested that an amalgamation of the four societies could be achieved within two years.

A year later, at another conference organised by the RACS Education Committee and Guild Council, Barnes acknowledged that there was a 'general apathy that prevented the consummation of the proposals'. Barnes suggested that 'the live elements of the four societies should get together and create special machinery for advancing the idea'. He placed great responsibility on RACS when he said that:

> Whether the amalgamation would come about depended largely upon the attitude of the RACS membership. The members of the London Society, for instance, had been more attuned to the process of amalgamation, and less likely to oppose a new proposition.[99]

Joe Reeves actively promoted the idea of the amalgamation of the London societies in a number of articles that he wrote in *Comradeship*.[100] But the matter dragged on. At a one-day school in April 1933, Reeves acknowledged that although the Management

Committees of the four societies had been considering the question for 'a number of years', they would only be able to move forward when they felt that they had 'the solid backing' of their members. Moreover, a number of objections had been raised and important among these had been the problem of harmonising the different practices of the four societies.[101]

We have already noted those which existed in RACS. They were paying a double dividend to staff, operating a system of proportional representation in its elections and having a full-time Board of Management. Moreover, RACS was the only one of the four societies that had affiliated directly to the Labour Party. The question of the double dividend looked likely to be the one most easily resolved. Although the three other societies no longer paid a double dividend John Corina, subsequently a notable figure in the RACS and wider Co-operative Movement, estimated that a Greater London Society could afford to continue the RACS practice and still maintain 'a dividend of 1s. 6d.'.[102] There appears to have been little public discussion about the other differences. It is likely, however, that they included that of political organisation and allegiances.

As we have seen, despite its current good relations with the Co-operative Party, RACS's prior political loyalty lay with the Labour Party. Indeed, a condition of its affiliation to the Co-operative Party had been that it would be allowed to continue to organise through local and Divisional Labour Parties. In sharp contrast the Political Committee of the London Co-operative Society continued to give its prior loyalty to the Co-operative Party, and its President, Alf Barnes, was also Chairman of the Co-operative Party. The LCS strongly resisted repeated attempts to persuade it to affiliate to the London Labour Party or to the national Labour Party. Herbert Morrison was associated with a number of these attempts and he was reputed to have had an eye to the £17,000 budget of the LCS Political Committee. When the LCS declined to be 'a milch cow to be milked on behalf of the LLP', Morrison organised a campaign by Labour Party members in LCS to press for a change. This also failed and worsened relations between Morrison and the LCS which protested at his 'underhand' methods. The LCS remained adamant that it would not directly affiliate to the Labour Party[103] and was, therefore, in sharp contrast with RACS.

The question of the possible amalgamation of the four London societies rumbled on during the 1930s. Seventy years later the issues still have contemporary significance. While arguing the need for rationalisation in their own areas, proponents also recognised the need for co-operative rationalisation in other parts of the country. They hoped that a London merger could set an example for societies in other large cities such as Manchester and Glasgow, but also recognised that such mergers would have implications for the Co-operative Wholesale Society.

In trying to sum up the debates over the proposed London merger there is a danger of over-simplification. It could be said, however, that the economic and trading cases for the merger were well made but that the societies lacked the political will to respond to them. One reason for this may have been that inherent in the proposition was the facilitation of expansion of co-operative trading into central London. While this seemed desirable to society leaders it may have been less relevant to ordinary members. It should be remembered that each of the four societies involved had taken root in working class communities on the edge of the metropolis. Three had originally been based on specific industries: RACS on Woolwich Arsenal; London on the London North Eastern Railway at Stratford; and Enfield Highway on the Ordnance at Enfield. Although those early links had weakened in the areas in which the societies were based they were still strongly working class.

It should also be remembered that a tenet of Rochdale Co-operation is that of sharing a common bond, 'namely that of self-interest to join together the means, the energies, and the talents of all for the common benefit of each'[104] (author's underlining). In the early days of each of the London societies members could very readily see how their self-interests were being met through the accessible and visible provision of services, and the tangible rewards of loyalty with the dividend. Generally speaking consumer co-operatives have become less successful as their relevance to members' self-interests have become less apparent. It may well be, therefore, that a reason for the 'apathy' among members to which both Barnes and Reeves referred was that they did not see that extending co-operative trade in central London was relevant to their immediate self interests.

As far as the RACS members were concerned they did not even welcome the chance of a smaller merger between the RACS and the South Suburban Society. A motion proposing this came before the RACS Annual General Meetings in 1934, but was defeated by 694 votes to 1,792 against,[105] even though it 'had been suggested by the Woolwich administration'.[106]

For RACS the debate climaxed in 1937. We have noted how Joe Reeves had argued for the merger. So, too, had William Neville, Secretary of the Society. Indeed, the above comment about the proposed RACS/South Suburban merger came from a letter that he wrote to *Comradeship* in January 1937. Earlier, in 1935, Neville had published *A Metropolitan Survey of Co-operation in London* outlining the economic and trading advantages that he believed would arise from the proposed merger.[107] The 1937 letter mentioned above was his most powerful appeal, however.[108] At the end of it Neville provided a series of tables which showed the relative positions of the four societies on membership, annual trade, capital, reserve funds, investments etc. These are reproduced as an Annex to this Chapter.

The merger failed to materialise and in June 1937 W B Neville resigned as General Secretary of the Royal Arsenal, the Society he had served for over 25 years. The position of General Manager of the London Co-operative Society had become vacant and he accepted an invitation to take it.[109] In 1938, after 20 years at RACS as Education Secretary and Editor of *Comradeship*, Joe Reeves also left. He became the Secretary/Organiser of the Workers' Film Association then being formed as a co-operative by the Trades Union Congress.[110] While neither Neville nor Reeves ever suggested that disappointment over the failed merger influenced their decisions to leave, it seems reasonable to speculate that it did. Both had been prominent advocates of the merger and had been so for a period of over ten years.

The years immediately before the second world war were possibly the high water mark of RACS. Although the Society continued to grow, and was to remain prominent in the British

Co-operative Movement for decades to come, changes were afoot that would eventually transform it and its environment.

The coming war would be the main catalyst for change. As a left-wing people's organisation, RACS had voiced its concerns about the spread of fascism in Italy, Germany, Spain and Austria. In September 1934 the RACS Political Purposes Committee publicised a Manifesto issued by the Joint Committee of the London Labour Party and Trades Council on *Labour and Fascism*.[111] It also joined with the Society in condemning the 'Armaments Race'[112] and in helping refugees from the Spanish Civil War. A number of these were invited to stay at Shornells[113], the country house which RACS had purchased in 1919 as a residential Co-operative Education Centre. In December 1938 the Political Purposes Committee strongly supported the Labour Party's policy on Peace and Security. In connection with this, *Comradeship* published an article by Herbert Morrison on *Labour's Lead for National Security* with the sub-heading 'Economic Anarchy Breeds War; Our Resources Must be Organised for Peace'. In the same edition Walter Green gave a long commentary on the Labour Party policy.[114] Anti-war and pro-peace articles proliferated in *Comradeship* in the countdown to the outbreak of the second world war. In addition the Political Purposes Committee was active in the National Peace Council to which it had first appointed representatives in 1935.[115] It passed resolutions condemning situations like that in Abyssinia in September 1935.[116]

Alongside such activities the Committee's more traditional activities continued. Walter Green had been elected a Labour and Co-operative MP for Deptford in 1935, his Tory opponent being Sir Malcolm Campbell, the holder of many world speed records. Green's majority of 6,892 overturned the Conservative's 1931 majority of 4,314.[117] It had previously been agreed that he would remain the Society's Political Secretary but on a reduced salary. It was thought that 'owing to the considerable amount of leisure available to MPs he would still be able to give considerable time in the Royal Arsenal Society's duties'.[118] Three years later Mrs Jennie Adamson, who had unsuccessfully stood in the 1935 General Election for Dartford, successfully contested the seat in a by-election. Like Walter Green she had been a member of the

RACS's Parliamentary Panel as well as that of the Co-operative Party. Thus, by the close of the inter-war years, and after 17 years of life, the Political Purposes Committee had assisted the return of two MPs and numerous members of the London County Council and local Councillors.

Conclusion

This Chapter has been concerned with RACS's development of significant political relationships that laid down patterns for the next fifty or sixty years. Because there was no merger of the four London Societies, RACS continued to base its political organisation on its affiliation to local, divisional and London Labour Parties. It may not have done so had the merger proceeded. Its affiliation to the national Labour Party took place after the concluding of the Cheltenham Agreement between the Co-operative Movement and Labour Party in 1927. This Agreement paved the way for pressure to be brought on RACS to affiliate also to the Co-operative Party. However, RACS had waited to see whether the Co-operative Party would be absorbed by the Labour Party. Only when it became apparent that it would not, and only after reference to the Labour Party's National Executive Committee, did the RACS affiliate also to the Co-operative Party. Nevertheless RACS's prior loyalty remained with the Labour Party.

ANNEX TO CHAPTER FIVE
REPRODUCTION OF TABLES FROM LETTER OF W B NEVILLE ON RELATIVE POSITIONS OF FOUR LONDON SOCIETIES IN 1936

Statistics Showing the Position of the Four London Societies

TABLE I
TRADE

Society.	Annual Trade.	Period Ending.	Weeks.
	£		
ENFIELD	1,070,104	9th Sept., 1936	53
LONDON	12,843,252	5th Sept., 1936	52
ROYAL ARSENAL	8,319,789	4th Jan., 1936	52
SOUTH SUBURBAN	3,829,468	5th Sept., 1936	52
	£26,062,613		

TABLE II
CAPITAL

Society.	Shares and Interest Accrued.	Loans and Deposits.	Total Members' Capital.	Employees' Superannuation Reserve Fund, Insurance Fund, &c.	Total.
	£	£	£	£	£
ENFIELD	685,611	159,810	845,421	133,023	978,444
LONDON	8,369,919	1,231,039	9,600,958	1,138,100	10,739,058
ROYAL ARSENAL	4,308,295	578,427	4,886,722	1,088,242	5,974,964
SOUTH SUBURBAN	2,565,397	469,676	3,035,073	344,630	3,379,703
	£15,929,222	2,438,952	18,368,174	2,703,995	21,072,169

TABLE III
RESERVE FUNDS
After additions or withdrawals made as a result of the year's working for the period stated in Table I.

Society.	Dividend Equalisation Fund.	Other Funds.	Total Funds.	Percentage to Members' Capital.	Percentage to all Capital, including Superannuation Funds, Insurance Funds, &c.
	£	£	£		
ENFIELD	1,396	74,198	75,594	8·9	7·7
LONDON	100,000	482,107	582,107	6·1	5·4
ROYAL ARSENAL	79,009	634,971	713,980	14·6	11·9
SOUTH SUBURBAN	25,000	167,651	192,651	6·3	5·7
	£205,405	£1,358,927	£1,564,332	8·5	7·4

TABLE IV
ADDITIONS TO RESERVE FUNDS DURING THE YEAR INCLUDING APPROPRIATIONS FROM THE SURPLUS OF THE YEAR STATED IN TABLE I

Society.	Reserve Funds.	Insurance and Death Benefits.	M/C. Funds.	Developments and Estates. &c.	Repairs Funds.	Profit Reserved not Allocated.	Dividend Equalisation Funds Withdrawn.	*Net Additions.
	£	£	£	£	£	£	£	£
ENFIELD	2,449	2,059	859	9,630	—	—	1,036	13,961
LONDON	22,667	—	—	—	—	22,429	—	45,096
ROYAL ARSENAL	24,961	11,878	244	539	—	—	22,547	15,075
SOUTH SUBURBAN	13,640	910	—	—	6,145	—	—	20,695
	£63,717	14,847	1,103	10,169	6,145	22,429	23,583	94,827

* Net additions from, and as a result of, one year's trading only.

TABLE V

LAND, BUILDINGS, FIXTURES, MOTORS AND HORSES
(as per Balance Sheets)

Society.	Total Original Expenditure.	Depreciation and Sales, &c., to date.	Percentage of Original Expenditure Extinguished by Depreciation, &c.
	£	£	
ENFIELD	535,603	263,902	49
LONDON	5,653,415	2,188,067	39
ROYAL ARSENAL	3,205,126	1,214,088	38
SOUTH SUBURBAN	1,477,826	531,077	36
	£10,871,970	4,197,134	39

TABLE VI

INVESTMENTS—MONEY IN LOANS, DEPOSITS AND BANK BALANCES

Society.	Shares.	Loans.	Mortgage.	Cash and Bank Balances.	Estates and House Property.	Halls.	Total.
	£	£	£	£	£	£	£
ENFIELD	97,241	428,519	97,753	17,717	5,976	3,385	650,591
LONDON	1,564,277	4,076,595	1,013,179	228,024	50,742	—	6,932,817
ROYAL ARSENAL	774,288	2,578,616	20,470	111,159	382,586	50,265*	3,917,384
SOUTH SUBURBAN	428,855	1,341,237	552,922	44,906	59,506	—†	2,427,426
	£2,864,661	8,424,967	1,684,324	401,806	498,810	53,650	13,928,218

* Includes " Shornells."
† Value of Halls not carried forward from year to year in the Balance Sheet of South Suburban Society.

TABLE VII

INVESTMENTS IN C.W.S. AND OTHER SECURITIES, AND PERCENTAGE TO CAPITAL

Society.	C.W.S.	Other Investments (including Bank Balances).	Total Investments.	Percentage of Investments to Share and Loan Capital.
	£	£	£	
ENFIELD	465,069	178,912	643,981	76
LONDON	5,416,779	1,516,038	6,932,817	72
ROYAL ARSENAL	3,215,721	692,153	3,907,874	80
SOUTH SUBURBAN	1,135,482	1,288,581	2,424,063	80
	£10,233,051	3,675,684	13,908,735	76

TABLE VIII

CONTRIBUTIONS TO EDUCATIONAL, POLITICAL AND HALLS FUNDS
FOR THE YEAR STATED IN TABLE I

Society.	Educational Grant. (a)	Political Grant. (b)	Halls Fund Grant. (c)	Total. (d)
	£	£	£	£
ENFIELD	1,800	238	283	2,321
LONDON	35,353†	in (a)	3,190	38,543
ROYAL ARSENAL	17,057	7,924	5,400	30,381
SOUTH SUBURBAN	7,727	—*	1,500	9,227
	£61,937	8,162	10,373	80,472

NOTE.—The London Society also contributes ¼d. per £ Sales to *Reynolds* (£13,000 per year).

* Subscription to the Co-operative Party, £281, is not included in this Table. † Includes political grants.

TABLE IX

ANNUAL WAGES AND INSURANCE STAMPS AND R.A.C.S. BONUS ON WAGES

Society.	Wages and Insurance Stamps Total. (a)	Bonus Additional to Wages Charged in (a).
	£	£
ENFIELD	153,368	—
LONDON	2,277,497	—
ROYAL ARSENAL	1,247,307	80,232
SOUTH SUBURBAN	509,315	—
	£4,187,487	80,232

TABLE X

AMOUNT OF BONUS ON WAGES IF PAID BY OTHER SOCIETIES AT THE SAME AVERAGE RATE AS R.A.C.S.

Society.	Amount.	Expressed as Pence per £ Sales.
	£	d.
ENFIELD	9,863	2·1
LONDON	146,520	2·7
SOUTH SUBURBAN	32,762	2·1
	£189,145	2·6

The R.A.C.S. bonus for the year ended January 4th, 1936, was 1s. 6d. per £ on wages paid, but not all wages qualify for bonus under the rules. The actual rate when taken over the whole of the wages was only 1s. 3·4d. per £.

The figure of 1s. 3·4d. is the basis of the above calculation. It is, of course, hypothetical for the reason that Enfield and London societies paid less dividend than the R.A.C.S. The figures are only useful as showing what bonus would have to be paid if the system became general in London, and all societies paid the same dividend rate as mentioned in the calculation.

TABLE XI

CALCULATION OF GRANTS TO EDUCATION, POLITICAL OBJECTS AND HALLS FUND, AND ADJUSTMENTS ON A BASIS COMMON TO THE HIGHEST AMOUNT NOW GRANTED

Society.	Present Grants to Educational, Political and Halls Funds.	Rate per £100 Sales.		Additional Sum Required to Equal 1s. 3·7d. per £100 Sales.
	£	s.	d.	£
ENFIELD	2,321	4	4·0	1,596
LONDON	38,543	6	0·0	8,402
ROYAL ARSENAL	30,381	7	3·7	—
SOUTH SUBURBAN	9,227	4	9·8	4,770
	£80,472		—	£14,768

TABLE XII

ADDITIONAL CHARGES FOR ONE YEAR IF ALL THE SOCIETIES CONTRIBUTED TO "REYNOLDS" ON THE LONDON SOCIETY BASIS FOR THE PERIOD MENTIONED IN TABLE I

Society.	Additional Charges.
	£
ENFIELD	1,115
ROYAL ARSENAL	8,667
SOUTH SUBURBAN	3,990
	£13,772

117

TABLE XIII

MEMBERSHIP AND PURCHASES

Society.	Membership to Begin.	Membership to End.	Mean Membership.	Trade Account Sales.	Purchases per Member per Week.
				£	s. d.
ENFIELD	35,034	37,696	36,365	1,070,104*	11 1
LONDON	574,921	631,464	603,192	12,843,252	8 2
ROYAL ARSENAL	317,624	318,960	318,292	8,319,789	10 1
SOUTH SUBURBAN	149,236	163,442	156,339	3,829,468	9 5
	1,076,815	1,151,562	1,114,188	£26,062,613	9 0

* 53 Weeks.

TABLE XIV

DISTRIBUTIVE AND PRODUCTIVE EXPENSES

Including charges for depreciation and interest

Society.	Distributive Expenses.	Rate per £.	Productive Expenses.	Total Expenses.
	£	s. d.	£	£
ENFIELD	213,859	3 11·9	21,507	235,366
LONDON	2,904,301	4 6·3	610,179	3,514,480
ROYAL ARSENAL	1,424,897	3 5·1	481,737	1,906,634
SOUTH SUBURBAN	685,622	3 7·0	96,303	781,925
	£5,228,679	4 0·1	1,209,726	6,438,405

NOTE.—The figures in this table, whilst being useful as general information, should not be regarded as an absolutely reliable comparison of working expenses. The practice in the societies varies as to splitting the charges between " production " and " distribution." Also it should be very carefully noted that the extent of productive operations undertaken by the respective organisations is not consistent with the sales of the societies.

TABLE XV

AGGREGATION OF DIVIDEND (ON PUBLISHED FIGURES)

Society.	Sales Qualifying for Dividend.	Amount Appropriated for Dividend.	Rate per £.
	£	£	s. d.
ENFIELD	1,048,800	65,550	1 3
LONDON	12,738,800	636,940	1 0
ROYAL ARSENAL	7,962,026	597,152	1 6
SOUTH SUBURBAN	3,812,440	285,933	1 6
	£25,562,066	1,585,575	1 2·9

NOTE.—Royal Arsenal dividend is now 1s. 5d. This reduction has the effect of bringing the average of 1s. 2·9d. down to 1s. 2·6d.

TABLE XVI

THE AMOUNT OF THE RESERVE FUNDS (SEE DETAILS IN TABLE III) EXPRESSED AS PENCE IN RELATION TO DIVIDEND PAID AWAY FOR ONE YEAR

(1d. in the £ on Sales for one year—£109,000)

Society.	Dividend Equalisation Funds.	Cover—for Dividend in Pence.	Other Reserves.	Expressed as Equivalent to the Pence Stated, on Annual Sales.
	£	d.	£	d.
ENFIELD	1,396	0·3	74,198	16·6
LONDON	100,000	1·9	482,107	9·0
ROYAL ARSENAL	79,009	2·3	634,971	18·3
SOUTH SUBURBAN	25,000	1·6	167,651	10·5
	£205,405	1·9	£1,358,927	12·5

NOTE.—Amount required to pay 1d. on the Annual Sales is £109,000. This sum ignores the Woolwich practice of paying to the staff the same rate per £ on wages as is paid on sales.

The above figures indicate that in the Dividend Equalisation Fund the combined societies would have a sum equal to a dividend for one year of 1·9 pence on all sales, whilst the other reserves, though not in practice used for dividend are equal to 12·5 pence in the £ on Annual Sales.

TABLE XVII

CAPITAL USED IN TRADE

Society.	Land and Buildings.	Fixtures, Motors, and other Trade Equipment.	Stock.	Members' Debts, including Mutuality and H.P.	Total.	Annual Trade per £100 of Capital Employed.
	£	£	£	£	£	£
ENFIELD	184,290	78,050	106,131	25,062	393,533	272
LONDON	2,588,180	877,168	744,887	566,790	4,777,025	269
ROYAL ARSENAL	1,284,478	706,560	611,079	358,717	2,960,834	281
SOUTH SUBURBAN	640,240	247,003	253,174	104,843	1,245,260	308
	£4,697,188	1,908,781	1,715,271	1,055,412	9,376,652	278

TABLE XVIII

NOMINAL VALUE OF LAND, BUILDINGS, AND EQUIPMENT, AND DEPRECIATION FOR THE YEAR STATED IN TABLE I

Society.	Land, Buildings, Fixtures, Motors, &c.	Depreciation for Year.
	£	£
ENFIELD	271,701	17,311
LONDON	3,465,348	260,000
ROYAL ARSENAL	1,991,038	116,412
SOUTH SUBURBAN	946,749	70,451
	£6,674,836	464,174

DECEMBER, 1936.   WILLIAM B. NEVILLE.

Notes

References to Minutes are to RACS Minutes held by the CWS SE Archive. *Comradeship* was published by RACS Education Department.

1   Davies, A J, *To Build a New Jerusalem*, Abacus, London, 1996, p.118.

2   Snell, Lord, *Men, Movements and Myself*, J M Dent and Sons Ltd, London, 1936.

3   *Comradeship*, January 1924, p.2.

4   CWS SE Archive, Minutes, Political Purposes Committee, 13 November 1923.

5   *Comradeship*, July 1925, p.iii.

6   *Comradeship*, May 1924, p.ii.

7   *Comradeship*, July 1924, p.ii.

8   Cole, G D H, *A Century of Co-operation*, Co-operative Union Ltd, Manchester, 1944, p.321.

9   Minutes, Political Purposes Committee, 14 October 1924

10   Davies, A J, op. cit., p.147.

11   Ibid., p.154.

12   Donoughue, Bernard and Jones, G W, *Herbert Morrison - Portrait of a Politician*, Weidenfeld and Nicholson, London, 1973, p.98.

13   Minutes, Political Purposes Committee, 13 January 1925.

14   *Comradeship*, January 1927, p.vi.

15   *Comradeship*, December, 1929, p.xv.

16   *Comradeship*, January 1928, p.vii.

17   Phillips, Gordon, *The Rise of the Labour Party 1893-1931*, Lancaster Pamphlets, Routledge, London, p.42.

18   Minutes, Political Purposes Committee, 11 November 1924.

19   *The Wheatsheaf*, July 1923, p.106.

20   Rhodes, Geoffrey W, *Co-operative-Labour Relations 1900-1962*, Co-operative College Paper No 8, 1962, pp.25-27.

21   Cole G D H, op. cit., p.317.

22   Rhodes, Geoffrey W, op. cit., pp.25-26.

23   Ibid., p.29.

24   Ibid., p.28.

25   *Comradeship*, October 1926, p.vi.

26   *Comradeship*, December 1926, p.iv.

27   *Comradeship*, December 1927, p.xviii.

28   Rhodes, Geoffrey W, op. cit., p.29.

29 International Co-operative Alliance, *Results of State Trading*, London 1933. A study of state and municipal enterprises to assess their value, estimate their effect on the Co-operative Movement and to determine a line of demarcation between such enterprises and co-operatives.

30 Rhodes, Geoffrey W, op. cit., p.28.

31 Co-operative Union Ltd, *Report of 1926 Congress, Belfast*, p.94.

32 Co-operative Union Ltd, *Report of 1927 Congress, Cheltenham*, pp.413-433.

33 Ibid., p.414.

34 *Comradeship*, February 1927, p.ii.

35 *Comradeship*, July 1927, p.i.

36 Minutes, Political Purposes Committee, 26 July 1927.

37 Co-operative Union Ltd, *Report of 1927 Congress, Cheltenham*, p.413.

38 Ibid., p.414.

39 Ibid., p.419.

40 *Comradeship*, May 1927, pp.iii-xii.

41 *Comradeship*, April 1928, p.iii.

42 *Comradeship*, December 1928, p.iii.

43 *Comradeship*, November 1931, p.iv and p.vi.

44 Minutes, Political Purposes Committee, 1 November 1927.

45 *Comradeship*, February 1928, p.viii.

46 Minutes, Political Purposes Committee, 1 November 1927.

47 Minutes, Political Purposes Committee, 15 November 1927.

48 Minutes, Political Purposes Committee, 21 December 1927.

49 Minutes, Political Purposes Committee, 31 December 1927.

50 *Comradeship*, January 1928, p.ix.

51 *Comradeship*, November 1928, p.vi.

52 *Comradeship*, December 1926, p.iii.

53 Carbery, Thomas, *Consumers in Politics*, Manchester University Press, Manchester, 1969, pp.35-49, and Rhodes, Geoffrey W, op. cit., pp.32-33.

54 Cole, G D H, op. cit., pp.324-325.

55 *Comradeship*, April 1926, p.ii.

56 Minutes, Political Purposes Committee, 28 August 1928.

57 Ibid.

58 Minutes, Political Purposes Committee, 18 December 1928.

59 Minutes, Political Purposes Committee, 16 April 1929.

60 Minutes, Political Purposes Committee, 1 June 1929.

61 Minutes, Political Purposes Committee, 15 October 1929.

62 Minutes, Political Purposes Committee, 18 February 1930.

63 Minutes, Political Purposes Committee, 12 April 1930.

64 Minutes, Political Purposes Committee, 30 May and 17 June 1930.

65 Minutes, Political Purposes Committee, 17 June 1930.

66 Minutes, Political Purposes Committee, 6 July 1930.

67 Co-operative Union Ltd, *Report of 1930 Congress, York*, pp.95-97.

68 *Comradeship*, July 1929, p.xvi.

69 Minutes, Political Purposes Committee, 18 November 1930.

70 Minutes, Political Purposes Committee, 20 January 1931.

71 Minutes, Political Purposes Committee, 3 February 1931.

72 Minutes, Political Purposes Committee, 17 February 1931.

73 Minutes, Political Purposes Committee, 17 March 1931.

74 *Comradeship*, May 1931, p.xx.

75 CWS SE Archive, Meeting of RACS Joint Committee, 31 March 1931.

76 Minutes, Political Purposes Committee, 21 April 1931.

77 Minutes, Political Purposes Committee, 8 June 1931.

78 *Comradeship*, July 1931, pp.iv and v.

79 Minutes, Political Purposes Committee, 21 September 1931.

80 *Comradeship*, September 1931, p.i.

81 *Comradeship*, August 1931, p.viii.

82 A V Alexander justified his action in an article in *The Co-operative Review* which was reprinted in *Comradeship* in October 1931 under the title of *The Crisis - A Call to Co-operators to Resist Dictation*.

83 Co-operative Union Ltd, *Report of 1932 Congress, Glasgow*, pp.103-105.

84 Minutes, Political Purposes Committee, 29 September 1931.

85 Minutes, Political Purposes Committee, 10 October 1931.

86 Minutes, Political Purposes Committee, 10 November 1931.

87 Phillips, Gordon, op. cit., pp.62-64.

88 *Comradeship*, July 1932, p.xii.

89 Minutes, Political Purposes Committee, 11 January 1932.

90 Minutes, Political Purposes Committee, 14 December 1931.

91 *Comradeship*, July 1932, p.xii.

92 *Comradeship*, December 1931 and November 1932.

93 Donoughue, Bernard and Jones, C W, op. cit., p.180.

94 Snell, Lord, op. cit., p.253.

95 *Comradeship*, November 1935, p.xi.

96 Attfield, John, *With Light of Knowledge*, London, 1981, p.54.

97 Newens, Stan, *Working Together - A Short History of the London Co-op Society Political Committee*, p.6.

98 *Comradeship*, November 1929, p.xi.

99 *Comradeship*, December 1930, p.xxii.

100 *Comradeship*, November 1929, p.i-ii, December 1930, p.xxii, November 1933, p.iii and April 1934, p.xv.

101 *Comradeship*, June 1933, p.vii.

102 *Comradeship*, May 1934, p.xiv.

103 Donoughue, Bernard and Jones, G W, op. cit., pp.211-212.

104 Bonner, Arnold, *British Co-operation*, Co-operative Union Ltd, Manchester, 1961, p.48.

105 *Comradeship*, April 1934, p.xi.

106 *Comradeship*, January 1937, p.iv.

107 Reprinted from *Tradition* and featured in *Comradeship*, July 1935, pp.v-vi.

108 *Comradeship*, January 1937, p.iv.

109 *Comradeship*, July 1937, p.iv.

110 *Comradeship*, September 1938, p.i.

111 *Comradeship*, September 1934, p.vi.

112 *Comradeship*, May 1934, p.xv.

113 *Comradeship*, July 1937, p.xxi.

114 *Comradeship*, December 1938, p.xii. and pp.iii-iv.

115 Minutes, Political Purposes Committee, 14 January 1935.

116 Minutes, Political Purposes Committee, 14 September 1935.

117 *Comradeship*, December 1935, p.1.

118 *Comradeship*, July 1921, p.ii.

CHAPTER SIX

RACS, the Second World War and Labour's Post-War Governments

Introduction

If we look at the war and the immediate post-war years we see that they differed markedly from the inter-war years. As far as this history is concerned, the main difference was that the years 1939 to 1951 saw Labour come to power, first in coalition government and then in two administrations of its own. The period, therefore, forms a distinct background against which to view political changes within the RACS. At the outset we should note the considerable disruption that the war brought to the Society. Although RACS objectives and structures remained unaltered, its environment was considerably affected. The blitz destroyed housing. In the short term this caused a displacement of population through extensive evacuation; in the long term, it led to rebuilt housing often in new forms and new locations, thus changing trading patterns and the Society's catchment area. We should begin, though, by looking at the more immediate problems caused by the war.

Wartime Dislocation to RACS

In the first world war the Society had had to adapt to an influx of workers and customers. This did not happen to nearly the same extent in the second world war. Instead, a loss of trade was threatened by bombing and evacuation displacing people. Moreover, problems of rationing did not arise to the same extent as they had in the 1914-18 war. Although most commodities became scarce, a system of national rationing was introduced soon after Labour joined the wartime coalition government.

Writing in *Comradeship*, Walter Green said that Labour had joined the Government because it had been 'inspired by loyalty to the most vital interests of the workers and concern for the future of socialism'.[1] Those 'vital interests' included fair supplies of foods and basic goods and so a national system of rationing was soon introduced. This helped RACS to avoid introducing its own schemes, as it had in the first world war. The national scheme, which began in 1940, eventually required shoppers to register with particular shops for basic food items. To some extent this froze trade which, in the case of RACS, helped to compensate for the loss of customers through bombing, evacuation and enlistment in the armed forces. Nevertheless, the Society experienced a decline in trade.

Problems in managing this were worsened by difficulties in maintaining the Society's system of distribution. The blitz damaged or destroyed property. At the same time supplies were uncertain or restricted and staff were being mobilised. By the end of 1944, RACS's staff numbered 6,743. Of these only 2,624 were permanent. Most of the others were temporary and covering for those who had been called into the armed services, or drafted into civil defence and other work of national importance.[2]

Besides problems in maintaining its distributive capacity, the Society also had financial difficulties. As early as July 1940 it became apparent that the RACS's trade was being hit by the war and members feared that the dividend of around 1s. 6d. in the £ could not be sustained. At the same time the Society's role as a workers' savings institution was being undermined by competition from National Savings and loans made on 'Government security' which had been introduced to assist the war effort.

It was, therefore, not surprising that, at members' meetings in June 1940, a decrease of 3.91 per cent in members' share accounts was reported. Although the Board attributed this to members leaving the Society's area 'either permanently or temporarily', the decline fuelled rumours of a dividend reduction to 6d. The Society's Chairman, F J Comerton, assured members that their money was as safe in RACS as 'in any financial organisation in this country ... Provided there is no financial collapse ...' He also assured members that the limitation of dividends paid on shareholdings that had recently been proposed by the Chancellor of the Exchequer would not apply to the dividends paid by co-operatives on their members' purchases.[3]

Nevertheless, when sales in 1941 declined by 21.32 per cent, over the corresponding period in the previous year, a dividend of only 6d. in the £ was, in fact, declared.[4] Happily an improvement in sales soon followed, although they were not to return to their previous levels until after the war. In the meantime, it became possible to return the dividend to the more respectable level of 1s. 1d. in the £.[5]

In view of all these difficulties the Political Purposes Committee felt it wise to suggest that the political grant be reduced by one-third.[6] This was not entirely altruistic. The war had reduced political activity. Labour had declared an electoral truce, which the Committee had endorsed in the Society's area.[7] Moreover, it believed that even with a reduced grant it could continue to meet the Society's affiliation fees to local Labour Parties. Grants for electoral purposes could, however, be safely reduced.

Throughout the war the Political Purposes Committee monitored the state of local Labour Parties to which the Society was affiliated. Many of these had difficulties in meeting because of the bombing and the blackout. After dark there could be no street lights and lights within buildings had to be hidden behind black curtains. On top of these difficulties, membership rolls, and lists of delegations, soon became out of date as civilian casualties grew or people were moved elsewhere. At the height of the blitz, Anthony Bingham, who had succeeded Joe Reeves as RACS Education Secretary, wrote:

> It is very difficult for those living outside London to realise the actual extent of the damage to property and the effect upon the lives of the people. Nevertheless, during the past weeks the magnificent spirit of Londoners, trapped in a situation of unparalleled horror, has been an inspiration to the whole country.[8]

The Society's democratic processes were also badly affected.

Sometimes members' meetings could not be held because there was not a quorum.[9] Where this happened the Board of Management, and other committees, could not be held accountable to RACS members. The Society, therefore, sought the advice of the Chief Registrar of Friendly Societies as to what it should do in these circumstances. Recent legislation had empowered him to 'give directions dispensing with or varying any rule or enactment requiring meetings of a society to be held at specified times or periods'. The Chief Registrar could also authorise the continuance in office of officials and committee members, who could be granted the ability to amend rules by the resolution of a committee of management, and the exercise by a management committee of the functions of a co-operative society that would normally be carried out by a meeting of the society.[10] Thus, with the agreement of the Chief Registrar of Friendly Societies, it was decided that the Society's committees, elected in 1939 and including the Political Purposes Committee, would remain in office for the rest of the war.

Political Purposes Committee During the War

Despite all the disruption, the Political Purposes Committee maintained regular meetings throughout the war. However, these tended to be moved from the evenings to Saturday afternoons, particularly during the winter months. Although the Committee continued its customary functions of liaising with local Labour Parties, it also became concerned with war issues, including how the war should be financed. At the beginning of the war a flat rate purchase tax had been proposed but the Labour Party and Co-operative Movement opposed it through the National Council of Labour.[11] Walter Green wrote in *Comradeship* in September 1940 that:

> the bulk of the people are prepared to pay to the point of sacrifice in order that the war may by successfully prosecuted but ... Many of us object altogether to an increase in indirect taxation in any form.[12]

Labour opposition led to changes in the structure of the tax but not its withdrawal. Green regretted that 'Labour did not oppose the tax as a whole',[13] a view held also by Co-operative MPs, the rest of the Co-operative Movement, and the London Vigilance Committee. This comprised representatives of the London Labour Party, the London Trades Council and the metropolitan Co-operative Societies and was set up to monitor war-time domestic conditions in London.[14] Co-operative opposition to purchase tax continued until the 1942 Budget extended exemptions from it but ceased thereafter, although the tax remained unpopular with co-operatives.[15]

Another war-time financial issue was the Keynes Plan which proposed meeting the costs of the war through taxes, partly through borrowing, and partly through deferred pay or compulsory savings by individuals. In March 1940 the Committee organised a Conference to discuss the Keynes proposals at which the main speaker was Barbara Wootton, later Baroness Wootton. The Committee had reservations about the Keynes Plan. Like the Labour Party, it disliked its compulsory saving element which would mean that the burden was not equally distributed. Walter Green wrote: 'At one end of the scale a small section will still be living in great luxury while at the other end many are living in dire poverty'.[16]

The Political Purposes Committee was far more enthusiastic about the Beveridge Report on social security published in December 1942. Walter Green welcomed it and the fact that 'the socialist, co-operative and trade union movements have declared in favour of its general principles'.[17] Throughout 1942 he widely reported the progress of the Beveridge proposals in Parliament, and elsewhere, in *Comradeship*.

The Political Purposes Committee itself organised a number of conferences on the Report[18] at which the main speakers were two MPs, James Griffiths and George Riddley, as well as Morgan Phillips who was then Secretary to the Labour Party's Research Department but was shortly to become the Party's General Secretary. In addition, the Political Purposes Committee organised a petition calling 'for the implementation of the general principles of the Beveridge Report'. In support of this the Management Committee provided tables at the Society's shops, and

Guildswomen collected 24,000 signatures. These were then presented to Clement Attlee, the Deputy Prime Minister.[19] In the House of Commons Walter Green, supported by Manny Shinwell, asked a question about the progress on preparing legislation to implement the Beveridge Report.[20]

Besides questions of how to fund the war and plans for post-war reconstruction, there was also the question of what kind of peace should follow. On this, the Political Purposes Committee fell easily into line behind the Labour Party's policy issued in the early months of the war and summarised as follows in *Comradeship*:

1 No dictated peace.
2 Recognition of the right of each nation to develop its characteristic civilisation.
3 Complete abandonment of armed force as an instrument of policy.
4 Recognition of the right of national, racial and religious minorities.
5 Recognition of an international authority superior to the individual States.
6 Abandonment of Imperialism. There must be equal access for all nations to markets and raw materials.[21]

The Co-operative Movement produced its own peace policy. This was wholly in line with the above but placed greater emphasis on the co-operative contribution to peace. Among other things it declared:

> The existing competitive system cannot give mankind peace, security and social well-being. The Co-operative Movement has, therefore, always sought a new social order based on Co-operation. The history of the last century, and especially the last 25 years, has shown how essential it is that the ideal of a Co-operative Commonwealth must be made a reality if permanent peace is to be assured ...
>
> The experience of the Co-operative Movement

especially in the economic field, convinces us that exaggerated economic nationalism prejudices the welfare of the whole world. The time is fully ripe for a serious attempt to establish a United States of Europe or some form of federal union between erstwhile competing States.

Tariff and other barriers to trade should be immediately reduced ... Economic disarmament should be substituted for the present era of economic nationalism. Nations should maintain close collaboration on all problems of trade, employment, production, and distribution. Freedom of trade and freedom of travel should be added to the other basic liberties of a democratic world ...[22]

Within the Labour Party and RACS, the peace issue became clouded by communist pressures for a Peace Conference and a Second Front in the West by which the German advance on the USSR might be deflected. We have previously noted how RACS, under its policy of open membership, could not exclude communists. This meant that, on these issues, the Society became a vehicle for communist demands. Judging from their actions, it seems likely that two communists, or communist sympathisers, were members of the Political Purposes Committee at this time. Their names were William Trott and Vincent Cheek. Consequently Walter Green, the Committee's Secretary, and the rest of the Committee, were forced into resisting communist moves, just a other parts of the Labour Movement were also doing. As early as January 1941, Walter Green wrote in *Comradeship*:

There are some amongst our people who, for varying reasons, are advocating the calling of a peace conference. We believe they are profoundly mistaken if they think that such a step would produce any result other than a betrayal of the high purpose for which we entered the war.[23]

In the next issue of *Comradeship* Green reported Herbert

Morrison's reply to a question in the House of Commons on other communist proposals for a people's convention. Morrison emphasised that the Communist Party would be organising this and added that 'One of the disadvantages of prohibiting the meeting is that such a course would not be likely to contribute to the enlightenment of those whom the organisers hope to beguile'.[24] At the end of this report Walter Green observed:

> I am frequently asked by guild secretaries whether this or that organisation or appeal originates from a certain source. When endeavouring faithfully to answer such queries, I also advise the inquirers to adopt a policy which has generally been approved by the Political Purposes Committee, that is, only respond to appeals for the appointment of delegates to conferences etc, when those appeals come from either the Labour or Co-operative Parties or the National Council of Labour.[25]

Of the communists or communist sympathisers on the Political Purposes Committee, Trott proposed a resolution at a meeting of the Committee as early as October 1939, calling for an International Peace Conference. It failed to get a seconder and was, therefore, dropped. Cheek was absent. In view of their possible communist sympathies, it is interesting to note that Trott and Cheek were both appointed delegates to the 1940 Co-operative Party Conference.[26] The Political Purposes Committee appointed delegates on a rota system. At one of its meetings in March 1941, the Committee learned that Cheek had been expelled from the Bexley Labour Party because he had attended the People's Convention. The Committee took no action other than to note that it would now be necessary to appoint another Society representative to the Bexley Labour Party. Although expelled from that, Cheek remained a member of the Political Purposes Committee. As such he proposed a motion calling for a Second Front in the West.[27] On this occasion Trott was absent and, there being no seconder, the motion fell.

The strength of communist support within RACS can be gathered from a vote taken at Society members' meetings in June

1943. Once again the Communist Party was trying to affiliate to the Labour Party and a motion supporting this had been proposed. Despite the fact that the Political Purposes Committee read out a statement to each members' meeting opposing the motion, it was passed by 435 to 340. It should be noted, however, that over 900 had attended the meetings. The fact that only 775 voted could have been due to the fact that because of an air raid, a number had left the largest meeting at Woolwich before the vote there was taken.[28]

In any event, it seems likely that the question of Communist affiliation to the Labour Party became confused with popular war-time sympathy for Russia. The strength of this can be judged from the fact that when the National Council of Labour set up a Help for Russia Fund, it received tremendous support from RACS members. Many donated their 'metal checks' on which their dividend would have been computed. In mid-1943 £934 was raised in this way during one four-week period.[29]

Although the Committee became active on some new issues, particularly those relating to the war and the peace to follow, it retained some of its earlier preoccupations. One of these was its relations with the Co-operative Party.

Committee's Relations with the Co-operative Party

Tensions increased once more during the war between the RACS Political Purposes Committee and the Co-operative Party. Just as the 1927 Cheltenham Agreement between the Co-operative Movement and the Labour Party had failed to provide a permanent settlement, so neither had RACS's affiliation to the Co-operative Party in 1930.

The two sets of relationships were linked in various ways. For example the Labour Party had gone on record as stating that 'it has always been the desire of the Labour Party that relations of the two Movements should become so close as to lead to affiliation in some form ...'[30] That had not happened and during the 1930s, relations between the Labour and Co-operative Movements became complicated by questions of the financing of candidates and agents, and who should control and hold accountable the latter. The convoluted course of relations and the failure to reach a satisfactory conclusion before the beginning of the war are admirably charted by Geoffrey Rhodes in his Co-operative College Paper *Co-operative Labour Relations 1900-1962*.[31]

One complicating factor was the Labour Party's continuing attempts to persuade the London Co-operative Society to follow RACS's lead and to affiliate directly. The Labour Party had always hoped that RACS would offer a model which other co-operative societies would follow, and this was more likely to happen if the London Co-operative Society also affiliated. Affiliation to the Labour Party could be shown to have brought benefits to RACS. For example, Walter Green represented it on the Party's Executive. In 1941 he was elected the Labour Party's Chairman and presided over its Annual Conference the following year.[32]

Not only were the Labour Party's attempts to persuade London Co-operative Society members to vote for affiliation unsuccessful but they also provoked a strong reaction. This led to the annual Co-operative Congress at Margate in 1939 passing a resolution expressing 'its opposition' to such moves and calling 'upon all co-operators to give effective resistance to this proposal'.[33] Such a resolution made it less likely that other co-operatives would follow RACS's lead.

Similarly, the Co-operative Party's hopes that when RACS affiliated to it relations would improve also failed to materialise. As Alf Barnes, Co-operative Party Chairman, acknowledged, the Party had hoped 'that time would have modified the agreement reached when RACS affiliated to the Co-operative Party'.[34] In particular, the Co-operative Party had hoped that RACS would follow the pattern of other societies in encouraging Party branches to develop within its area. This had not happened because RACS kept firmly to the agreement that affiliation to the Co-operative Party would not entail this. The main vehicle of its local organisation continued to be local and divisional Labour Parties.

It should be emphasised that, despite their respective disappointments, there were still successful and ongoing relations between the Co-operative Movement and the Labour Party, and between the RACS and the Co-operative Party. Co-operative MPs at Westminster accepted the Labour whip and became part of the Parliamentary Labour Party. Good relations were also assisted by the decision of the 1941 Co-operative Congress that the Co-operative Movement would join the National Council of Labour,[35] previously comprising representatives of the Trades Union Congress, the Labour Party and the Parliamentary Labour Party. Ironically, when the co-operative representatives first took their place they were welcomed on behalf of the Labour Party by Walter Green![36]

Similarly, there had been good ongoing relations between RACS and the Co-operative Party. RACS delegates regularly attended London and national Co-operative Party Conferences. However, tensions arose after the Co-operative Party introduced a new Constitution in 1938 which was designed to take account of the Party's recent organisational development. Initially, the National Committee of the Co-operative Party had comprised representatives drawn from sections of the Co-operative Union together with those from national Co-operative organisations and auxiliaries, as well as societies which had joined the Party and were grouped on a Sectional basis. Provision had not yet been made to include representatives of local Co-operative Parties on the Party's National Committee. However, these were the ones who were now tending to become the most politically active and vocal element in the Party, particularly at the Co-operative Party's Annual Conference. Another reason for updating the Party's Constitution was that it had now been in force over 21 years, and under it, the Annual Conference had no independent or binding power. This remained vested with the Annual Congress of the Co-operative Movement as the Party was still a Department of the Co-operative Union.

Under a new Constitution agreed by the Party Conference and the Annual Co-operative Congress in 1938, however, the Party's relations with the Co-operative Union and the Co-operative Congress were redefined. While the Party remained accountable to both, its Annual Conference was given increased importance through the enlargement of the Party's National Committee which was now to include eight representatives nominated by Society Parties on a sectional basis. This enlarged National Committee would report to the Party's Annual Conference.[37]

Such a development appeared to hold little interest for the RACS Political Purposes Committee. So far, neither it nor the Society had nominated anyone for election to the Party's National Committee, although Joe Reeves had sat on it as a representative of the National Education Executive of the Co-operative Union. Of more concern to RACS was an initiative undertaken by the Party in the wake of its new Constitution which was to attempt to increase the Party's individual membership. It was in connection with this that the Party approached the Political Purposes Committee in December 1940 to ask if it could set up machinery through which it could contact co-operative auxiliaries within RACS.[38] The Committee decided to defer consideration of the matter.[39]

Other issues also remained unsettled. Earlier in July 1940 the Co-operative Party had written to the Political Purposes Committee asking it to reconsider a decision it had taken not to allow Co-operative Party Councils to be set up under the Party's new Constitution. The Committee decided to hinge its reply on whether, under the new Constitution, the Party would recognise the Committee as a Society Party.[40] This was highly unlikely, though, because the Political Purposes Committee encouraged no Party membership or branches. Moreover the Committee itself could hardly be said to constitute a Society Co-operative Party. These inter-related matters dragged on with the Political Purposes Committee threatening to withdraw from the Metropolitan Co-operative Political Federation, comprising delegates from the main London societies, 'until such time as the Co-op Party Executive recognised the Political Purposes Committee as a Society Co-op Party'.[41]

In May 1941, the Committee sought a meeting with the Executive of the Co-operative Party. At this Alf Barnes, the Party's Chairman, outlined the Party's position. It had honoured the agreement under which RACS had affiliated to the Party, but times and conditions had changed and difficulties had arisen as a result. One of these was RACS's failure to conform with the Party's new Constitution and allow Party branches. Another was that RACS had not encouraged links between Guilds in the Society and the Party. A third problem was that RACS continued to maintain its own Parliamentary Panel.

In reply James Newman, Chairman of the Political Purposes Committee, stated that the Committee's actions were bound by the Society's Rules and Standing Orders and these did not provide for the setting up of Party branches in the Society's area. Even if they had he felt that such branches could cause 'chaos, confusion and overlapping'. Walter Green assured the Party Executive that the Committee had tried to overcome the difficulties mentioned by the Party. For example, on the question of the Guilds, it had tried to bring them into closer touch with the Party through the Metropolitan Federation. On the question of RACS's Parliamentary Panel, Green suggested that if the Co-operative Party would endorse the candidatures of Joe Reeves and Mrs Adamson, the Political Purposes Committee would promise, until 'the next General Election, to submit any future candidates to the Co-operative Party for endorsement'. It may be recalled that Mrs Adamson was the MP for Dartford and Joe Reeves was Prospective Candidate for Greenwich. As a member of the RACS Political Committee, Mrs Adamson was present at the meeting. At the time she was also Parliamentary Private Secretary to the Minister of Pensions.

Related to the question of Parliamentary Candidates were the difficulties that Barnes believed had arisen from the 1933 Hastings Agreement. At a wider level these had also proved to be a stumbling block in negotiations between the Labour Party and Co-operative Movement. Of particular difficulty were those aspects dealing with the percentage of costs to be met by sponsoring organisations, and the direction and accountability of Labour Party agents. Green disagreed with Barnes on the supposed problems of the Hastings Agreement. He said that as far as RACS was concerned, the Committee had found that the Agreement 'did not in any possible way interfere with or alter arrangements with regard to finance in operation for many years in the Parliamentary divisions' within the RACS area. In other words, the Committee did not share the difficulty that the Co-operative Party, and the rest of the Co-operative Movement, had with the Hastings Agreement

At the end of the meeting Barnes promised that the Party Executive would consider the points raised, but he had little hope that the Party Executive would agree to endorse RACS Parliamentary candidates.[42] After the meeting there appeared to be little follow up by either side. One reason may have been, as Alf Barnes had said, that a 'settlement was not urgent' because of the 'political lull' caused by the war. Another reason may have been that both sides were shadow boxing with neither having much hope of accommodation; the differences on both sides had become entrenched over the years and yet had been treated with a fair degree of tolerance by either side. It had been the advent of the Co-operative Party's new Constitution, and its attempt to encourage Society Parties and Party branches, that had disturbed those fudged relations.

Neither did the meeting appear to cause changes in the way the Committee worked. Later in 1941 at one of its Conferences, Walter Green urged the Guilds to appoint representatives to local Labour Parties[43] but made no similar appeal on behalf of the Co-operative Party. It is, therefore, perhaps not surprising that when, four months later, S F Perry wrote on behalf of the Party Executive to suggest that discussions 'should stand adjourned till the end of the war without prejudice to either party', the Political Purposes Committee readily agreed.[44]

Some of the questions rumbled on, however, particularly those relating to the issue of affiliation. For example, the Women's Guild at New Cross tried to affiliate to the Co-operative Party but was not accepted because of the 'difficulties' between the Party and the Political Purposes Committee. The Guild then invited Walter Green to attend one of its meetings to explain these difficulties.[45] There was also the question of whether RACS was really affiliated to the Co-operative Party. Reports began circulating within RACS that Percy Harnwell, Political Secretary of the London Co-operative Society, had written to the Abbey Wood Guild stating that RACS was not affiliated to the Co-operative Party. Worried about the 'confusion this would cause in Guild circles, if circulated',[46] the Committee sought a copy of the letter. This, in fact, asserted that 'RACS was not affiliated to the Co-operative Party but the sum paid to that body each half-year was only regarded as a donation',[47] Green quickly wrote to Harnwell objecting to the inaccuracy of his statement.

The episode is interesting because it reveals how others viewed RACS's affiliation to the Co-operative Party, and how sensitive the Committee was on the subject.[48] Both episodes also suggest that the Committee attached considerable importance to the Guilds within RACS. There were two main reasons for this. First, they formed an important constituency in Society elections, including those to the Political Purposes Committee. Second, they also provided many of the Society's representatives to local Labour Parties.

Besides difficulties in its relations with the Co-operative Party, the Committee also found that those with the Society's Management Committee were less close than once they had been, despite the fact that the Management Committee still appointed two of its members. For example, the Management Committee had nominated Alf Barnes for the National Committee of the Co-operative Party without reference to the Political Purposes Committee. The stated reason was that there had not been sufficient time to consult the Committee,[49] but this seems strange given that the Society had delegated its political business to the Political Purposes Committee and that the two committees functioned within the same organisation. On top of that, given the Committee's difficulties, Alf Barnes might not necessarily have been its choice.

Another example of relations being less close between the Management and Political Purposes Committees came shortly afterwards, at the Co-operative Party's Annual Conference. At this a member of the Management Committee intervened in a debate contrary to the line agreed by the Political Purposes Committee. This episode led the angry Committee to seek a meeting with the Management Committee to ask for a reconsideration of 'the procedure to be followed at future Conferences of the Co-operative Party and other political Conferences by delegates representing it and other committees of the Society'.[50]

Generally speaking, though, the Committee's views on a political issue prevailed. For example, when the Management Committee suggested that the Society should raise again the issue of whether the Co-operative Party should affiliate to the Labour

Party,[51] the Political Purposes Committee managed to persuade it that it was 'inadvisable to raise this important matter at the present time'.[52]

Nevertheless, the question of whether RACS should seek to encourage the Co-operative Party's affiliation to the Labour Party soon became caught up with renewed negotiations between the Party and the RACS Political Purposes Committee. In early 1944 the Party Executive had sought a meeting with the Committee. Its main purpose was to discuss once more the setting up of local Co-operative Party organisation in RACS's area. Alf Barnes began by saying that he had hoped that time would have 'modified the agreement reached when RACS affiliated'. However this had not happened and now new difficulties had arisen from the fact that some 70 people had requested Party organisation in the Society. The Society through its Political Purposes Committee had failed to respond to these requests, and was thus the only one failing to observe Congress decisions on Co-operative Party development. Barnes continued that the Co-operative Party 'could not agree to the indefinite continuance of such a position'.[53] From this it can be deduced that the Party's position had hardened, perhaps to head off renewed calls for its affiliation to the Labour Party but, more likely, in anticipation of the negotiations for a new Co-op/Labour Agreement that would resume after the war.

During the meeting the eight of the twelve members of the Political Purposes Committee present remained intransigent, largely repeating their previous arguments: the setting up of Co-operative Party organisation would cause dissension; it would be against RACS Rules and members were unlikely to agree to changes; and the Committee itself should be recognised as the Co-operative Party in the Society's area. The only new argument was that, in view of the Society's 'unusual position politically', the Co-operative Party should treat the Committee under the section of its constitution which allowed for 'Special Circumstances'. In closing for the Committee, its Chairman, James Newman, suggested that as many as 600 local Co-operative Parties could be set up in the Society's area but they would be, 'If not in opposition to local Labour Parties, at least ostensibly existing for the same purpose'.[54] It would appear that this was the crux of the position as far as the Committee were concerned. For over 20 years they had directed their political capital towards the Labour Party, and this was now proving too big an investment to jeopardise.

While this might seem a reasonable argument in the political context of south-east London, it was at odds with Co-operative Party experience in other metropolitan co-operatives; also in the rest of the Co-operative Movement where individual Party membership was increasing. Until the 1938 Constitution the only membership category provided for was that of affiliated co-operative societies. In 1944 this stood at 82.5 per cent of UK Co-operative membership or 7,392,242 members.[55] In practice, however, individual members did join and, as we have noted, these were becoming the most vocal and politically active parts of the Co-operative Party. The 1938 Constitution had been intended to recognise this and to make provision for them so as to encourage an increase in their number throughout the Movement. Even in RACS there was an apparent demand for local Co-operative Party organisation, which the Society was not allowing.

At this point we should perhaps remind ourselves that RACS had proved that it could sustain, over long years, a distinct position on a number of issues such as paying a bonus to labour, creating a full-time Board, and instituting a system of proportional representation in Society elections. It was, therefore, reasonable to expect that, given its local traditions and local electoral strength, it could also maintain a political tradition slightly at variance with that of the rest of the Movement.

It should be emphasised, however, that it was a slight variance. The Co-operative Movement conducted its relations with the Labour Movement at one remove through the alliance and electoral arrangement of the Cheltenham Agreement. It had also joined the National Council of Labour in 1940.[56] Royal Arsenal, on the other hand, had affiliated directly to the Labour Party. The difference might only be a matter of degree but it had considerable implications for what kind of organisation should exist at local level, and whether a secondary left-wing party should seek individual members within a co-operative society.

With this kind of background it is perhaps not surprising that there was no satisfactory outcome to the meeting between the Co-operative Party Executive and the RACS Political Purposes Committee in February 1944. Soon after that, moves began to renew Co-op/Labour negotiations which had been suspended 'for the period of the war'. This had been, though, 'on the understanding that the position of the Co-operative Party in relation to the Labour Party should be that applying prior to 1933', and that this should be held until normal electioneering could begin again.[57]

In 1944 the Co-operative Party suggested that the time had come to resume negotiations because the absence of an agreement could prove 'inimical' to both the Labour and Co-operative Parties. It is likely that before restarting discussions the Party had hoped to bring RACS into line with other co-operative societies. Quite apart from the question of unanimity, RACS provided a precedent that encouraged Labour politicians, such as Herbert Morrison, to believe that other co-operative societies might also be persuaded to affiliate directly to the Labour Party. We have noted the ill-feeling that Morrison aroused by his attempts to appeal directly to members of the London Co-operative Society.

Returning, though, to the question of RACS/Co-op Party relations we should note that the Political Purposes Committee, after its meeting with the Party Executive in February 1944, wrote to the Party reaffirming its position. The Committee was not prepared to become responsible for the setting up of local Co-operative Parties nor, indeed, to recognise them. It would only allow them to be set up if the Co-operative Party recognised it as a Society Party which covered the whole of the RACS area.[58] There was still failure to agree and the Committee wrote:

> For reasons given in our letter of 24th April we are still of the opinion that not only would it be undesirable for us to operate Section A rules of your Constitution but under our Society's Standing Orders we have no power to do so.
>
> We are reluctantly forced to the conclusion that as

your Executive are not able to accept our Society's Rules and Standing Orders and as we are unable to fall in with the wishes of your Executive, the wiser course will be to leave matters as they are, and while recognising the differences between us, continue the friendly relations which have existed in the past.[59]

The suggestion 'to leave matters as they are' was hardly realistic. With an eye to the coming Co-op/Labour negotiations, both the Co-operative Party and the RACS Political Purposes Committee were trying to get each other to shift. Indeed, far from leaving matters as they were, the RACS Political Purposes Committee began another move in a new direction.

It started with a joint meeting with the Society's Management Committee. This decided that the Political Purposes Committee should publish a statement 'outlining the methods of the Society's political activity and stressing the desirability of direct affiliation to the Labour Party'. Moreover, copies of the statement should be sent to all the national organisations within the Co-operative Movement as well as to 'members of the National Executive of the Co-operative Party, Secretaries of Federations and Co-operative Parties, Secretaries of all Retail Societies in the country, Secretaries of RACS Guilds and Labour Parties' to which RACS was affiliated. The statement was also to be included in the Committee's Report to the coming RACS members' meetings. In addition, the joint meeting decided that the Society would submit 'a motion in favour of affiliation to Labour Party' to the next Co-operative Party Conference.[60]

The report, submitted to all RACS members' meetings, was accepted,[61] thus giving greater weight to the RACS motion submitted to the 1945 Conference of the Co-operative Party. This read:

> This Conference, recognising that in regard to politics and industry people can be divided into two main classes
> 1   Those who believe in the profit motive as a primary factor in wealth production, and who support monopoly, cartelisation, and production planned not for abundance but maximum profits;

142

2   Those who believe in co-operation and socialism and
     the planning of industry for the production of
     abundance;
expresses its opinion that, in order to plan successfully
for abundance and to ensure the rightful position of the
consumers' co-operative movement in the post-war
world, the co-operative movement and the Labour Party
should be in close alliance, that the Co-operative Party
should affiliate to the Labour Party, and that negotiations
to discuss the conditions of affiliation should take place
without delay.

At the Co-operative Party Conference this motion was headed
off by an amendment which read:

This Conference calls upon the Co-operative Party
Executive to take all immediate practical steps to negotiate
with the Labour Party such modifications of the
Cheltenham Agreement as seem desirable in the light of
experience and practice. It, therefore, welcomes the
decision of the National Co-operative Authority[62] to
reopen negotiations with the Labour Party on a basis
which will ensure (1) the continued unity of the co-
operative movement (2) the further development of the
Co-operative Party as a body primarily responsible to
the Co-operative movement, and (3) effective co-operation
and the maximum agreement between the two parties
on the political field.

This amendment, supported by the National Committee of the
Co-operative Party, was not merely intended to head off the
original motion but to leave it dead in the water. That intention
was realised when it was carried by 5,488,000 votes to 1,247,000.[64]
Inasmuch as this vote was reported to, and accepted by, the
annual Co-operative Congress in Nottingham in 1945, it became
official co-operative policy on the eve of negotiations with the
Labour Party.
    These led to the conclusion of a new Agreement in 1946.

Again, this fell short of direct national affiliation by the Co-operative Movement to the Labour Party. Instead the Co-operative Party was now to 'encourage the affiliation of the electoral units of the Co-operative Party to the Labour Party'. Local units were not defined as co-operative societies or society parties, but rather the constituency parties formed under societies' rules. The co-operative aim appeared to be not so much the strengthening of local Labour Parties, as it had consistently been in RACS from 1922, but the improvement of co-operatives' ability to nominate Co-operative Parliamentary candidates to Labour selection conferences.

A pamphlet, published by the Co-operative Party to help explain the new Agreement, suggested that it had five advantages. First, it could help to avoid local frictions. Second, it provided the right of co-operative representation on Labour Parties' governing bodies. Third, it offered rights of nominating for Parliamentary and local elections. Fourth, it enabled nomination of co-operative candidates for office within local Labour Parties, and fifth, it conferred the right for Co-operative Constituency Parties to assist in Labour policy making.[65]

The new framework for Co-operative/Labour relations left unchanged RACS's relations with the Labour Party. It also had little bearing on RACS's relations with the Co-operative Party. For the time being these followed the course suggested by RACS in June 1944: '... to leave matters as they are, and while recognising the differences between us, continue the friendly relations which have existed in the past'.

By the time the new Co-op/Labour Agreement had been concluded the 1945 General Election had been held. It proved a triumph for Labour and led to the first majority Labour Government. Before examining the role of RACS in this, and its relations with the new Labour Government, we should conclude consideration of the war years by noting their effect on members of the RACS Political Purposes Committee.

Personal and Personnel Matters

Throughout the war the Political Purposes Committee held regular meetings. Their Minutes give some insight into the effects of the war on Committee members. None escaped its dangers and dislocation but some fared worse than others. For example, James Newman, the Committee's Chairman, had his home bombed four times,[66] and Mrs Trueman, a Committee member, was injured in an air raid.[67] Jennie Adamson MP, a member of the Committee, had a son in the Air Force. In June 1943 the Committee congratulated her on his being decorated with the DFM.[68] A year later they were commiserating with her on his being killed in action and her home being bombed.[69] Shortly after the war her husband also died.[70] Originally elected to Parliament for the Dartford Division, Jennie Adamson was to be re-elected in 1945 for the newly formed Bexley Constituency. Shortly after her husband's death, though, she resigned to become deputy chairman of the Assistance Board. Within a few months of that she retired from the Political Purposes Committee on which she had served for 13 years.

The Committee was also to lose other senior and long-standing members. Shortly after the war its Chairman, Councillor James Newman, a member for nearly 24 years, and Mrs Chapman and Mrs Truman all retired.[71] Together with Mrs Adamson's retirement this meant that a third of the Committee had departed. Thus, the post-war Committee was likely to be different from that in the inter-war years. This prospect was also underlined by the imminent departure of Walter Green and the appointment of a new Political Secretary.

In March 1943 Walter Green had reached retirement age. At that point the Political Purposes Committee unanimously agreed that he should retire but they immediately reappointed him as Secretary in a 'temporary capacity' until the end of the war.[72] In January 1945 Green also announced that he would not contest the Deptford constituency in the coming General Election.[73] To mark the end of his political career the Borough of Deptford conferred on him the Freedom of the Borough.[74]

That the old order was changing was underlined, shortly after the war, by the death of Charles Grinling at the age of 86.[75] He had been the Committee's first Chairman for three years. He had also served on the Special Political Committee whose report had led to the setting up of the Political Purposes Committee in

1922, and to the Society's affiliation to the Labour Party. As the war came to an end, however, the RACS Political Purposes Committee was preparing for the General Election that must follow.

The 1945 General Election

In March 1945 the Political Purposes Committee decided to limit its financial responsibility to four Parliamentary Candidates.[76] These would be Mrs Adamson and Joe Reeves from the pre-war panel plus Mr H Berry and Herbert Morrison who would go on Panel A. One further name, Mr T C Pannel, went on to a new panel, Panel B. The Committee agreed:

> That in respect of those placed in Section A, financial responsibility be undertaken by the Committee within the limits laid down by the Hastings Agreement in operation at the time of the General Election. With regard to those placed on Panel B, the Committee does not necessarily assume any financial responsibility in respect of their candidatures adopted.
>
> In each case the nominee before being placed on the Panel, must either be endorsed by the National Executive of the Labour Party, or placed by them on their panel ...[77]

Three points should be noted here. The first is that no reference is made to Co-operative Party endorsement; acceptability by the Labour Party was the chief consideration. Second, the conditions were to be under the Hastings Agreement, the Agreement with which the Co-operative Party and the wider Co-operative Movement had had much difficulty. Third, one of the four candidates was to be Herbert Morrison.

Morrison had decided to leave South Hackney for East Lewisham[78] where he lived. RACS's nomination of him, and his subsequent selection, strengthened still further his links with the Society. To some extent this was ironic because Morrison was a strong advocate of municipal and state ownership rather than of co-operative collective social ownership. RACS, on the other hand, was still a leading example of Co-operation. Nevertheless, its

146

Political Purposes Committee, and the Parliamentary Candidates it sponsored, were strongly identified with state socialism. Such a dichotomy had arisen from the left-wing culture of the inter-war years and was reinforced by RACS's strengthened political organisation. The latter was reflected in the tribute that F R Cooper, the Society's first part-time Political Secretary, wrote to Walter Green on his retirement:

> When Walter Green accepted the appointment there was nothing to be seen of the edifice which was to arise in the next few years. Indeed, the original committee members had to proceed warily, almost stealthily, lest the imagined prejudices of those who did not approve of the society 'going into politics', might be aroused to the detriment of the society's trade.[79]

Given the Society's strength in the inter-war years it did not seem that its politics adversely affected its trade. Indeed, the two seemed to go remarkably well in hand. The 1945 General Election illustrated this. All four of its main candidates were elected: Herbert Morrison for East Lewisham, Mrs Adamson for Bexley, Joe Reeves for Greenwich and H Berry for West Woolwich. Triumphantly, Walter Green wrote that 'Labour now marches towards the Socialist State ...'[80] Labour had won 393 seats against the Conservatives' 213. Only two of the latter survived in the RACS's area which now produced six senior Ministers in the new Labour Government - Herbert Morrison, Ernest Bevin, George Isaacs, Lewis Silkin, Ben Smith and John Wilmot - and two Parliamentary Secretaries, George Strauss and Jennie Adamson. Moreover, the swing to Labour was sustained in the Society's area when, in the following November, local elections also produced 'colossal victories'. Nearly all the Society's 130 candidates were elected, and eight of them went on to become Mayors of their boroughs.[81]

In the General Election the Co-operative Party achieved its highest number of MPs before those gained at the 1997 General Election. In 1945 23 Labour/Co-operative candidates were elected, including Alf Barnes, who became Minister of Transport, and A V Alexander, who remained First Lord of the Admiralty, but who was later to move to the Ministry of Defence.[82]

The course of the 1945 Labour Government has been well recorded elsewhere. Our prime concern is with its impact on the Royal Arsenal Co-operative Society's Political Purposes Committee. This, like the rest of the Labour Movement, had to adapt to a new and heady situation. Against expectations there was a Labour Government that, unlike its predecessors, had a massive majority and which was, therefore, likely to complete its term of office. The elation felt by many was well captured by Hugh Dalton, who had lectured frequently in RACS during the inter-war years, and had also written in *Comradeship*. Dalton recorded:

> That first sensation, tingling and triumphant, was of a new society to be built, and we had the power to build it. There was exhilaration among us, joy and hope, determination and confidence. We felt exalted, dedicated, walking on air, walking with destiny.[83]

While the Labour Government got on with building the welfare state and struggling with the economic aftermath of the war, Labour Party activists had to adapt to being a part of government rather than one of opposition. There had already been some adjustments during the war-time coalition, but greater demands on loyalty were made in the later 1940s when the economy worsened, rationing continued for longer than expected, and the Cold War developed. The RACS Political Purposes Committee adapted well from opposition to government. In the post-war years, it built up a reputation for being centre-right in Labour politics despite having an active left-wing element in its membership.

Its parent organisation, the Royal Arsenal Co-operative Society, also had to make post-war adjustments. Over 2,500 of its 3,269 employees mobilised in the war effort returned to the Society's employment and had to be reassimilated. The Society gave them a warm reception, holding welcome-home parties for over 2,200 at Tooting, Peckham and Woolwich. At each an MP who was prominent in the Society spoke, including Herbert Morrison and Joe Reeves.[84]

In addition to these adjustments Walter Green was now able to retire. His successor was to be Edwin Furness who came from outside the Society. Throughout what was now becoming a long history, RACS had been prepared to appoint officials from elsewhere in the Co-operative Movement. Notable examples had been the General Secretary, W B Neville, from Nottinghamshire, and the Education Secretary, Arthur Hainsworth, from Yorkshire. Furness came from Manchester and his move to Woolwich began in late 1945 when the post of Political Secretary was advertised in the *Co-operative News* and the *Labour Organiser*.[85]

The Political Purposes Committee had already agreed that the starting salary should be £400, rising to £500 by annual increments of £25, together with the 'prevailing Co-operative war bonus'. It had also appointed a sub-committee to make a short-list of at least six candidates.[86] The full Committee also set other terms and conditions which reflected a change. For example, the hours of the new Political Secretary were to be 9.30am to 4.30pm Monday to Friday and the appointment was to 'be regarded as one demanding full-time service. The person appointed shall devote such full-time service to the position. No appointment or service shall be undertaken which interferes with this principle'.[87]

Walter Green's position had become less than full time with his local government and Parliamentary responsibilities and service on the Labour Party Executive. Nevertheless, there had never been signs of dissatisfaction with his position as it had evolved. He had undoubtedly done all that had been asked of him, and had also proved to be a lively and frequent political columnist in *Comradeship*. Sixty applications to succeed him were received. Of the six shortlisted only two came from the Society's area; the other four came from Manchester, Warrington, Leicester and West Bromwich. Their ages ranged from 31 to 43.[88] Furness was the oldest. On 15th December 1945 he was appointed by a meeting of the Political Purposes Committee that was also attended by the Society's Chairman and Secretary.

Furness brought with him a distinction that was then fairly rare among co-operative officials, namely a degree. He had graduated in Economics at Leeds University in 1931 and had subsequently served as a WEA class tutor. His work before joining the army during the war had been as secretary and chief agent to the City of Manchester Labour Party. He took up his appointment at RACS in February 1946, at about the time that electoral activity in RACS was able to resume.

We have already noted that departures from the Political Purposes Committee created clear vacancies. In 1946 the new Committee members elected directly by RACS members included Joe Reeves, now MP for Greenwich who was proposed by F R Cooper, the Committee's first Secretary. Elected also was Jeremiah Duggan, who had been a member of the Society 10 years but whose previous voluntary activities had been in trade unions. Another elected for the first time in 1946 was Mrs Shade. A member of the Society for 26 years she had a rich background in the Co-operative Women's Guild, the National Union of Distributive and Allied Workers and the Labour Party. It is interesting to note also that in the 1947 elections a new candidate was John Cox. He had been an RACS member for 17 years but with no previous committee experience in the Society, although he had been heavily involved in the Labour Party in East Lewisham and had the distinction of being proposed by H Morrison and J Adamson. The former was presumably Herbert Morrison, in view of the East Lewisham link, and the latter Jennie Adamson who had just resigned from the Committee. It was likely, therefore, that with such backers John Cox was to the centre of the Labour Party rather than the left.

Another new member was Walter Spencer. Like other new members he had been a long-time member of the Society but not previously a member of any of its committees. He had, however, taken a number of Co-operative Union examinations and had been active in the National Guild of Co-operators, as well as a trade union member for 26 years. His subsequent actions in the Political Purposes Committee, and those of Jeremiah Duggan, suggest that they were members, or sympathisers, of the Communist Party. Cheek, who had previously been identified as such, also returned briefly to the Committee after demobilisation from the RAF.[89]

Besides a third of the Committee's membership changing, its Chairman also changed. First Jennie Adamson was elected following James Newman's retirement.[90] Then, when she left the Committee, Mrs E V Coyle became the Committee's Chairman.[91]

In addition to these changes, the end of the blackout meant that the Committee could return to monthly evening meetings. Then, in May 1946 the Committee decided to reconstitute the Society's Parliamentary Panel[92] and to increase its number to six, including the three remaining MPs, Morrison, Reeves and Berry. New financial arrangements were agreed:

> That no RACS candidate be sponsored in any Parliamentary division unless 75% of such a division is within our trading area.
>
> That for the next Parliamentary General Election or by-election our grant on behalf of RACS candidates be not more than £250 and that the organisation grant be £50 each half-year, with a further £20 grant on the employment of a full-time agent. This information be given forthwith to sitting Members.[93]

It was also decided that the Panel would be unified rather than having Panels A and B. In November 1946, after a due process of nomination, three names were added to the Parliamentary Panel: John Corina, a member of the RACS Board of Management and recently elected Vice Chairman of the Co-operative Union,[94] Alderman T C Pannel and Arthur Skeffington.[95]

For the existing RACS Labour MPs it had been assumed that they would be considered part of the Co-operative Parliamentary Group. This proved not to be the case and when, in December 1945, the Co-operative Wholesale Society invited Co-operative Members of Parliament to a lunch but 'ignored the four RACS representatives' the Political Purposes Committee protested to the Wholesale. Thereafter, an informal arrangement developed under which RACS Members could attend meetings of the Co-operative Parliamentary Group but as observers and not as full members.

However, the Committee's protest to the CWS earned a

rebuke from F G Burch, RACS's Secretary, because it had not been sent through the Society's Management Committee. Burch reminded the Committee that that was the correct route for any correspondence with the CWS.[96] While this underlined the fact that the Political Purposes Committees was junior to the Management Committee, the Committee began to assume greater importance in providing links between the Management Committee and local authorities in the Society's area.

Such links became important as the new Labour Government increasingly used local authorities to step up post-war house building, local planning and development. Since the inception of the Political Purposes Committee, RACS had had institutional links with local Labour Parties, but now it began to develop a wider approach in its relations with councillors. In addition to the customary periodic conferences which brought together members of the Management and Political Purposes Committee with the Society's representatives to local Labour Parties, their whips, and local councillors, the Committee began to organise social events. One kind was the Annual Reunion for 'those serving the Co-operative and Labour Movements' that had been held before war and was resumed in June 1947. That was held at Shornells, the Society's Adult Education Centre at Abbey Wood where 'Tea was served on the lawn while the Catford Co-operative Orchestra' played and members of the Management and Political Committees, together with the Society's Parliamentary Panel, met with mayors in the Society's area.[97]

In addition to these Reunions a new type of gathering was also held. This was a Dinner/Meeting and the first, for County Councillors, was also held in 1947. For this it was agreed 'That a hot dinner be arranged ... That wines and beer be available at the Dinner ... That a printed programme be got out for this Dinner/Meeting'.[98] During this time little wine was drunk by the working classes. Neither did many have cars, even fewer chauffeur-driven ones. Yet, during this period, the Political Purposes Committee decided that 'Committee members shall be picked up from their homes, or other places within the RACS trading area, to bring them to Committee meetings and return them home following such meetings'. Moreover, travelling to conferences outside London was to be by First Class rail at a time when Third Class was still the mode for most working class people.[99] Such practices, at a time of unparalleled peace-time austerity, suggest that contemporary consumer co-operatives were creating working class élites.

Another indication of expansive feelings within the Political Purposes Committee was its new interest in international travel, possibly sparked off by the Management Committee's decision to 'investigate modern methods of food production and distribution, store design and dairy and bakery plants, rolling stock, and food by-products ... outside Britain'.[100] Whatever its origin, the Political Purposes Committee wrote to the Management Committee in June 1947 asking 'whether, under our Rules, it is possible ... to send deputations to foreign countries'.[101] Burch, the Society's Secretary, replied that the matter would be considered when changes to Rules were contemplated.[102] The Political Purposes Committee was not satisfied and proposed that the Society's Management Committee should approach 'the Metropolitan Co-operative Societies and the Co-operative Union for consideration of Joint International Goodwill Delegations to foreign countries, whenever the opportunity arises'.[103]

While there was thus some post-war innovation in the Political Purposes Committee, it resumed most of its pre-war activities including considering the agendas of the Annual Conferences of the Labour and Co-operative Parties and the London Labour Party; appointing and mandating delegates to these; holding periodic joint meetings with the Society's Management and Education Committees; convening quarterly conferences of Society whips and representatives on local Labour Parties; and holding other conferences at which Government Front-Bench Ministers were speakers. These included Herbert Morrison, Lord President of the Council, James Griffiths, Minister of National Insurance, and Lewis Silkin, Minister of Town and Country Planning. John Strachey, the Minister of Food, was to have spoken at one Conference but ill-health prevented him from doing so and Dr Edith Summerskill, his Parliamentary Private Secretary, deputised for him.

Generally speaking, the RACS Political Purposes Committee

did not take positions, or campaign, on issues arising during the 1945 Labour Government. In this they contrasted sharply with the Political Committee of the London Co-operative Society, just across the Thames at Stratford, which became increasingly left-wing.

Two main reasons can be deduced for the RACS Committee's lack of direct involvement. One was that this was the province of the Society's delegates to local and London Labour Parties. The other was that, essentially, the Committee had always been a functional committee administering affiliation fees and grants, Parliamentary and Local Panels and delegations, and - more recently - acting as an intermediary between the Society and County and Borough Councillors. Its support for the 1945-50 Labour Government was taken for granted and was reflected in articles that its Political Secretary wrote in *Comradeship* and the Committee's conferences.

The 1950 and 1951 General Elections

As we have seen, the direct political action occurred elsewhere. Thus the Committee's Minutes make only a few references to major political events such as General Elections; they were much more concerned with organisational questions. This was certainly true in the late 1940s when the main issues were the changing relations with the Co-operative and Labour Parties and the Committee's financial and constitutional position within RACS. Each of these were inter-related and the Committee's handling of them reflected change in its membership and in the Political Secretary, as well as a changing environment. The old certainties about the relationship with the Labour Party were still strong but problems were arising.

At the same time there was a gradual improvement in relations with the Co-operative Party. For example, there were fewer setpiece meetings between the Political Purposes Committee and the Executive of the Co-operative Party of the kind previously described. Instead there were more meetings between the 'two Secretaries',[104] Edwin Furness and Jack Bailey. The Co-operative Party had also seen changes in personnel. In 1942 S F Perry had retired as the Party's Secretary and had been followed by Jack

Bailey. Originally a Welsh miner, Bailey had been Secretary of the Bradford and District Co-operative Party from 1925 to 1936 and a National Organiser of the Party in the North Eastern and North Western Sections of the Co-operative Union between 1936 and 1942.[105] Alf Barnes had also relinquished the Party's Chairmanship when he entered the Labour Government in 1945, and was followed by Will Coldrick, the Labour/Co-operative MP for Bristol North.[106]

Improving relations between the Co-operative Party and the Committee were also assisted by the 1946 Agreement between the Labour Party and the Co-operative Movement.[107] It had reformulated arrangements for Parliamentary and local candidates, constituency agents and affiliation fees and created a National Organisation Committee, comprising four representatives each from the Co-operative Movement and the Labour Party; its meetings were to be called only when either side requested them. A measure of the success of the new Agreement was that it met only nine times in as many years.[108] The new Agreement also set up a National Policy Committee consisting of representatives from the Labour Party and the Co-operative Movement, and this was intended to smooth policy differences. An example occurred when the Government proposed bringing the private insurance industry, including the Co-operative Insurance Society, under state control. Co-operative opposition prevented this but aroused strong feelings in parts of the Labour Party, including the RACS's area. This issue became one of the points of tension in relations between the Political Purposes Committee and local Labour Parties. Before looking at others, though, we should examine other aspects of the improving relations with the Co-operative Party.

We have noted that there were more informal meetings between Bailey and Furness which Mrs Coyle, Chairman of the RACS, sometimes attended.[109] Generally speaking, though, the Political Committee appeared content to retain its ultimate control through Furness's detailed reporting back. Within this more relaxed atmosphere changes began to occur. When formal meetings did take place they were used to confirm or ratify understandings that had developed between the two Secretaries.

An example came in December 1948, when the joint meeting of Committee and Party Executive resulted in an agreement under which both sides shifted from earlier positions. The Political Purposes Committee would now allow the Co-operative Party to recruit individual members in the Society's trading area. For its part the Party agreed to disband the South London Voluntary Co-operative Party that it had set up and agreed that the Political Purposes Committee should become a Society Party and so take its place. The RACS Society Party would then become responsible for existing members, creating new Individual Members Sections within the Society's area, and affiliating RACS Guilds to the Co-operative Party. Having concluded the agreement the Political Purposes Committee was then happy for Edwin Furness 'to take up further conversations with the Secretary of the Co-operative Party, Mr Jack Bailey, for the implementation' of the new measures.[110] It is debatable though whether the Political Committee was keen to make a success of the new Individual Members Sections. It decided that membership fees should be one shilling (5p) per year and that the Political Secretary would deal with their administration; moreover, that members joining them should be given the 'facts as to the relationship between the Co-operative Party and the RACS Political Purposes Committee'.[111] The Committee also agreed that individual members' meetings would be held only twice a year at Woolwich, Peckham and Wimbledon.

Perhaps because of this infrequency, or the fact that individual members could not elect their own branch officials or decide their programmes, meetings of individual members were not successful. Only small numbers attended.[112] Nevertheless, the Political Committee's willingness to shift on the question seems to have prompted the Co-operative Party to offer an accommodation on the question of Parliamentary candidates. In 1948 it proposed that there should be a dual panel. The Political Purposes Committee felt that it needed to ask if its existing candidates would agree. Morrison and Berry declined outright. Reeves and Skeffington were more receptive to the idea but expressed doubts whether their Constituency Labour Parties would agree.[113]

In September 1949 the Political Purposes Committee delegated Edwin Furness and the Committee's Vice-Chairman, Councillor J W Andrews, to meet the Co-operative Party Executive to discuss the matter. This lead to Skeffington applying to become a member of the Co-operative Party's Parliamentary Panel. At the same meeting questions were raised about when RACS Individual Members Sections would be allowed to elect their own officers or to arrange their own meetings. The Committee decided to defer a decision on these points.[114]

In October 1949, with a General Election approaching, the Committee reaffirmed the members of its own Parliamentary Panel.[115] Thus, in the General Election of February 1950, its candidates were all sitting members: H Berry for West Woolwich; Joe Reeves for Greenwich; Arthur Skeffington for West Lewisham; and Herbert Morrison for South Lewisham. Morrison's constituency had been renamed after boundary changes. The swing against Labour resulted in the Government being returned with a majority of only six, and also to Skeffington and Berry losing their seats.[116] While all four RACS candidates, and their agents, wrote to thank the Political Purposes Committee for its financial help, the Committee was concerned that only two, the successful Morrison and Reeves, had mentioned this support in their election addresses.

After the Election the Political Purposes Committee agreed to continue its financial responsibility for Morrison and Reeves but deferred decisions on Berry and Skeffington; Berry was ill and the latter was under consideration for membership of the Co-operative Party's Panel. At the same time the Political Purposes Committee agreed to initiate talks between the officers of the Greenwich Labour Party and Joe Reeves to see whether the latter would be agreeable to Reeves becoming a member of the Co-operative Parliamentary Group.[117]

As relations between the Political Purposes Committee and the Co-operative Party continued in a relatively more amicable vein, those with local Labour Parties became more problematic. Although still generally good, small points of friction began to arise. One was the Committee's difficulties in continuing to fund at existing levels the *Citizen*. This was a nationally produced

Labour monthly newspaper printed by the Co-operative Press with pages for local constituency news, introduced in the late 1940s. From the start the Political Purposes Committee had heavily subsidised constituencies' purchase costs of the paper. These proved heavy because RACS covered many constituencies, and started to be questioned when the Committee began to feel financial pressures.[118] The Committee was anxious that its 'grants and payments to the Labour Party should stay as they are' until after the coming General Election. Therefore something else, such as payments for the *Citizen*, were under threat. This prospect alarmed many Constituency Labour Parties who found the *Citizen* a valuable propaganda vehicle. For its part, though, the Committee had begun to feel that the Society's long-standing financial support for local Labour Parties might be coming to be taken for granted, a view reinforced when Berry and Skeffington failed to mention it in their 1950 General Election addresses.

At a meeting of the Political Purposes Committee in September 1950, Edwin Furness attributed the Committee's financial difficulties to 'rising prices'.[119] Trying to overcome them, though, could raise constitutional issues because the Committee might find it necessary to seek 'an increase in the half-yearly political grant from the Society, or an alteration in the activities and grants on which the fund is expended'. Either could involve a change to RACS Rules. Furness went on to suggest that:

> It may be time to consider the effect in South London political life of the financial contribution made by the Royal Arsenal Co-operative Society Limited. Does it stand for anything in the way of moral leadership or is it merely using the facilities of a co-operative trading organisation to provide payments to the Labour Party? Does the present set up give us the political organisation and representation to put over a co-operative contribution to socialist thought inside the Labour Party
>
> The Labour Party rules limit the number of delegates to a General Council. Roughly a payment of about £1 gives one delegate and five times this sum 5 delegates which is the usual maximum. No Trade Union in South

London compares to the payments made by RACS. For example, to one Party in 1949 Affiliation Fees were paid to the amount of £628.15.4d ... eleven Guilds in addition paid £2.9.4d, whilst 64 Trade Union branches and clubs paid £230.3.8d. Another Party received a total of £99.4.10d in fees of which £76.14.3d was paid by the RACS.[120]

For the immediate future Furness proposed that either the charge to Labour Parties for the *Citizen* be increased, or that the *Citizen* should be cancelled except in those constituencies where the Society was funding Parliamentary Candidates.

The Committee decided to delay consideration, possibly until after the next Committee elections, then six months away. These, however, produced no significant change in the Committee; only one new member was elected directly by RACS members. In passing, however, we should note that there was still considerable competition for these places and that among the unsuccessful were Richard Marsh and Arthur Palmer.[121] Both subsequently became Labour MPs, the latter also a Co-operative MP. Marsh, who went on to become Chairman of British Rail, was, at 22, already making a mark in RACS. In 1949 he had won a Society scholarship to study for a year at Ruskin College, Oxford. Candidates for this scholarship had to be from families who were trading members of the Society.[122]

Before then, however, the strain in RACS/Labour relations showed itself in a row in the Committee. A recorded row is unusual in its annals. At one meeting, Arthur Skeffington, MP for West Woolwich, asked if he might pass to members a memorandum he had written on 'RACS-Labour relations'. Furness advised Committee members that they should not 'duplicate documents which purport to give an account of the proceedings of Committee meetings and that it is not regarded as good form to publish the name of Committee members as having voted one way or another'. It was, therefore, decided that Skeffington's memorandum should be placed on the table for members to take as they might wish.[123]

Earlier at the same meeting, Skeffington had admitted to a breach of confidentiality on Committee voting. Another member,

Councillor Arthur Chrisp, had claimed that this had been 'a wrongful action and a personal attack on himself'. Arthur Skeffington apologised, and said that what he had believed to be a private conversation had been overheard. Worse was to follow. The Skeffington memorandum, left literally to lie on the table, had been circulated beyond members of the Political Purposes Committee. This had come to the notice of the Committee of Management and F G Burch, the Society's Secretary, had written to the Political Purposes Committee to say that:

> ... It is not the practice in the Society for records to be kept of the way in which members of a committee vote at committee meetings, and I feel that circulation of such information is very undesirable, leading as it must inevitably do to friction not only between members of the Committee but amongst members of the Society who cannot have knowledge of the full facts; and the issue of such a document is in my opinion not calculated to preserve harmony between the local Labour Parties and this Society'.[124]

It emerged that Skeffington had allowed a copy of his memorandum to be read at a meeting of the South Lewisham Labour Party, Herbert Morrison's constituency. At this point we should note that there was already tension between this Labour Party and the RACS as to whether Morrison could continue to be an RACS sponsored candidate.

However, the Political Committee took greater exception to Skeffington's references in his memorandum to his own constituency of West Lewisham. It went on record to say:

> That we must deplore his reference to West Lewisham Labour Party as the Political Purposes Committee has been extremely generous to this constituency (which is barely in our trading area) and its Parliamentary Candidate. Had Mr Skeffington any appreciation of the traditions of the RACS he would now be a member of the Co-operative Parliamentary Panel and getting the

resources from our movement, with goodwill all round, as in Merton and Morden, to make a certainty of success in the General Election ...

... we regret the complete failure of Mr Skeffington to appreciate that the RACS has a dual affiliation - one to the Labour Party and one to the Co-operative Party - and which requires Committee members to be prepared to work loyally with both bodies.[125]

Two quick points should be made here. The first is to note that Skeffington had not gone on to the Co-operative Party's Parliamentary Panel. The second is that Arthur Palmer, as a member of that Panel and nominated by RACS, had recently been selected as the Prospective Labour/Co-operative Candidate at Merton and Morden.[126] A more substantial point is that Skeffington appeared to be fighting a rear-guard action against the Committee's closer relations with the Co-operative Party, although other issues were undoubtedly involved. In November 1950 he moved the following motion at a Committee meeting:

That this Committee reaffirms its loyalty to the Labour Party and places on record its determination to continue in closest harmony with it, so that the good work which has gone on for the last thirty years may continue. Further it desires that its political activities shall add to the strength of the Labour Party throughout the RACS area, which in turn will strengthen co-operative influence in South London.[127]

The Committee voted against this motion, and went on to reaffirm its dual affiliation to the Labour and Co-operative Parties.

It was against this background that Herbert Morrison ceased to be an RACS candidate. There had been long drawn out, and sometimes complicated discussions, about a new agreement between RACS and his constituency of South Lewisham.[128] On the eve of the 1951 General Election RACS acknowledged failure to get a new agreement.[129] Thus in the 1951 General Election RACS had only one sponsored candidate, Joe Reeves for

Greenwich, who held the seat. Arthur Palmer, whom the Political Purposes Committee had nominated to the Co-operative Party's Panel, was unsuccessful in Merton and Morden.[130]

On the eve of the 1951 General Election, the Political Purposes Committee had approached the RACS Management Committee with a suggested change of Rule to allow an increased Political Grant. A report from the Committee stated that:

> ... the division of the Political Fund into two parts with the earmarking of Part I to local Labour Parties is now too rigid. Circumstances today enable Labour Parties to raise income through their increased membership much more easily than in the 1920s. Therefore, the large payments made by the RACS bring no greater political influence than would smaller payments more nearly comparable to those of the trade union movement.

The Committee, therefore, proposed a change to the Society's Standing Orders to widen Part I to include payments to the national and regional Labour Parties. Otherwise it feared that a shortage of funds could lead to reduced payments to the 'National and London Labour Parties', which would 'not ... be desirable'. A further change proposed was that of 'an increase of ½d. to the Political fund to provide for the Co-operative Party affiliation fees in accordance with the decisions of the Annual Congress of the Co-operative Union Limited ...'[131] Such changes to Rules were likely to take time. In the meantime the Political Purposes Committee attempted to secure its standing with organisations such as the London Labour Party. It also tried to gain some acknowledgment from them of the financial contributions that RACS had made to them.[132] At the same time the Committee was increasingly questioning the returns the Society's links with Labour had brought. For example, it concluded its Report on the Political Purposes Fund which it submitted to the RACS Management Committee between the 1950 and 1951 General Elections with the following:

> One interesting comparison of RACS and LCS methods

of political working may be seen from recent election results.* In looking at these results one should bear in mind that London only pay fees to local Labour Parties for actual voting strength whereas RACS pays on a membership basis without comparable voting rights. In the London Society's area there are nine Co-operative Party MPs and Co-operative Party nominees have been adopted in another six constituencies. In the RACS area we have no Co-operative Party MPs, but one elected on a Labour/Co-operative label, Mr J Reeves, another elected Labour Candidate, Mr H Morrison nominated and supported financially, and one nominee adopted as a prospective candidate, Mr A Palmer. It would appear that the larger payments to the Labour Party made by the RACS have not secured a similar allocation of Parliamentary seats as obtained by the London Society.[133]
*1950 General Election

We can see RACS's financial contribution to Labour Parties in its area in 1950 from the table it presented to the Management Committee. This is reproduced as an Annex at the end of this Chapter.

Conclusion

The period 1939-1951 was one of upheaval for the RACS Political Purposes Committee. During the early part of it there had been dislocation brought about by the war. The resumption of electoral activity in the Society in 1946 had brought new members on to the Committee when about one third of its existing members retired. It could be said that those who retired had constituted an old guard that had been dedicated to RACS's traditional links with Labour. New members, and a new Political Secretary, might have continued this tradition had changes not occurred in local Labour Parties, and if there had not been increasing financial difficulties within the Committee. Alongside these changes, better relations developed with the Co-operative Party with some degree of rapprochement taking place. In repositioning itself the Committee was not afraid to draw invidious comparisons between itself and the Political Committee of the London Co-operative Society. It had obviously begun to feel that, so far as political activity was concerned, there was merit in falling into line with the rest of the Co-operative Movement and Co-operative Union Congress decisions.

In 1951 the Labour Party went into opposition once more. Our next Chapter will see whether the trends appearing in the late 1940s in the RACS Political Purposes Committee continued.

ANNEX TO CHAPTER SIX

Comparisons
1950 Financial Statements
RACS Trading Area

Labour Parties		Total Income £	TU etc £	RACS £	M. Subs £
Battersea		2,476	100	9	275
Bermondsey		2,478	98	69	428
Camberwell					
Dulwich		1,877	39	132	312
	Peckham	3,459	40	133	882
Dartford		1,461	138	37	485
	Erith	609	10	100	196
	Crayford	608	11	11	285
Bexley		2,928	50	301	1,124
Chislehurst DLP		802	19	26	510
Deptford		1,518	66	130	558
Greenwich		1,599	63	144	770
Lambeth	Brixton	3,634	72	132	503
	Norwood	689	28	12	256
	Vauxhall	1,491	25	71	92
Lewisham	North	4,194	36	108	743
	West	1,970	32	66	755
	South	3,209	31	71	1,110
Merton & Morden		1,736	20	131	479
Surbiton		580	1	83	219
Southwark		1,665	22	103	135
Wandsworth	Central	1,287	34	134	333
	Clapham	1,808	44	27	525
	Streatham	367	4	21	139
Wimbledon	Wimbledon)	752	28	114	212
	Malden & Coombe)				
Woolwich		6,237	232	604	1,911

Extend outside RACS Trading Area

		Total Income £	TU etc £	RACS £	M. Subs £
London		8,222	2,500	451	999
Southern Regional Council		2,124	319	40	235

Political Fund – RACS Trading Area
Affiliation Fees to Labour Parties

Labour Parties	1925 £	1935 £	1950 £
Battersea	–	–	9
Bermondsey	20	88	69
Camberwell	114	315	264
Dartford	82	293	148
Bexley	–	–	293
Chislehurst/Sidcup	–	–	26
Deptford	68	173	130
Greenwich	61	135	144
Lambeth	55	167	132
Merton & Morden	–	–	131
Mitcham	10	87	76
Surbiton	–	29	63
Southwark	48	160	103
Wandsworth	56	203	206
Wimbledon	29	172	114
Malden & Coombe	9	45	54
Woolwich	273	323	604

Notes

References to Minutes are to RACS Minutes held by the CWS SE Archive.
Comradeship was published by RACS Education Department.

1   *Comradeship*, July 1940, p.iv.
2   *Wheatsheaf*, April 1945.
3   *Comradeship*, July 1940, p.v.
4   *Comradeship*, October 1941, pp.i-ii.
5   *Comradeship*, April 1942, p.1.
6   Minutes, Political Purposes Committee, 27 March 1941.
7   Minutes, Political Purposes Committee, 19 April 1940.
8   *Comradeship*, December 1940, p.1.
9   *Comradeship*, July 1940, p.v.
10 *Comradeship*, December 1940, p.ii.
11 Co-operative Union Ltd, *Report of 1941 Congress, Edinburgh*, p.50.
12 *Comradeship*, September 1940, p.ii.
13 *Comradeship*, October 1940, p.iv.
14 *Comradeship*, May 1941, p.iii.
15 Co-operative Union Ltd, *Report of 1943 Congress, Edinburgh*, p.95.
16 *Comradeship*, June 1940, p.ii.
17 *Comradeship*, February 1943, p.ii.
18 Minutes, Political Purposes Committee, 18 February 1943 and Special Conferences 18 February 1943 and 20 March 1943.
19 Minutes, Political Purposes Committee, 25 March, 13 April and 25 May 1943.
20 *Comradeship*, September 1943, p.iii.
21 *Comradeship*, January 1940, p.ix.
22 *Comradeship*, May 1940, p.vii.
23 *Comradeship*, January 1941, p.ii.
24 *Comradeship*, February 1941, p.ii.
25 Ibid.
26 Minutes, Political Purposes Committee, 11 March 1940.
27 Minutes, Political Purposes Committee, 20 November 1941
28 *Comradeship*, June 1943, p.iii.
29 *Comradeship*, May 1943, p.iii.
30 Rhodes, Geoffrey, *Co-operative-Labour Relations 1900-1962*, op. cit., p.47.
31 Ibid, pp.33-61.
32 *Comradeship*, August 1942, p.iii.
33 Co-operative Union Ltd, *Report of 1942 Congress, Margate*, p.67.

34 Minutes, Political Purposes Committee, 17 February 1944.

35 Co-operative Union Ltd, *Report of 1942 Congress, Edinburgh*, p.84.

36 *Comradeship*, September 1941, p.ix.

37 Co-operative Union Ltd, *Report of 1939 Congress, Margate*, p.121.

38 Minutes, Political Purposes Committee, 10 December 1940.

39 Ibid.

40 Minutes, Political Purposes Committee, 15 July 1940.

41 Minutes, Political Purposes Committee, 8 November 1940.

42 Minutes, Political Purposes Committee, 8 May 1941.

43 Minutes, Political Purposes Committee, 16 August 1941.

44 Minutes, Political Purposes Committee, 11 September 1941.

45 Minutes, Political Purposes Committee, 19 February 1942.

46 Minutes, Political Purposes Committee, 19 November 1942.

47 Minutes, Political Purposes Committee, 15 December 1942.

48 Minutes, Political Purposes Committee, 21 January 1943.

49 Minutes, Political Purposes Committee, 25 March 1943.

50 Minutes, Political Purposes Committee, 22 June 1943.

51 Ibid.

52 Minutes, Political Purposes Committee, 13 April 1943.

53 Minutes, Political Purposes Committee, 17 February 1944.

54 Ibid.

55 Co-operative Union Ltd, *Report of 1945 Congress, Nottingham*, pp.100-101.

56 Co-operative Union Ltd, *Report of 1940 Congress, Glasgow*, pp.60-61.

57 Co-operative Union Ltd, *Report of 1945 Congress, Nottingham*, p.66.

58 Minutes, Political Purposes Committee, 20 April 1944.

59 Minutes, Political Purposes Committee, 17 June 1944.

60 Minutes, Joint Meeting, 20 July 1944.

61 *Comradeship*, June 1945, p.ii.

62 The National Co-operative Authority was the Central Co-operative Organisation representative of the Co-operative Union, the two Wholesales, the Co-operative Productive Federation, the Co-operative Party and the Co-operative Press. Its role was to discuss and decide co-operative policy on current national issues affecting the Movement between Congresses. The Co-operative Union implemented its decisions and its reports were included in those of the Union's Central Board presented to annual Congresses.

63 *Comradeship*, June 1945, p.ii.

64 Co-operative Union Ltd, *Report of 1945 Congress, Nottingham*, p.106.

65   Rhodes, Geoffrey, op. cit., p.79.

66   Minutes, Political Purposes Committee, 17 June 1944.

67   Minutes, Political Purposes Committee, 19 October 1944.

68   Minutes, Political Purposes Committee, 22 June 1943.

69   Minutes, Political Purposes Committee, 20 July 1944.

70   *Comradeship*, December 1945, p.iii.

71   Minutes, Political Purposes Committee, 8 December 1945.

72   Minutes, Political Purposes Committee, 15 December 1942.

73   Minutes, Political Purposes Committee, 18 January 1945.

74   Minutes, Political Purposes Committee, 16 March 1944.

75   *Comradeship*, July 1947, p.iii.

76   Minutes, Political Purposes Committee, 15 March 1945.

77   Minutes, Political Purposes Committee, 26 April 1945.

78   Donoughue, Bernard and Jones, G W, *Herbert Morrison - Portrait of a Politician*, op. cit., p.336.

79   *Comradeship*, February 1946, p.iv.

80   *Comradeship*, August 1945, p.ii.

81   *Comradeship*, December 1945, p.iii.

82   Carbery, Thomas F, *Consumers in Politics - A History and General Review of the Co-operative Party* , op. cit., p.50.

83   Dalton, Hugh, *High Tide and After*, Muller, London, 1962, p.3.

84   *Comradeship*, April and November 1946.

85   Minutes, Political Purposes Committee, 17 July 1945.

86   Minutes, Political Purposes Committee, 30 August 1945.

87   Minutes, Political Purposes Committee, 15 November 1945.

88   Minutes, Political Purposes Committee, 5 December 1945.

89   *Comradeship*, January 1947.

90   Minutes, Political Purposes Committee, 15 March 1946.

91   Minutes, Political Purposes Committee, 21 March 1947.

92   Minutes, Political Purposes Committee, 23 March 1946.

93   Minutes, Political Purposes Committee, 10 October 1946.

94   Minutes, Joint Meeting, 15 August 1946.

95   Minutes, Political Purposes Committee, 25 November 1946.

96   Minutes, Political Purposes Committee, 6 October 1945.

97   *Comradeship*, August 1947, p.iv.

98   Minutes, Political Purposes Committee, 2 May 1947.

99   Minutes, Political Purposes Committee, 2 May 1947 and 17 March 1950.

100 *Comradeship*, July 1947, p.ii.

101 Minutes, Political Purposes Committee, 6 June 1947.

102 Minutes, Political Purposes Committee, 5 September 1947.

103 Minutes, Political Purposes Committee, 5 December 1947.

104 Minutes. Political Purposes Committee, 3 September 1948.

105 Co-operative Union Ltd, *Report of 1943 Congress, Edinburgh*, p.86.

106 Co-operative Union Ltd, *Report of 1946 Congress, Blackpool*, p.103.

107 Ibid., pp.63-66.

108 Rhodes, Geoffrey, op. cit., p.92.

109 Minutes, Political Purposes Committee, 3 September 1948.

110 Minutes, Political Purposes Committee, 3 December 1948.

111 Minutes, Political Purposes Committee, 25 March 1949.

112 Minutes, Political Purposes Committee, 5 May 1950 and 3 July 1950.

113 Minutes, Political Purposes Committee, 1 October 1948 and 3 December 1948.

114 Minutes, Political Purposes Committee, 7 October 1949.

115 Ibid.

116 Minutes, Political Purposes Committee, 3 March 1950.

117 Ibid.

118 Minutes. Political Purposes Committee, 3 June 1949, 19 August 1949, 21 September 1949 and 1 September 1950.

119 Minutes. Political Purposes Committee, 25 September 1950.

120 Ibid.

121 *Comradeship*, January 1951, p.vi-x.

122 *Comradeship*, September 1949, p.iv.

123 Minutes, Political Purposes Committee, 28 November 1950.

124 Minutes, Political Purposes Committee, 1 December 1950.

125 Ibid.

126 Minutes, Political Purposes Committee, 25 September 1950.

127 Minutes, Political Purposes Committee, 3 November 1950.

128 Minutes, Political Purposes Committee, 1 December 1950, 5 January 1951, 4 May 1951 and 20 July 1951.

129 Minutes, Political Purposes Committee, 13 October 1951.

130 Minutes, Political Purposes Committee, 2 November, 1951.

131 Minutes, Political Purposes Committee, 7 September 1951.

132 Resolution proposed by Political Purposes Committee at meeting of Executive Committee, London Labour Party; Minutes, Political Purposes Committee, 2 February 1961.

133 Minutes, Political Purposes Committee, 2 February 1951.

CHAPTER SEVEN

Opposition Years 1951-1964

Introduction

The years 1951 to 1964, when Labour was in opposition, were relatively quiet years, politically, both nationally and within RACS. In the General Election in October 1951 Labour won 295 seats against the Conservative's 321. Although the Party thus went into Opposition, the first time fully in over 10 years, its supporters were not too downhearted. They considered the election an aberration because Labour had gained the highest number of votes, 48.8 per cent against the Tories' 48 per cent, making it likely that Labour would be returned at the next election. Such hopes proved wrong in 1955 and again in 1959. However, the expectation of a return to power helped to shape Labour actions and attitudes in the 1950s.

Another factor shaping them, and helping to make the fifties less divisive than the 1930s, was that there was a fair degree of consensus between the parties on central issues such as the Welfare State and major industries operating under state control. It had been a Conservative Government that had passed the Railways Act in 1921, organising the railways into four regional groups. In general, the Conservative Party was not opposed to the increasing state control of the mines. It shared the widely held dissatisfaction with their performance between the wars and in the second world war when private mining companies had seemed unwilling or unable to carry out necessary reforms. Moreover, an influential minority of the party that included Harold Macmillan, Prime Minister 1957-1963, favoured corporatist solutions to industrial problems and did not rule out nationalisation as a last resort.[1] There was also a fair measure of agreement between the parties on education. R A Butler had steered the 1944 Education Act on to the statute book with Labour support.

Thus there was varying degrees of consensus over a wide range of issues which meant that Labour was not going to be as confrontational in opposition in the 1950s as it had been in the 1930s. This spilled over into RACS where the tone of Edwin Furness's Political Notes in *Comradeship* were noticeably less strident and class conscious than Walter Green's had been in the inter-war years.

The Political Purposes Committee itself remained concerned mostly with relations with the Labour and Co-operative Parties. In the early 1950s, those with the Labour Party continued to be affected by problems of finance.

Problems of Finance and the Labour Party

The proposals that the Political Purposes Committee had made to change the RACS's Political Purposes Fund,[2] had been turned down by the Society's Management Committee and the Committee's financial position had continued to deteriorate. By 1952 there was an annual deficit of nearly £800. When a further attempt to achieve changes was blocked by opposition at RACS members' meetings, the Committee was forced to consider a reallocation of funds rather than seeking their increase. It therefore proposed a new amendment to Rules which would 'merely reduce the 1d. on Part I Political Purposes Fund to ⅔d. and to increase the 2d. in Part II Political Purposes Fund to 2⅓d.'. Its effect would be to transfer one third of the grant available to local Labour Parties to the Committee's General Fund, or Part II Fund, and reduce the Society's affiliation fees to Constituency Labour Parties by one-third. Payments to the National and Regional Labour Parties would be similarly affected.[3]

The Committee began a series of consultations to explain its proposals and why they had become necessary. The first, held at Church House, Great Smith Street, on 7th November 1952, was with the Labour Party's General Secretary, Morgan Phillips, and National Agent, Len Williams. The Committee presented the following arguments. Its proposals would:

> ... leave the global amounts still to be determined on a RACS membership basis. These arrangements would give

the Labour Party as a whole roughly one-third of the Political Purposes Fund Grant as affiliation fees. In addition further payments would be made to the Labour Party in support of co-operative candidates. If looked at reasonably these proposals are certainly not ungenerous and could no doubt be blessed as a not unfavourable compromise by both Labour Party and RACS Members.

On the question of delegates the Committee believed that:

The matter of maximum co-operative representation might be left for consultation, negotiation and local agreements based on mutual goodwill. It is felt that a measure of agreement on this matter might be reached over a period of one or two years. It is of importance both to the Labour Party and the RACS that a body of co-operators in every constituency are ready to voice the consumers point of view equally with a trade union group voicing a producers point of view.

In view of its rising deficit the Committee suggested that:

The only way out of this immediate problem, it seems to us, is for the National and London Labour Parties for the present half year to agree to forgo affiliation fee payments.[4]

The Committee also asked the National Executive of the Labour Party to suggest to Constituency Labour Parties that it was 'essential that both the RACS and the TU Group should each have a nominee in the shortlist in order that both the Co-operative and Trade Union case might be stated, otherwise our arguments about a trinity of Co-op, TU and Socialist is a sham ...'

In reply Morgan Phillips, the Party Secretary, assured the Committee that it was highly regarded by the Party's National Executive as the 'political link between RACS and the Labour Party'. For this reason he felt 'it would be unwise' to reduce

RACS's national affiliation fees to the Labour Party, although he agreed that those for the current half year could be cancelled.

From comments elsewhere by P H Daines, Secretary, London Labour Party, it seems that the suggestion had been made that the Labour Party should try to influence the vote of RACS members on the question of its Political Fund. In this connection, and possibly with memories of the troubles caused by Herbert Morrison's attempts to sway decisions in the London Co-operative Society, Morgan Phillips observed that 'It would be difficult for the NEC to agree to intervene ... in order to guarantee success'. He planned, however, that the Joint Organisation Committee, created under the Co-operative/Labour Agreement of 1946 should consider the decisions of RACS members' meetings on the Society's Political Fund once these had been taken.

Indicative of the interest that the Labour Party Head Office maintained in the financial side of RACS political activities, Morgan Phillips queried whether the Political Purposes Committee was 'spending money wisely in supporting the issue of editions of the *Citizen*, or in payment of Agent's Grants, or even in making local government election grants on behalf of RACS Panel Candidates'. More significant is the fact that these comments were taken on board by the Committee and these were the areas in which it subsequently made cuts. In his closing comments Morgan Phillips agreed that it was desirable that both trade union and RACS candidates should be considered at selection conferences. He promised to ask the National Executive Committee to consider the question.[5]

Morgan Phillips had suggested reductions in local expenditures and this was the direction in which the Committee sought to balance its budget. For example it decided to continue support for the Citizen in only one constituency, that of Joe Reeves at Greenwich. Together with various other cuts it was also able to decide not to 'pursue the question of amendment to the RACS Standing Orders ... at the present time'.[6]

Local economies led to local tensions and these were not helped when Walter Green's old constituency of Deptford selected a new candidate without any consultation with RACS. This caused the Committee to protest to the National Labour Party and to voice its 'displeasure at the discourtesy shown to our Society ...'[7] We have already noted the failure to conclude a new agreement in Herbert Morrison's seat of South Lewisham. Despite these local difficulties the RACS retained its seat on the Labour Party's National Executive: Arthur Skeffington was elected in 1953.[8]

Problems for RACS Political Secretary

Strangely, during this period, the Committee did not seek to reduce its affiliation fee to the Co-operative Party. Indeed, it increased it. This leads us to speculate whether there was an attempted swing in RACS away from the Labour Party to the Co-operative Party.

As we have seen, relations between the Committee and the Co-operative Party had improved after Furness's arrival. This had ramifications not least in the wider relations between the Labour and Co-operative Movements. The member of the Committee most identified with wanting to maintain the status quo in RACS's relations with the Labour Party was Arthur Skeffington. He now became Furness's main protagonist in moves which today might be construed as grounds for constructive dismissal. Something of a power struggle can be sensed from the Committee's Minutes although these seldom attributed proposals or moves. However, it is possible to deduce positions, and those of Furness can be sensed by the way by the way he wrote the Minutes, or inserted comparisons to illustrate arguments. An example of the latter which we have seen already occurred when he drew comparisons between the effectiveness of the Political Purposes Committee and the Political Committee of the London Co-operative Society in gaining the election of Co-operative Members of Parliament.[9] Another, also mentioned in Chapter Six, was the handling of the Skeffington memorandum. This highlighted a feature of Furness's Minutes which were his bracketed asides. It will be recalled that the Committee decided that the Memorandum should literally lie on the table. Furness's Minutes then included a bracketed warning that documents should not be duplicated, and that the Committee's voting figures should not be published. It is possible that Furness gave the warning to keep himself procedurally correct and on the right side of the anticipated admonition from the Society's Secretary, F G Burch.[10] For whatever reason, Furness experienced increasing difficulties in his work including a reduction in secretarial assistance. His one clerk was reduced from full-time to two-thirds time, despite the fact, as the Minutes noted, that there was now a 'shorter working week and the increased requirements of the Political Purposes Committee which are at least equivalent to pre-war operations ...'[11] In brackets in the Minutes Furness made comparisons with the staff in other political offices: twelve in the office of the London Labour Party, five in that of the Labour Party Southern Region, four in the office of the Woolwich Labour Party and twelve, including seven typists, in the office of the London Society's Political Committee.[12]

Furness's estimated expenses were also reduced by £50. Thus in brackets, the Minutes noted that these were already 'at a much lower rate of expenses than is allowed generally in comparable staff positions in either the Trade Union or Labour Party Movements'.[13] At the same time the Committee did not reduce its expenses. These had been set three months earlier at £2 per day when delegated to Labour and Co-operative Party Conferences, with three additional days for five-day conferences, and two additional days' expenses for three and four-day conferences. Rail travel was still to be First Class and RACS chauffeur-driven cars were to be provided when Committee members attended Society meetings, Committee Conferences and other events.[14]

As part of the cost reduction exercise Furness was also required to limit postage and printing costs and also to provide a 'quarterly itemised financial statement' and 'an annual budget'. Two members of the Committee were delegated to 'conduct a monthly examination of the (Committee's) accounts': Their reports were to be 'circulated at each monthly meeting of the Political Purposes Committee'. It was also decided to examine 'the conditions of service of the Political Secretary'.[15] The Committee later decided that the Political Office's 'Petty Cash Book should be laid on the table, available for inspection at each meeting of the Committee'.[16] During what was obviously a contentious period, the Committee decided for the first time that its Chairman should receive a copy of the Committee's Minutes prior to their being circulated.[17] Although this practice finished a few months later, it seems part of a concerted move to put pressure on Furness.

On the question of his conditions of service it will be recalled that these stipulated, when drafted in 1946, that the appointment should be full-time and that no external commitments should be undertaken.[18] This meant that Furness's conditions were different from those of Walter Green. In practice Furness had taken on a number of external commitments that differed little from those taken by Green and later Political Secretaries. When the Committee re-examined his conditions in September 1953, the Minutes were unusually brief. They merely stated that the Committee received the 'Regulations relating to the employment of the Full-Time Political Secretary' and that these were 'Noted'.[19]

The matter, however, was not allowed to rest, and was raised again by a new Committee member, T W Agar. He wrote a letter that came before the Committee's next meeting. It asked that reference should be made in the Minutes to the 'discussions on the matter of the conditions of service of the Political Secretary'. The outcome of this request was that the Committee resolved:

> That following a lengthy discussion at the September meeting on the conditions of service of the Political Secretary, during which questions were asked about absences from the office during the day, to which the reply was given that absences were due to speaking engagements on behalf of the Committee or on the average a day a week attending meetings of the Kent County Council which was actually time allowed off to compensate for evening and Saturday attendances on committee work; these explanations were accepted and it was further agreed to receive and note the conditions of service under which the political secretary is satisfactorily operating.[20]

It should be noted that, in fact, Furness had followed Walter Green into wider political activity. While he did not become an MP or a member of the Labour Party's National Executive Committee, as Green had, he was elected to the Kent County Council in 1952[21] and became prominent on the Southern Regional Council of the Labour Party, becoming its Chairman in 1954.[22] Furness was also active in the London Labour Party. The Committee had endorsed these appointments. Moreover in a half-yearly report to the Society it requested that 'an expression of appreciation to the Political Secretary be recorded ... for his services for seven years as a member of the London Labour Party Executive Committee'.[23]

Furness undoubtedly had his supporters as well as his detractors. Nevertheless, some of the latter continued to snipe. An example of the latter was Arthur Skeffington's proposal 'That the Political Secretary should telephone to the Chairman at 9.30 am on a definite day each week'. Another member, Mr Spencer, intervened to say that such a motion would represent 'a vote of no confidence in the Secretary and would leave him with no option but to resign'. The Committee chose a middle course and left it to the Chairman and Secretary to 'reach a mutual agreement' for the conduct of business which should be reported to the next meeting of the Committee.[24]

It is suggested, however, that the Committee's new closeness to the Co-operative Party was only one factor in Furness's difficulties. At about the same period he became controversial through his active support of Moral Rearmament, and there were no doubt other reasons for the problems he encountered.

Besides Furness's difficulties there is other evidence of a tendency within RACS during this period for a shift away from Labour. For example, in March 1955 an article appeared in the Kentish Mercury which purported that RACS was shifting from the Labour Party to the Co-operative Party. Some suspected that a member of the Political Purposes Committee had leaked information, although this was denied and never proved. At its meeting the following month the Committee issued a disclaimer:

> There is no foundation whatsoever for the allegation made in the article that a new Co-operative Party machine would be set up; and at no time has there been any proposal before the Political Purposes Committee advocating a split with the Labour Party.[25]

However, relations with the Labour Party had the ability to embarrass the Committee and the Society. We noted, in connection with discussions with Morgan Phillips on the question of payments to the Party, that the suggestion had been made, but rejected, that Labour Party votes should be used in favour of an alteration to RACS Rules. Nevertheless, in 1957, an attempt was made by the Secretary of the Bermondsey Labour Party to canvass Labour Party members to support six candidates in elections to the Political Purposes Committee, namely Keen, Skeffington, Andrews, Kennard and Collins, and Mrs Burgess. Such action contravened RACS Standing Order No 36 in regard to written canvassing and the case was referred to the Society's Arbitrators. From there it was reported to the Chief Registrar of Friendly Societies who declared the six candidates disqualified, even though they had not known about, or approved, the appeal to Labour Party members.[26] Various moves followed, including Committee lunches with the Labour Party's General Secretary, Morgan Phillips,[27] and Herbert Morrison.[28] An appeal was also made to the High Court[29] and this proved partially successful. Mr Justice Vaisey ruled:

> ... that the circular letter issued by Mr Thomas of the Bermondsey Labour Party last February was to be regarded as solicitation for support to no other candidate than Mr J Keen. In these circumstances it follows that Messrs Andrews, Kennard and Skeffington and Mrs Burgess are properly elected to serve on the Political Purposes Committee until March, 1960.[30]

This case illustrated how far the Political Purposes Committee was tied to the Rules of the Royal Arsenal Co-operative Society. It also reflected the concern that Labour Parties within the Society had to secure the return of candidates likely to be favourable to the Society's continuing links with the Labour Party. We have previously noted that the Society's major Committees - General, Education and Political Purposes - represented different groups among Society members. This was one of the rare occasions when the workings of one of these could be so clearly seen, and six out of the twelve members of the Political Purposes Committee identified with it.

Later we will note the problems that arose out of members elected from another group. In the meantime, though, we should return to the question of the Committee's closer relations with the Co-operative Party.

Relations with the Co-operative Party

Relations with the Co-operative Party might have improved but they were never to be wholehearted. Some improvement was, however, reflected in the Committee's decision in August 1953 to raise the Society's affiliation fee from £200 to £250 per half year, despite its financial problems.[31] This was still below the current rate recommended by the Co-operative Union as agreed at Co-operative Congresses.

Moreover, the Committee was hesitant to commit itself solely to the Party's Parliamentary Panel. In 1953 it accepted a compromise proposal of its Sub-Committee which was to create a panel with two sections. The first would comprise candidates who, having been interviewed and endorsed by the Committee and the Party's National Committee, would be 'nominated and fully supported in suitable constituencies in accordance with the agreements between the Labour Party and the Co-operative Party': an immediate nominee would be Joe Reeves, the sitting Member for Greenwich. The second section would allow some vestige of an RACS Panel to remain and would comprise:

> Nominees to be qualified in accordance with RACS Standing Orders. Nominees will be expected to prove exceptional co-operative loyalty and service and at the discretion of the Political Purposes Committee may be required to be interviewed. A minimum of three years co-operative membership to be expected. Consideration to be given on merit to service with another Co-operative Society. Grant up to £100 at a Parliamentary Election. To secure a grant there must be an acceptable reference to the Co-operative Movement in the election address. A limit of this Section to five people. All nominees to be

acceptable to the RACS Joint Meeting of Committees and Members' Council.[32]

The Committee accepted the above proposal although the last provision was later strengthened by the requirement that the candidate's election address must also make an acceptable reference to RACS.

In passing we can, perhaps, mention that one of the first nominees to the second panel was Freda Corbet, who was already the MP for Peckham.[33] From her time as a member of the London County Council, an Executive Member of the London Labour Party, and her early days in the House of Commons, she had been closely associated with Herbert Morrison[34] who may, therefore, have suggested her nomination. He still appeared to be a powerful influence behind the scenes in RACS. It had been in his constituency of South Lewisham that the Skeffington Memorandum had been read out and he proposed Skeffington when he stood for re-election to the Political Purposes Committee in 1955. Morrison may also have prompted the RACS nomination of Hugh Gaitskell as Labour Party Treasurer in 1954[35] when, in a strongly fought election, Gaitskell's opponent was Aneurin Bevan; Morrison had been a long-time opponent of Nye Bevan. While he was still likely, however, to have been an influence in RACS, it is not likely that he would have approved the Political Purposes Committee's continued use of First Class rail travel. When he travelled to marry his second wife at Rochdale in January 1955, Morrison went by Third Class rail![36]

Returning though to relations with the Co-operative Party, the Committee continued to organise meetings of individual RACS members and invited the Party's Secretary and Assistant Secretary, Jack Bailey and Harold Campbell, to speak at them. The number of individual members rose from 81 in 1949 to 169 two years later. Moreover, the Committee acknowledged 'These numbers could be increased by more active propaganda at any time.'[37] By 1954, in addition to the ordinary meetings, Annual Meetings with prominent Party speakers were also being held at Woolwich, Wimbledon and Peckham.[38] Amicable relations with the Party were also underlined by the Committee's continued active role in the Metropolitan Federation of the Party. John Andrews, the Committee's Vice-Chairman, became the Federation's Chairman in 1952.[39]

In Parliament, Joe Reeves and Arthur Skeffington were invited to attend meetings of the Co-operative Parliamentary Group in an ex-officio capacity.[40] Skeffington had been returned to Parliament in 1953 in the Hayes and Harlington by-election. It was, however, in the area of policy that the improved relationship between the Party and RACS could best be seen. By the early 1950s there was growing unease in the Co-operative Movement that post-war nationalisation was falling short of expectations in a number of areas, including benefits to consumers and the ability of consumers to influence the control of national corporations. At the Co-operative Party's Annual Conference in 1952 the Political Purposes Committee joined in the endorsement of the Party's new pamphlet, *The People's Industry*. This acknowledged the role of nationalisation in certain basic industries and supported its extension to the arms and aircraft industries. It also recognised the spheres in which municipalisation was appropriate, with perhaps some mixture of co-operative ownership. But the pamphlet also reasserted the values of Co-operation as a distinct form of social ownership.[41]

At the Labour Party Conference the following year the Political Purposes Committee submitted the following resolution:

> This Conference, recognising that Co-operation is public ownership, is public control and is in the public interest, urges all members of the Labour Movement to give practical support to the Co-operative Movement by trading with and actively assisting its various enterprises whenever possible.[42]

The fraternal greetings of the Co-operative Party to that Conference, conveyed by Jim Peddie, a member of its National Committee and a Director of the Co-operative Wholesale Society, contained the warning:

> Do not be misled. The Co-operative Movement has no intention of taking part in its own funeral, however

friendly the undertaker might be. There may be some, I regret to say, who believe that co-operative organisations are a useful prelude to the development of some system of State control which would absorb existing co-operative organisations. That view is wrong, dangerous, and based upon an abysmal ignorance of co-operative principles and organisation. The destruction, or even weakening of the absorption through nationalisation - would be a disaster. It would take the economic power of the people out of their hands. The whole purpose of socialism should be to expand not curtail opportunities for direct participation in economic affairs.[43]

Peddie's words reflect co-operative concern that the Co-operative Insurance Society had nearly been absorbed into a nationalised insurance business. They also reflected a growing recognition of the need to remind others in the Labour Movement that Co-operation was a distinct, voluntary and successful form of social ownership pre-dating nationalisation. Linked to this argument was that, to remain successful, Co-operation needed trade union and Labour Party members' trade: that had been the burden of the RACS resolution at the same conference.

Not surprisingly, in view of the reconstruction of large parts of South East London after the war, the RACS and its Political Purposes Committee fell in line with the rest of the Co-operative Movement on the question of shop sites. At the 1953 Annual Conference of the London Labour Party the Political Purposes Committee supported a resolution proposed by the Political Committee of the London Co-operative Society on shop sites. This was in line with the policy of the Co-operative Union which demanded a fair and reasonable allocation of shops, the ability of consumers on housing estates to choose between co-operative and private stores, and the allocation of shop sites through negotiation rather than through tendering or premium payments. The Co-operative Union policy, although recognising that local authorities needed to negotiate for economic rents to cover their costs, warned that such rents should not be inflated. Otherwise they would become an extra burden on shoppers.[44]

In line with this, at the 1954 Co-operative Party Conference, the Political Purposes Committee proposed a resolution which demanded the withdrawal of restrictive covenant agreements enforced by some local authorities when letting shops.[45]

The questions of co-operative social ownership vis-a-vis nationalisation, and shop sites in redeveloped areas and new towns, were high among the concerns of the post-war RACS and the wider Co-operative Movement. Both contained threats to the Movement's continued expansion at a time when the rate of growth was beginning to slow down.

RACS at its Height

The difficulties RACS experienced in the 1950s probably seemed temporary and likely to be overcome by the Society's sheer size and strength. It had a long record of success and now had over 370,000 members and around 9,000 employees.[46] Its achievements were celebrated in big ways. In October 1952 the Society hired the newly opened Royal Festival Hall for a Members' Rally at which the main speaker was Clement Attlee, who had been Prime Minister until the General Election a year earlier. Over three thousand members attended together with MPs, leaders of the London County Council, civic heads of South London and adjoining boroughs in Kent and Surrey, and representatives of other co-operative societies.[47] A year later the Society achieved annual sales of over £25 million for the first time. This was celebrated by large-scale concerts at Peckham, Woolwich, Greenwich, Wimbledon, Lewisham and Tooting but only those who had been RACS members for over 40 years were invited: 5,043 attended, 80 of whom had been members for more than 60 years.[48] Employees with over 15 years' service, together with their partners, were invited to celebrate this achievement at the Royal Albert Hall with dancing to Geraldo's Broadcasting Orchestra.[49] Such events underlined the importance the Society attached to member and employee loyalty.

An event open to all was a Co-operative Exhibition in 1956. For this the Woolwich Stadium was hired. Memories of the Society's earlier exhibition in 1927 are likely to have been promoted. This time over 160,000 people attended.

Despite such triumphalism, worrying trends were beginning to develop in the Society. One was that member's meetings were becoming less well attended.[50] Another was that gross surplus margins on trade were declining during a period of rising prices. We have noted the problems that these were causing for the Political Purposes Committee. On the Society's trading side they meant that members' dividend was being calculated on increased prices: thus it became more difficult to sustain earlier rates of dividend. As costs rose the Society's size and diversity made things worse and appeals were made to members to show 'the highest degree of loyalty to the society' to help overcome the problems.[51] Although the continued expansion in sales volume made it possible to limit expense rates, costs still rose. In 1953, compared to the previous year, rents and rates rose by £450 per week, electricity by £400 per week, and wages by £2,300 per week.[52]

Moreover, there were times during the 1950s when the withdrawal of share capital exceeded members' deposits either through contributions or the transfer of interest and dividend to their share accounts.[53] Building societies and National Savings were becoming effective competitors for working class savings which had earlier traditionally gone to co-operatives. This increasing unreliability of members' share capital, compounded by its easy withdrawal, impacted on co-operative societies at a time when they were beginning to need more capital to lease or build new and larger stores. Although it was not yet understood as such, a new revolution in retailing was beginning. This time it would not be led by the Co-op.

Within RACS itself doubts began to appear about its continued expansion:

> In the 1930s we travelled fast. Under wise and far-seeing leadership we made tremendous progress, and while we have by no means yet reached saturation point, it is obvious that the rate of development must to some extent decelerate.[54]

So wrote the Society's new Secretary, W J Morton, in September 1955. Although the Society continued to expand through the 1960s it was mainly due to its amalgamation with smaller societies. The impetus for these mergers came not only from the RACS's internal needs but also from the push for rationalisation within the wider Co-operative Movement. We now need to examine this because, as we have previously noted, there is a close link between co-operative politics and co-operative trading structures. In earlier times the RACS had been known as the Woolwich Society and had been closely identified with Woolwich politics. Geographical expansion was weakening the links with Woolwich and thus the links with its political traditions.

Co-operative Regionalisation

We have already referred to the first signs of a new retailing revolution. Full employment and rising wages during the 1950s changed consumer expectations and demands. At the same time co-operatives' competitors began to regroup and to become larger scale. Some co-operatives found it difficult to adjust to the new competition. On top of this, greater price competition became possible when resale price maintenance began to be phased out. As a result the levels of co-operative dividend came under attack. RACS itself was still adjusting to new shopping patterns after damage to so many of its stores during the war. Increased town planning brought new procedures and sometimes delays in building or leasing new stores.

There were also problems about internal relations within the Movement, including the future role of production in modern co-operative retailing. In its early days the Movement's ability to integrate vertically had brought the benefits of economies of scale to local retail societies and their members. From the late 1950s these became less certain when wholesaling declined in the wider retailing sector. Some of the larger multiple traders which ceased to be family firms and became public limited companies grew big enough to deal directly with manufacturers and so cut out wholesaling costs. Together with rationalising their stocks, reducing ranges and advertising them more heavily, such retailers became better able to use price cutting as a competitive weapon. Multiples' increasing market share was also assisted because, having gone public and now gaining access to larger amounts of capital, they could improve their sites in town centres.

The co-operative position was under attack. Although there were still increases in co-operative trade they were at a slower rate. In this new and unfamiliar situation the role of the two Co-operative Wholesales in the Movement began to be questioned. Old ties of loyalty were weakening as local societies complained that the wholesales were not fully meeting their requirements. In return the wholesales complained that retail societies were being insufficiently loyal, with the result that the wholesales' factories were running at under capacity.

In 1954 the Co-operative Congress called for a Special Committee to look into closer co-operation between the two wholesales and the Co-operative Productive Federation, the body which brought together independent producer co-operatives. The aim was to develop the marketing of co-operative productions on a joint national basis. A year later, Congress endorsed the view put forward by the three productive federations, that what was required was an independent commission to 'examine every facet of co-operative structures'.[55] It had been recognised that the problem was not only one of co-operative production but also of distribution; the wholesales were required to supply over a thousand retail societies, some of them very small, with a vast range of goods.

Consequently Congress set up an Independent Commission which which was chaired by Hugh Gaitskell, the Labour Leader. Its Secretary was Anthony Crosland, a leading Labour politician and author. The Commission reported in 1958 and that part of its report which has the greatest relevance to this study was its proposal that there should be a major reduction in the number of retail societies. To help implement this the Co-operative Union was asked to conduct a National Amalgamation Survey which was completed in 1960.[56] Progress remained slow however and attempts to speed mergers were made in 1969 and again in 1974 by Regional Plans drawn up by the Co-operative Union. The second of these proposed the formation of 26 regional societies based on the largest and strongest co-operative societies. The society proposed to be assembled around the Royal Arsenal Society would include the South Suburban Society and others at

Ashford, Chatham, Dover, Sittingbourne and Dartford. Of these the Royal Arsenal Society was by far the largest with an annual turnover of £68.2 million. South Suburban came next with £21.8 million.[57]

The creation of such a regional society would have had political implications. It could have brought into one society co-operatives which had Society Parties operating under the Co-operative Party. How these would then have operated, alongside the RACS tradition of giving greater prominence to relations with the Labour Party, would have been problematical.

A Regional Society along the lines proposed by the 1974 Regional Plan did not however materialise. Instead there was a gradual amalgamation between RACS and smaller societies but never with its nearest and largest neighbour, South Suburban. Political choices were, therefore, never quite as sharp as perhaps they might have been under the 1974 Regional Plan. Even so, RACS became caught up once more in Co-operative and Labour relations.

A New Co-op/Labour Agreement
Defeat in the 1955 General Election caused the Labour Party to cast around for reasons. There was increasing focus on the Party's organisation and a sub-Committee was set up under Harold Wilson to look into the Party's organisation. Its report, published in late 1955, made observations on the working arrangements between the Labour Party and the Co-operative Movement and commented favourably upon the direct affiliation of the Royal Arsenal Society. The Wilson Report suggested that 'it would be to the benefit both of the Labour Party and of the Co-operative Movement if more societies were to affiliate direct to the Party'.[58] Jack Bailey, Secretary of the Co-operative Party, riposted in the Co-operative Party's *Monthly Letter* that this would be 'unacceptable to the Co-operative Movement' because 'the Local Co-operative Party is the vehicle of affiliation to the Labour Party', a view endorsed by various other co-operative leaders and the Co-operative Party's Annual Conference in 1956.

It is possible, therefore, that the Wilson Report was a factor in the surprise decision of the Labour Party in 1957 to terminate the 1946 Agreement. We can only speculate about this because the Labour Party never subsequently explained its move. However, Professor Tom Carbery, in his history of the Co-operative Party, suggested four possible reasons. The first was the Labour Party's concern at the potential growth of the Co-operative Party. Second, the Labour Party's leadership had been pressured by trades unions who were becoming unhappy at the increasing success of co-operative candidates at selection conferences. Third, there was unease about the position of the Parliamentary Co-operative Group within the Parliamentary Labour Party: at the height of the Cold War there had been threats of indiscipline on foreign affairs. Fourth, the Wilson Report, having drawn attention again to the 'money-bags of the Co-operative Movement', had stimulated renewed pressure to gain the direct affiliation of more co-operative societies.[59] Carbery placed little weight on this last argument, suggesting that, on the basis of the Co-operative Movement's current membership of around 10 million, there was a risk of swamping 'the Trade Union element ...'

The Co-operative Movement did approve a new Agreement in 1958 but it did so reluctantly, as was reflected in the Co-operative Union's Report to the 1959 Co-operative Congress:

> ... it must be appreciated that the new agreement has not been entered into with any degree of enthusiasm by the Central Executive. It is believed, however, that the agreement represents the utmost the Labour Party was prepared to concede.[60]

Carbery refers to the new Agreement's essential feature as being a 'containment policy' as far as the Co-operative Party was concerned. This was reflected in the new Agreement's restriction on the number of delegates a local Co-operative Party could have at a Constituency Labour Party, and in the number of Co-operative sponsored candidates at any General Election. At that held in 1959 the number agreed was 30 and this remained the figure thereafter. In 1960 the Labour Party added new clauses that had the effect of channelling Co-operative candidates into 'constituencies with the same degree of hopefulness as those contested in 1959'.[61] Despite the Co-operative Movement's reluctance to enter into the 1958 Agreement it proved to be one in which both Parties were able to operate.

Conclusion

We can see that as the Royal Arsenal Political Purposes Committee entered the 1960s its environment was changing. The most significant part of that was the underlying trends and changes in the Society's trade and its geographical expansion. Smaller societies merging with RACS would bring in different political traditions and usually stronger allegiances to the Co-operative Party than had traditionally been the case in RACS. However at this time this was significant in only two cases, namely with the Woking and Sheerness Societies. Thus there was scope for new tensions.

Notes

References to Minutes are to RACS Minutes held by the CWS SE Archive. *Comradeship* was published by RACS Education Department.

1   Millward, Robert and Singleton, John: *The Political Economy of Nationalisation in Britain 1920-1950*, Cambridge University Press, 1995.

2   See Chapter 6, p.162.

3   Minutes, Political Purposes Committee, 17 October 1952.

4   Ibid.

5   Minutes, Political Purposes Committee with representative of the Labour Party, 7 November 1952.

6   Minutes, Political Purposes Committee, 24 November 1952.

7   Minutes, Political Purposes Committee, 13 October 1951 and 6 December 1951.

8   Minutes, Political Purposes Committee, 24 April 1953 and 1 January 1954.

9   See Chapter 6, p.163.

10   See Chapter 6, p.160.

11   Minutes, Political Purposes Committee, 18 June 1953.

12   Ibid.

13   Ibid.

14   Minutes, Political Purposes Committee, 7 March 1953.

15   Minutes, Political Purposes Sub-Committee, 23 June 1953.

16   Minutes, Political Purposes Committee, 8 August 1953.

17   Minutes, Political Purposes Committee, 10 April 1953.

18   See Chapter 6.

19   Minutes, Political Purposes Committee, 4 September 1953.

20   Minutes, Political Purposes Committee, 9 October 1953.

21   *Comradeship*, May 1952, p.v.

22   *Comradeship*, July 1954, p.vi.

23   Minutes, Political Purposes Committee, 10 April 1953.

24   Minutes, Political Purposes Committee, 1 January 1954.

25   Minutes, Political Purposes Committee, 1 April 1955.

26   Minutes, Political Purposes Committee, 5 April 1957.

27   Minutes, Political Purposes Committee, 27 June 1957.

28   Minutes, Political Purposes Committee, 12 July 1957.

29   Minutes, Political Purposes Committee, 14 August 1957.

30   Ibid.

31   Minutes, Political Purposes Committee, 8 August 1953.

32   Minutes, Political Purposes Committee, 4 December 1953.

33   Minutes, Political Purposes Committee, 3 December 1954.

34   Donoughe, Bernard and Jones, G W, *Herbert Morrison - Portrait of a Politician* pp.213, 538 and 543.

35   Minutes, Political Purposes Committee, 8 October 1954.

36   Donoughe, Bernard and Jones, G W, op. cit., p.532.

37   Minutes, Political Purposes Committee, 4 January 1952.

38   *Comradeship*, January 1954, p.xi.

39   *Comradeship*, June 1952, p.v.

40   *Comradeship*, August 1955, p.vi.

41   *Comradeship*, May 1952, p.v.

42   Minutes, Political Purposes Committee, 4 September 1953.

43   *Comradeship*, November 1953, p.v.

44   *Comradeship*, May 1953, p.vi.

45   *Comradeship*, April 1954, p.vi.

46   *The Co-operative Way - The History and Practices of a Great Co-operative Society*, published by RACS Education Committee in the 1950s.

47   *Comradeship*, November 1952, p.iii.

48   *Comradeship*, December 1955, pp.vi-vii.

49   *Comradeship*, April 1956, pp.iv-v.

50   *Comradeship*, October 1952, p.1.

51   *Comradeship*, September 1952, p.1.

52   *Comradeship*, September 1953, p.i.

53   *Comradeship*, March 1952, p.i.

54   *Comradeship*, September 1955, p.1.

55   Bonner, Arnold, *British Co-operation*, Co-operative Union Ltd, Manchester, 1961, p.280.

56   Ibid., p.182.

57   Co-operative Union Ltd, *Regional Plan 2*, 1974, p.4.

58   Carbery, Thomas F, *Consumers in Politics - a History & General Review of the Co-operative Party*, Manchester University Press, 1969, pp.114-115.

59   Ibid., p.115.

60   Ibid., p.118.

61   Rhodes, Geoffrey, *Co-operative–Labour Relations 1900-1962*, Co-operative College Paper, 1962, p.113.

CHAPTER EIGHT

In and Out of Government

Introduction

The main focus of this Chapter will be the period 1964 to 1979 during which the Labour Party was in and out of Government. It is difficult to make sharp distinctions between one period and another, however. Usually there are trends and dynamics that overlap untidily. We therefore begin this Chapter by noting two dynamics which had begun to develop in the 1950s and which were to have a profound effect on co-operative politics. These were changes in co-operative trade and in the Labour Party.

The organisation of co-operative trade was to change fundamentally in the final third of the 20th century. In the last Chapter we saw the beginning of those changes with the proposals of the Independent Commission and the two Regional Plans. These heralded moves towards the position which exists today, namely the predominance of two national co-operative retailing groups, the Co-operative Wholesale Society and Co-operative Retail Services, alongside several large regional societies in Scotland and in the English Midlands and North, with only a few local societies remaining. Such changes represented one dynamic. Another, and equally powerful one, was a turbulent, and later reforming, Labour Party.

From the mid-1950s the Labour Party became increasingly volatile. The departure of some to the SDP in the early 1980s was demoralising but morale was further weakened by General Election defeats between 1979 and 1992. Thereafter, Party reforms developed slowly under Neil Kinnock, gathered momentum under John Smith and culminated with Tony Blair.

Although there were various divisions in the Party, two major ones that developed in the mid-1950s were particularly disruptive. One was a basic split between left and right wings. A second

192

was between those advocating unilateral nuclear disarmament and those supporting a multilateral approach. Often the left-wingers were also unilateralists, and the right-wingers multilateralists. Nye Bevan, and those in the Tribune Group, were prominent among the left-wingers and unilateralists. It should be said, however, that before his early death, Bevan shifted towards a multilateral approach so as not 'to go naked into the conference chamber'. Hugh Gaitskell led the right wing of the Party and, in 1955, also followed Clement Attlee as the Leader of the Party.

Such Labour Party divisions had an effect on the RACS Political Purposes Committee. Until now it had been mainly concerned with its functions rather than Party policy. Now it became more caught up with the latter. One consequence was that the Labour group on the Committee became less cohesive than it had previously been. Moreover, the Committee also now became sometimes out of step with the rest of RACS.

We have already noted in Chapter Seven that the Committee had proposed Hugh Gaitskell for Labour Party Treasurer.[1] After he became Party Leader the Committee then supported George Brown, another right-winger, when he stood for that position. This decision, however, ran counter to the one taken by the Central Members' Council comprising representatives of the Management, Education and Political Purposes Committees, together with representatives of the Members' Council. That had voted in September 1956 to support Aneurin Bevan rather than George Brown for the position of Party Treasurer.[2] Nevertheless, the Committee persisted in its support for Brown.

Worse divisions were to occur over the question of nuclear disarmament. These reflected not only left-wing Labour Party pressures in the Society but also those of communists. Although the latter were always an element in RACS, they were sometimes more apparent than others. Earlier examples included attempts to gain Labour members' support for the Communist Party affiliation to the Labour Party in the 1920s.[3] Another was communist pressure during the Second World War for an International Peace Conference and a Second Front in the West.[4] However, it was not only issues which enabled communists to come to the fore but also those of their members who were particularly effective operators. One of these was Charlie Job. He had been elected to the RACS Management Committee and was, therefore, capable of influencing the Society's position, and *ipso facto* potentially that of the Political Purposes Committee, on matters such as nuclear disarmament. We should, therefore, examine the communist impact on this question within RACS.

RACS Communists and Labour Policies

Quite apart from his RACS activities, Charlie Job provides an important, but unwitting, footnote in history. In the 1951 General Election he had stood against the sitting Labour Member, Ashley Bramall, in the Bexley Constituency. Bramall was defeated by the future Conservative Leader and Prime Minister, Ted Heath, who took the seat for the Conservatives with the small majority of 1,639.[5] Many blamed the loss of this Labour seat on Charlie Job's intervention.

At the time when divisions deepened between the unilateral and multilateral nuclear disarmers within the Labour Party, the RACS General Committee appointed Job to sit on the Political Purposes Committee. It will be recalled that, from its inception, the Committee had comprised eight elected members and two members each appointed by the Society's General and Education Committee. Unhappy at its implications, the Political Committee asked the General Committee to reconsider Job's appointment,[6] but to no avail. Job's appointment stood.

News of a 'rift' between the two Committees leaked and was reported in the *Kentish Independent*. Under the heading 'Co-op Committees in Row over Red', this news item also identified another communist member of the Political Purposes Committee, namely 'Mr W Spencer of Abbey Wood'.[7] Following its failure to get the General Committee to recall Job, the Political Purposes Committee tried, again unsuccessfully, to get an alteration to the Society's Rules under which:

> No member shall be nominated for or be a member of the Political Purposes Committee who is ineligible to be a member of the Labour or Co-operative Parties.[8]

Throughout its history it is likely that the Political Purposes Committee never had more than two or three communist members at any one time: Labour Party members traditionally formed its majority. It was, therefore, through the Society's Quarterly Meetings, and the Central Members' Council, that the communists stood the most chance of creating political pressure. One such example occurred over the question of disarmament at the 1960 Labour Party Conference.

The RACS policy had been determined by a resolution in favour of unilateral disarmament which had been passed at the Society's Quarterly Meetings. However, the overall majority for this resolution was only ten, and this might not have been achieved had it not been for the alleged mishandling of the vote at the Woolwich meeting. The Political Purposes Committee subsequently claimed that at that, 'an honest decision of the members was not reached owing to the very prolonged nature of the ... Meeting'. Moreover, the Chairman of the meeting had not kept to an undertaking given by the General Committee that the Political Purposes Committee would be allowed to present a statement on the question at all quarterly meeetings. Most disturbing, though, had been the fact that 'thirty-nine people left the Woolwich meeting before the vote was taken without any advice from the Chair'.[9] This led the Political Purposes Committee to observe that:

> No-one can be happy other than pacifists, the unfortunate campaigners for nuclear disarmament and the communists who back Russia rather than Britain.[10]

The Society's vote in favour of unilateral disarmament, however slim and dubious, created difficulties for the Political Purposes Committee. In subsequent discussions it identified a number of options. One was not to vote on disarmament motions at the Labour Party Conference. A second was to support motions favouring unilateral nuclear disarmament or 'Neutralism'. A third option was to 'Support Labour Party National Executive Committee Statement on Defence on the grounds that the vote at the (RACS) September Meeting is not sufficiently decisive to cause the Political Purposes Committee to change from an advocacy of multilateral disarmament to unilateral disarmament policy ...' A final and most extreme option was to cancel the Society's delegation to the Labour Party Conference.[11]

Before the Labour Party Conference the Committee had to face a meeting of the Society Central Members' Council where it would need to report on what conclusion it had reached, and also take into account whatever position the Council Meeting subsequently took. The General Committee had already written to the Political Purposes Committee to express its view that the Disarmament motion passed at RACS Quarterly Meetings 'was binding on the Political Purposes Committee'.[12] Despite this, the Committee decided, by four votes to three, not to implement that decision at the Labour Party Conference. It then decided, by six votes to four, to recommend to the the Central Members' Council that Society delegates should vote in support of the Labour Party Defence Statement.[13] At the Council Meeting held some days later, this proposal was rejected by 41 to 27 votes.[14]

This made the Committee's position even more difficult. For the first time the Committee was poised to act counter to the views of the Society's Members' Council. At the 1960 Labour Party Conference at Scarborough it, therefore, convened a Special Meeting at 10 pm one night to reconsider the position. There it finally resolved:

> That we re-affirm our previous support for multilateral Disarmament and support for the Labour Party National Executive Committee Defence Statement.[15]

Such action reflects the Committee's assessment that, in the final analysis, it should resist communist attempts to influence Labour Party policy through the RACS; moreover, that it should do so even if this invited a vote of censure, as it certainly did at the next Central Members' Council by 59 votes to 15.[16] Even then the Political Purposes Committee refused to accept it, and it counter-attacked by arguing that the Central Members' Council had only the authority to recommend while final political decisions lay with itself.[17] The dispute looked set to rumble on until the General Committee called a halt. It decided that the:

> ... matter has now been discussed and commented upon for quite long enough and that it should now be dropped ... your Committee will appreciate that the sooner completely harmonious relations exist between the various committees and representative bodies, the better it will be for the Society generally.[18]

This incident has been dealt with at length because it illustrates the kind of left-wing pressures the Political Purposes Committee was coming under in the early 1960s. It also shows the Committee's right-wing stance, and the fact that it needed to operate within two frameworks, that of the Royal Arsenal Co-operative Society and that of the Labour Party. During the 1960s each would change and the Committee would have increasing difficulty in reconciling the two.

The Changing Labour Party

By the 1964 General Election the Labour Party had been in opposition for 13 years. Far from the 1951 General Election having been an aberration, it proved to have been the first of three General Elections won by the Conservatives. It was against a background of increasing Labour frustration that some of its leading figures changed. Elderly ones such as Herbert Morrison retired. A far bigger shock came with the unexpected death of Hugh Gaitskell, the Labour Leader, in 1963. Only a month earlier the Secretary of the Labour Party for 20 years, Morgan Phillips, had also died.

Within RACS Joe Reeves had retired at the 1959 General Election[19] along with Herbert Morrison. Although Morrison had no longer been an RACS candidate, he had become a member of Section Two of its Parliamentary Panel which entitled him to an RACS grant of £100 towards his election expenses. After the failure to renew the agreement under which Morrison had been a full RACS candidate,[20] there was no attempt to negotiate a new one for his successor. RACS Parliamentary roots were far stronger at Greenwich where Joe Reeves had, from 1935, been first RACS/

Labour candidate and then MP. On his retirement the Political Purposes Committee successfully nominated Richard Marsh, and he was elected at the 1959 General Election.

A year before, in 1958, another break with the past occurred. Walter Green, the RACS's first Political Secretary, had died.[21] He had already retired from Parliament in the 1945 General Election and, as we have noted, the Political Purposes Committee had not been consulted on a successor.[22]

Within the national Labour Party Harold Wilson followed Hugh Gaitskell and led the Party to an inconclusive victory at the 1964 General Election: Labour's majority over the Conservatives was 13 but overall only five. Another General Election was, therefore, likely and came in 1966. At this Labour increased its overall majority to 97. While the RACS held only Greenwich at both elections, 19 of the Co-operative Party's Labour/Co-operative candidates were elected at the 1964 General Election,[23] that figure being reduced by one in the following General Election.[24] During the two Parliaments, depending on reshuffles, the number of Labour/Co-operative MPs holding Government position averaged six.

Labour failed to retain power in the 1970 General Election, however, when the Conservatives gained a majority of 30. Ironically, they were now led by Ted Heath. Many in Co-operative circles believed that he had gained his seat through Charlie Job's intervention at Bexley in 1951. In the February 1974 General Election the Heath Government failed to achieve an overall majority and, when the Liberals declined to join it, made way for another minority Labour Government. That went to the country again the following October. Despite achieving an overall majority of only three, and facing increasing problems, this held power until May 1979 under Jim Callaghan. It was then defeated and Margaret Thatcher's first Government came to power with an overall majority of 44. Labour was to be out of office for the next 18 years. Thus it can be seen that from 1964 to 1979 the Labour Party was in and out of office, but when in power it lacked a commanding majority. The frustrations, disillusionments and the sheer pressure of problems during these years paved the way for the splits of the 1980s.

They were also years in which friction developed between the Co-operative Movement and Labour Governments over taxation policies. Labour's 1966 Budget announced a Selective Employment Tax. Intended to encourage a shift in employment from the service to the manufacturing sector, it was bound to increase retailers' costs. Moreover, it came on top of the Co-operative Movement's growing concern about the effect of other increases. In May 1966, the RACS Political Purposes Committee passed a resolution listing their effect on the Society. The combined effect of increased National Insurance, petrol tax, postal charges, redundancy payments, vehicle road tax and local rates, together with a reduction in Investment Allowances, meant an extra cost of £279,000 per year to RACS. The proposed Selective Employment Tax was likely to add a further £350,000, and this was 'almost equal to the total dividend returned to its 400,000 members last year'. The Political Purposes Committee's motion ended by calling:

> ... upon the Government to fully recognise the essential social role of the Co-operative Movement by treating its capital investment expenditure as falling in the category for full relief of taxation and exempting the Movement from the Selective Employment Tax.[25]

Copies of this resolution were sent to James Callaghan, Chancellor of the Exchequer, and to Labour MPs in the RACS trading area. The RACS was not alone in calling for the withdrawal of the Selective Employment Tax; the Co-operative Movement mounted a large campaign. Over 250 co-operative directors and chief officials, together with several hundred other co-operators lobbied MPs at Westminster. The Co-operative Party issued a leaflet called *This Stupid Tax* which was distributed to delegates attending the 1966 Labour Party Conference. Reprinted twice, some 118,000 copies of this leaflet were sold, giving some idea of co-operative hostility to the Selective Employment Tax.[26]

It should be remembered, though, that this tax came on top of other rising taxes which forced co-operatives to try to offset them through reducing costs. One way this could be attempted was by rationalising structures. In the 1960s RACS tried to do this in a number of ways including merging with smaller co-operative societies in Surrey, Kent and Berkshire.

The Changing RACS

Early mergers included those with the Godalming and Woking Societies in 1963[27] and Haslemere in 1965.[28] Others followed and had implications not only for the Society's trade but also for its Political Purposes Committee and its distinct tradition of direct affiliation with the Labour Party. All the incoming societies had had Co-operative Party branches. How the Committee achieved a relatively smooth transition, and acceptance of its way of working, provides interesting insights. These are brought into sharper focus by a number of contemporary sources, both oral and written, that now become available to supplement the written sources we have so far used. Two contemporary accounts have been given by members of societies which merged with RACS. Both became members of the Political Purposes Committee, and eventually chaired it. One was Hilda Smith from Woking and the other Colin Shrive from Sheerness. Hilda Smith gave a taped interview to Ron Roffey, the last General Secretary of RACS, in May 1992, in which she described the factors leading to the merger of the Woking Society with RACS in 1963. When asked if 'the Woking Board lay down ... any demands on the Royal Arsenal', Hilda Smith replied:

> Yes, one of the important ones was that we should keep the Co-operative Party. We were very concerned, as I have already mentioned. Board members were Co-operative Party members and I could show you the list, because I was secretary of the Co-operative Party at one time ... So we stipulated that we should keep our Co-operative Party and have activity through the Co-operative Party because we felt that it was important and of course one of the things that happened, not long after the merger ... was that Mr Furness ... came in and said to us you can't have a Co-op Party because this isn't our structure because we work through the Labour Party ...[29]

Mrs Smith suggests that the Woking Co-operative Party continued for a little while but that Co-operative Party delegates who went to the constituency were turned into Labour Party delegates.

Other people interviewed in connection with this study have also suggested that Co-operative Party branches in societies that merged with RACS were not encouraged. They were allowed to die although there were one or two exceptions such as in Gravesend. One reason was that, except for a brief period in the late 1940s and early 1950s, when the Committee had allowed twice-yearly meetings of individual members, they had not been encouraged within RACS. Even during the time when meetings were held they were called by the Committee, and allowed no scope for members to develop their own programme or appoint their own officers. These meetings appear to have died out in the mid-1950s, although Furness asserted that their attendances 'could be increased by more active propaganda at any time'.[30]

One reason why a full Co-operative Party structure was not allowed was that it could complicate the Committee's basis of affiliation to Constituency Labour Parties. This happened at Woking and the problem that arose led, in May 1965, to a meeting between the Political Purposes Committee and A L Williams, successor to Morgan Phillips as the Party's Secretary, and Sarah Barker, the Party's National Agent. Edwin Furness expressed the Committee's concern at:

> ... the way consultations took place at Woking Constituency Labour Party which is a new area through the Co-operative Society merging with the RACS. The Labour Party Regional Organiser assumed at the outset that we had to be treated on the basis of agreements reached with the Co-operative Union for Co-operative Party affiliations, and, in spite of the build up of our Political Fund, to be regarded as the equivalent of a single Trade Union Branch and not as a group of branches.[31]

'Branches' here meant the trading branches of the Society. In previous discussions on the Woking problems with Ron Hayward, Southern Region Labour Party Organiser, Furness had explained that:

Our payments are based on our Society membership within each Parliamentary Constituency, in which the RACS Ltd has trading branches. If we are regarded in the same way on the basis of branches as a Trade Union Organisation, then, for example, where we have ten branch trading points this would give us an entitlement of 50 delegates. We have never put out this kind of claim for full implementation, but rather as a basis for discussion, but as a body nationally affiliated to the Labour Party there seems no reason why the reasonable request of the RACS for increased representation should not be given favourable consideration by the Labour Party.[32]

At its meeting with Len Williams and Sarah Barker, the Political Purposes Committee argued that an existing Co-operative Party structure:

... could not be taken as defining the basis of the affiliation of the RACS to Constituency Labour Parties. Our association as we are nationally affiliated, must be based on a separate understanding reached with the Political Purposes Committee.

This point seemed to be accepted by Len Williams who agreed that:

... because the RACS was a directly affiliated body to the Labour Party nationally, obviously the agreements reached with the Co-operative Union on behalf of the Co-operative Party, were not applicable in matters of affiliation to the RACS Ltd. The Labour Party valued very highly and would wish to retain, the link which had existed for a very long time between the RACS Political Purposes Committee and the Labour Party.[33]

Thus we can see that the RACS affiliation to Constituency Labour Parties was linked to the Society's national affiliation to the Labour Party, and also to its membership in a given area. The latter began to be challenged as membership ties in co-operative societies gradually weakened from the 1960s onwards. They perhaps remained stronger in RACS than in most other societies, but this did not stop Ron Hayward, the Labour Party's Southern Regional Organiser, and later General Secretary, referring to RACS's membership in a CLP as 'notional membership', thus greatly annoying the Political Purposes Committee.[34]

Apart from problems arising from changing the basis of affiliation to Constituency Labour Parties, the Political Purposes Committee adapted well to a widening geographical area. Representatives from new areas were encouraged to seek election to it and, as we have noted, two of these eventually came to chair the Committee. One of these, Colin Shrive, gives a fascinating account of how he came to be a member of the Committee. In doing so he illustrates the interaction of various groups on the Committee:

> I remember the approach being made to me about standing for election to the Political Committee towards the end of 1971, the year the Sheerness Society transferred engagements to the RACS. At the time I was secretary of the Queensborough in Sheppey Labour Party and leader of the Borough Council ... I was invited to a meeting in County Hall in London.

There he met three members of the Committee, together with other well known Labour activists'. Shrive continued:

> Not having any experience of the single transferable vote system I was quite bemused by the technicalities of the allocation of candidates for first, second and third preference in areas to maximise the Party vote. Clearly the invitation to me was to pull out a party vote in Sheppey and so ensure second and third preferences to other better known candidates. The tactics were successful and I think the London Labour Party

203

establishment were surprised when I scraped in as the last successful candidate.[35]

Shrive's comments suggest that there were now geographical as well as the traditional groupings on the Committee. His reference to the 'London Labour Party establishment' also points to the fact that this was still a prominent force in the Committee. It was to become less so as the RACS, and its Political Purposes Committee, became less sharply focused on Woolwich. Moreover, as we should perhaps have mentioned when dealing with the changing Labour Party, the London Labour Party was itself declining in importance. As Donoughue and Jones point out, it was:

> … no longer the great electoral machine it had been in the years of Morrison's dominance. Membership fell in the mid-fifties, though not dramatically; in fact the Party's decline was more fundamental and less tangible than just a question of membership figures. The London Labour Party was very much Morrison's creation and, like himself, reflected and symbolised a phase in the growth of Labour to a mass national Party, adding the superstructure of urban local government to the original trade union foundations. That stage was now over, as the core of working-class communities dissolved under the social and economic pressure of a more affluent and mobile society.[36]

Another and subsequent factor in the London Labour Party's decline was the Conservative Government's proposal in 1962 to abolish the LCC and replace it with a Greater London Council in which the traditional inner Labour working-class boroughs would be offset by more affluent outer boroughs in which Labour had no natural majority. The Political Purposes Committee condemned the London Government Bill as being 'politically biased, ill-conceived and based upon a lack of understanding of local government in London.'

Nevertheless, the Bill proceeded and the Greater London

Council was created. In response the Labour Party set up its Greater London Regional Council to which, after much negotiation, the RACS Political Purposes Committee affiliated.[37] The new Greater London Regional Council continued alongside the longer established London Labour Party in which the Political Purposes Committee continued to play a full part.

Just how badly the Labour Party was subsequently to fare in the new Greater London Council was shown in the GLC elections in 1967. Then, with swings against the Labour Government, the Conservatives won 82 seats while the Labour Party held only 18: the creation of Aldermen raised these figures to 92 and 24 respectively. Staunchly, the Political Purposes Committee held that 'This vote can only be regarded as an anti-Labour Government protest token and had nothing to do with the work of the Greater London Council.' The Committee's earlier Chairman, John Andrews, was defeated at Greenwich, while Edwin Furness suffered the same fate at Bexley. However, another member and subsequently an MP, Harry Lamborn, was re-elected at Southwark.[38]

Besides changes in the RACS and the London Labour Party, the Committee was also set to experience more internal changes. In June 1966 Edwin Furness reminded its members of his impending retirement.[39] Arrangements were thus set in hand to appoint a successor. The Committee agreed that they would invite applications for the post of Political Secretary 'on similar conditions as agreed for the present occupant of this office' and that procedures previously used to make the appointment should apply again. What was different this time was that the National Organiser of the Co-operative Party, Louis Cornillie, was to be invited to participate in the shortlisting and interviewing of candidates[40] thus underlining the Committee's improved relations with the Co-operative Party.

Fourteen applications were received, compared with 171 when Green applied and 60 when Furness applied.[41] Of the six shortlisted in 1967 only one, John Cartwright, a full time Labour Party agent at Bexley, came from the RACS's area. Again, it was an all-male shortlist although, as we have seen the Committee from its start had always had a number of women members. Prior to the interviews the Committee resolved:

That the candidate appointed should be advised that he will not be expected to take up a prospective candidature for Parliament for at least a period of five years from the day of his appointment.[42]

At the end of January 1967 the interviews were held and a ballot vote resulted in a majority for 'Mr John Cartwright of Woolwich'. The Committee also resolved that his starting salary would be £1,268 plus half-yearly dividend bonus on salary, and a car allowance.[43] It is interesting to note that RACS still continued the practice of paying a dividend on the wages of employees.

John Cartwright became the Political Secretary on 1st May 1967, succeeding Edwin Furness who had held the position, sometimes with seeming difficulty, for 21 years. The Committee organised a reception for Furness and his wife in June 1967 which was attended by 'personalities from the Labour and Co-operative Parties, the Society Secretary and General Manager and members of the General and Political Committees'.[44]

We should perhaps pause here to reflect upon the consequences of age in RACS and its Political Purposes Committee. Furness was retiring at 65 but seemed little bowed by age. He had pursued his job energetically and brought about improved relations with the Co-operative Party although it could perhaps be said that these had more to do with spirit and intent rather than with substance. Furness had also pursued an active role in local government. Nevertheless, he was of an ageing generation. His Labour roots went back even farther: his mother-in-law, a Mrs Senton, had been the 'daughter of Mr Jim Hardaker, the first working man candidate with Trade Union support to stand in the City of Bradford in the 1873 Parliamentary Election'.[45]

RACS's roots went back even farther and in 1968 it was due to celebrate its centenary. Already, the Political Purposes Committee had proposed that this be commemorated by a 'Concert Meeting to be held at the Royal Festival Hall or another hall in Central London, with speakers such as the Prime Minister, Chairman of the Co-operative Party, Trade Union Congress and the Co-operative Wholesale Society'.[46] RACS could think in such grandiose terms because it was still one of Britain's strongest consumer co-operatives, but other aspects of age were more insidious. From the 1880s an important element in the Society had been the Co-operative Women's Guild. Their electoral importance in the Society was reflected by the fact that, from its inception, the Political Purposes Committee had regularly sent representatives to 'Guild Birthdays'. Rosters of them appear frequently in the Committee's Minutes. When John Cartwright agreed to be interviewed for this study, and was asked about the Guild Birthdays, he recalled that invitations included the instruction to the invitee to take along his or her own 'knife, fork and spoon'. While this provides an endearing and heart warming reminder of its practical nature, the Guild was nevertheless appearing old-fashioned in many respects by the late 1960s. The Guild had not only brought working-class women together under the aegis of co-operative societies, it had also campaigned on issues affecting all women such as health and divorce reform. By the later years of this century more narrowly-based, and even single issue, women's organisations had developed thus causing the Guild to appear anachronistic. It seemed even more so as its membership visibly aged and fewer young women, a greater number of whom were now benefiting from improved education and were heading for professional occupations, joined the Guild. Moreover, those who went into less skilled jobs appeared neither to have the time nor energy to go to Guild meetings. On taking over from Edwin Furness, John Cartwright found the Guild still an important resource although a declining and ageing one.

From all that has gone before in this Chapter, it is possible 'o see that Cartwright's arrival coincided with a number of changes affecting the RACS: the Society's geographical expansion, changes in the Labour Party and the incipient decline of the Guild. There were also changes among figures who had been influential in RACS politics: Joe Reeves and Herbert Morrison had retired in 1959, and Morrison died in 1965, the Society conducting his funeral. In 1971 Furness's long-time protagonist, Arthur Skeffington, also died.[47]

Changing Personnel
One effect of John Cartwright's arrival was that relations with

the Co-operative Party became less warm. When in July 1967 Don Storer, the Political Secretary of the South Suburban Co-operative Society, asked for names of individual Co-operative Party members in the Brixton area with a view to establishing a local Co-operative Party', Cartwright declined to provide them and the Political Purposes Committee endorsed this response.[48] It has to be said, however, that it might have been coloured by the traditionally awkward relations between the RACS and its immediate neighbour, the South Suburban Co-operative Society. Over the years there had been problems over boundaries and there were also political differences: whereas South Suburban had unreservedly affiliated to the Co-operative Party, the RACS had not and had retained its prior loyalty to the Labour Party. A number of attempts had been made to amalgamate the two South London co-operative societies but all had failed.

Elsewhere, the RACS was achieving successful mergers but with repercussions on its relations with the Co-operative Party. We have noted that mergers usually led to the demise of Co-operative Party branches. However, when the Gravesend Society discussed an amalgamation with RACS, its Board demanded that its traditional Co-operative Party organisation should be allowed to continue. The RACS Board agreed. John Cartwright immediately pointed out the financial and organisational implications for the RACS Political Purposes Committee which then protested to the Board declaring that it had been:

> ... disturbed that undertakings on political matters had been given to the Gravesend Society without prior consultation with the Committee and required that such commitments should not be given in the future without consultation with the Political Secretary or Chairman of the Political Committee.

The Political Purposes Committee now seemed to adopt a dual approach. On the one hand it agreed 'That the Political Secretary be authorised to hold informal discussions on the problems involved in granting a measure of local autonomy to local Co-operative Parties within the Society's enlarged trading area'. On the other it decided to re-open the questions of its relations with the Co-operative Party, and what affiliation fees it should pay to it.[49]

At this point we should perhaps note that there had also been changes in the officers of the Co-operative Party. In 1963 Jack Bailey had retired as the Party's Secretary. He had been much respected as a gentle, generous and philosophic man who was, nonetheless, an astute politician. Relations between him and Furness had been better than those between Perry and Green. Sir Jack Bailey, as he soon became, was followed by Harold Campbell who was no less a practical and enthusiastic co-operator. Both he and Bailey were members of the Board of the Enfield Highway Society, one of the four London societies that failed to merge in the 1930s. They, therefore, had a strong background in consumer co-operation. Despite having been the Party's Assistant Secretary since 1946, Campbell held the post of Secretary barely four years, leaving it in 1967 to take a position in co-operative housing. He was succeeded by Ted Graham, now Lord Graham of Edmonton. When young, Graham had been active in the Co-operative Youth Movement and was the first Secretary of the Party to have studied at the Co-operative College. Like Bailey and Campbell, Graham was also a member of the Enfield Society's Board. Prior to his appointment as Party Secretary he had been Secretary of the Southern Section of the Co-operative Union. In that position he had had much contact with RACS and had also been responsible for encouraging societies to merge under the Co-operative Union's regionalisation plans. Graham was, therefore, well acquainted with the RACS position.

He soon knew of the Committee's unease over the position at Gravesend, and also its wish to re-open the questions of affiliation fee and relations with the Co-operative Party. Graham, therefore, sought a meeting. This took place in July 1968 but with no immediate outcome.[50] However, at its next meeting, the Committee considered a 'detailed report from the Political Secretary' tracing the history of the relationship with the Co-operative Party and commenting on the level of affiliation fees paid to it. Cartwright's report also examined the future of four local Co-operative Party branches that now existed within the

RACS's trading area. It suggested that it was time to consider the reintroduction of a separate RACS Parliamentary Panel. Decisions on the first two of these, namely affiliation fees and the continuance of the four Party branches in the RACS area, were deferred because the Co-operative Party had just set up a Working Party to review its operations and it was, therefore, decided to await its outcome. In the meantime the Committee agreed that the four Party branches might continue to meet and could apply to the Committee for grants to cover their administrative costs. On the third point, however, the Committee decided that it did indeed wish to 're-establish an independent RACS Parliamentary Panel'. Once more a final decision was delayed until 'early 1968' so that it could be taken in the light of the Committee's financial position and the availability of suitable candidates'.[51] A year later the Committee resolved:

> That a return to the past practice of an independent RACS Parliamentary Panel separate from that of the Co-operative Party be approved in principle; that the Political Secretary notify interested organisations of the decision ...[52]

Not surprisingly, the Co-operative Party quickly sought another meeting with the Committee. This took place in November 1969 when the Party was represented by Ted Graham, its Assistant Secretary, David Wise and National Organiser, Louis Cornillie.[53] Despite their representations the Committee 'reaffirmed' its decision to re-establish a separate RACS Parliamentary Panel.[54]

The Committee made a rapid about turn, however. Only a month later it decided to take no action until after 'the General Election'. A likely factor was that John Cartwright had been nominated as the Prospective Parliamentary Candidate at Bexley and 'the Co-operative Party had offered official sponsorship which would involve financial support'. In these new circumstances the Committee agreed:

> That the offer be accepted; that the Political Secretary be nominated for the Co-operative Party Panel; and that the Committee accepts its share of the financial commitment

which would result from the selection of the Political Secretary.[55]

Cartwright was subsequently adopted as Prospective Labour and Co-operative Candidate at Bexley. In all this the Committee seems to have lost sight of its original condition that its new Political Secretary would not seek a Parliamentary nomination for five years 'from the day of his appointment'. But the Committee had been content for Cartwright to continue as a Woolwich Borough Councillor and for him subsequently to become Leader of the Council. As far as Bexley was concerned he was not successful but was later nominated for Joe Reeve's old constituency of Greenwich. A by-election occurred there in 1971 following Richard Marsh's resignation on becoming Chairman of British Rail.[56] But Cartwright failed to get the nomination and did not, in fact, contest a Parliamentary election until after he had stepped down as RACS Political Secretary in October 1972. His reason for resigning was that he had been elected to the Board of the RACS which was still a full-time position.

The post of Political Secretary was once again advertised, this time with an annual starting salary of £2,160, a car allowance of £340 and a staff bonus of 2½ per cent.[57] Fifteen people applied and the five shortlisted included one woman. They were interviewed in December 1972 and, after a ballot vote, 'Mr R A Balfe of Peckham' was appointed.[58] Colin Shrive, who was present, observed that he 'was easily the best candidate for the post'.[59] Just as Cartwright had at Woolwich, Balfe combined his Political Secretaryship with local government. He was elected to the GLC and became Chair of its Housing Development Committee in 1975.[60]

Within the Political Purposes Committee itself, we find two trends developing from the mid-1970s. One was a period of protracted and difficult relations with the Co-operative Party. This coincided with a change in the Party's Secretaryship. When Ted Graham was elected to Parliament in 1974 as the Labour/ Co-operative MP for Edmonton, his place was taken by David Wise. He was a Director, and later President, of the

211

Invicta Co-operative Society which was adjacent to RACS at Dartford in Kent. Wise went on to become a Director of the Co-operative Wholesale Society and Chairman of the Co-operative Insurance Society, thus continuing the tradition that Co-operative Party Secretaries had strong co-operative as well as Labour backgrounds. It was now Balfe and Wise who were the main negotiators

By 1975 the two main points of difference between the RACS Political Purposes Committee and the Co-operative Party were affiliation fees and RACS maintenance of an Independent Parliamentary Panel. A sticking point over the latter this time was the question of who was eligible to vote in selection conferences. Under the RACS's Rules this was anyone who was a member of the Society whatever their political persuasion. Under the Party's Rules it could only be someone who was a member of the Co-operative and Labour Parties. This had always been an inherent difference but the Political Purposes Committee had not previously made it a sticking point. Now they did and observed that RACS Rules did 'not allow for the exclusion of any member of the Political Committee from a meeting, whereas those of the Co-operative Party' did. In June 1975 the Political Purposes Committee took the unequivocal position that:

> ... Mr J C Cartwright, Mr H Lamborn and Mr A J Wellbeloved be placed on the new Parliamentary Panel without further consideration by the Committee.[61]

Each was a sitting MP for a constituency within the RACS area. Cartwright had been elected for Woolwich East, Lamborn for Southwark and Wellbeloved for Erith and Crayford. Moreover each had been, or would be, a member of the Political Purposes Committee.

It is likely that the costs of supporting three candidate shaped the Committee's views on the other main difficulty between it and the Co-operative Party, namely that of affiliation fees. It can be seen from the Table at the end of this study that during the mid-1970s, the RACS affiliation fee dropped dramatically. In 1975 it had been £1,815 but dropped to £900 the following year and

£450 the year after that. Only in 1979 did it rise to £1,000 and then increased dramatically in 1980 to £4,606. While some of the decrease could be explained by the Committee's commitment to its Parliamentary candidates, some of it also seems due to poorer relations with the Party. During the mid to late 1970s a number of abortive meetings between the Committee and Party were held and equally abortive correspondence exchanged.

The Changing Committee

The second important trend in the Committee was its move away from being a purely functional committee as it had been in its first 40 years. Now it became more involved with issues and even campaigning. The Minutes during the year 1977 reveal interests in a wide range of issues over and above its more traditional ones with RACS and the Labour and Co-operative Parties. These issues included the Royal Commission on the Health Service, Deportation Orders, World Development Movement, Public Transport Campaign, Wandsworth Development Agency, Meriden Motorcycle Co-operative, Grunwick Strike Appeal, Brixton Homeless Housing Society Ltd, Labour Abortion Rights Campaign, Area Health Authorities, All Britain Peace Liaison Group, South London Branch of Britain/ Cyprus Committee, National Council for Civil Liberties, Scottish Football Association's Visit to Chile, National Campaign for Nursery Education, Increase in Dental Charges, the journal *Liberation*, Industrial Common Ownership Movement, Trade Union & Co-op Esperanto Group, the Campaign for Labour Party Democracy, Clay Cross Defence Fund, Southwark Campaign Against Racialism and Fascism, Lewisham Campaign against Racialism, Co-operative Housing, Southwark Child Care Campaign, Campaign for Nuclear Disarmament, British Uganda Association, Southern Africa Solidarity Fund Committee, Trade Union, Labour and Co-operative Democratic History Society, Transport White Paper, Health Care for Women, Rally Against Racialism, Co-operative Development Agency, International Co-operative Alliance and Payment to Foster Parents.

This range of interests is not likely to be much different from those of the Political Committee of the London Co-operative Society during the same period. The big difference was, however, that that was a membership organisation whereas RACS Political Purposes Committee was not. With or without members, the point to note is that the Committee was increasingly seeing itself as a Political Committee.

The above list illustrates the Committee's concerns with wider co-operative issues. During the 1970s it also became involved with problems internal to RACS. One was how to improve member participation. Concern over the decline in this had led the Society in 1972 to set up a Special Committee to look into the question. When this reported, however, the Political Purposes Committee feared that its proposals 'would remove from the democratically elected Political Purposes Committee the right to decide how the Society vote is cast at the Annual Conferences of the Labour and Co-operative Parties'.[62] The Committee also feared that the proposed Area Councils would affect 'political activities within the Society'. It therefore requested 'a Formal Special Joint Meeting to discuss the powers, functions and constitution of the new Area Councils ...'[63] Membership participation in RACS had declined to a dangerous level with some Members' Quarterly Meetings failing to get a quorum.[64]

The Society also had problems in maintaining its traditional dividend. In 1970 the Board proposed the introduction of dividend stamps. The Political Purposes Committee was worried that a different computation of the dividend would adversely affect its Political Grant. In March 1970 it passed the following motion:

> That the Political Committee expresses its concern at the possible effect of the introduction of dividend stamps on the Political Grant and informs all concerned that it is opposed to the introduction of dividend stamps until such time as its objections are met.[65]

In the wider co-operative sphere the Political Purposes Committee campaigned for a government funded Co-operative Development Agency. It also decided to affiliate to the Industrial Common Ownership Movement.[66]

In RACS's own area the Committee was concerned at the rising 'level of unemployment'. That the Society itself might be forced to consider redundancies became clear as its central area at Woolwich experienced closures among traditional firms of boiler makers and cable makers, and those producing propellers. Besides the larger closures of Woolwich Arsenal and Siemens Bros, smaller riverside businesses such as barge-breaking, petrol refineries and paint works were also in difficulties.

In the wider political area the Committee voiced its concern on a number of occasions about the situation in Northern Ireland. Colin Shrive recalls that, at one Labour Party Conference at Brighton:

> ... Richard Balfe, a member of the RACS delegation was learned to have invited Gerry Adams to attend Conference as his guest. They were both barred at the doors. During the same Conference week members of the delegation prevented the Political Committee banner from being used at a fringe meeting at which Gerry Adams was the main speaker. The Political Committee had its 'Irish mafia' at one stage.[67]

In the political sphere the Committee actively campaigned against Britain joining the European Economic Community. RACS members had declared their opposition to this at a number of their Meetings in 1970, 1971 and 1974. The Committee not only campaigned against entry among Labour Parties, trade unions and other organisations in its own area, but also joined in a campaign opposing entry with the Political Committee of the London Co-operative Society. The growing closeness of the two Political Committees was reflected when, in 1975, the RACS Committee contributed towards the Alf Lomas Defence Fund. Lomas was then Political Secretary of the London Society and in May 1973 had visited Gibraltar at the invitation of the Gibraltar branch of the Transport and General Workers' Union to speak at their Bi-Annual Meeting. While there he was interviewed on Gibraltar television, and inadvertently gave incorrect information about prices and wages in a local store which held a franchise 'for mailing goods from a well-known British retailer'. Settling the matter out of court meant that Lomas had had to find almost £1,500. The Political Purposes Committee contributed £40.[68] At the same meeting the Committee also agreed to pay £40 to the Richard Balfe Defence Fund. Balfe had made an 'off the cuff' remark to a journalist about the conduct of a Housing Association involved in a dispute with its tenants. The Housing Association was then awarded damages of £500 plus costs of a further £500. There were dangers of bankruptcy proceedings against Balfe. Had Balfe been declared bankrupt he would have been unable to continue sitting on the Greater London Council.[69]

We thus find that in the 1970s the Political Purposes Committee became more concerned with wider political issues. Perhaps it could also be said that during this period it also became more flamboyant.

Conclusion

During this period 1964 to 1979 the Political Purposes Committee had three Political Secretaries: Furness, Cartwright and Balfe. In 1979 Balfe was to relinquish the position on being elected to the European Parliament. During the early part of the period the RACS had continued its geographical expansion. Although this continued during the latter part of the period, problems increased with declining membership participation and difficulties in maintaining the traditional form of dividend. The Woolwich area was becoming depressed as unemployment increased.

Despite a background of increasing tension in the Labour Party, the Committee's relations with that Party remained reasonably good. In the next Chapter, though, we will find that an RACS nominee could no longer expect automatic election to the Party's National Executive Committee. The Committee's relations with the Co-operative Party during the latter part of the period worsened. Problems arose over the selection of Parliamentary Candidates and the Society's affiliation fees to the Party. As always, though, relations with the Co-operative Party were a matter of degree. Despite the difficulties, the RACS and its Political Purposes Committee still continued to play a full part in the Party's Annual Conference and many of its other events. Another feature of this period was the Committee's shift away from being a purely functional Political Purposes Committee to one with wider actions. Although still to the right of its counterpart in the London Co-operative Society, it drew closer to that Committee.

Notes

References to Minutes are to RACS Minutes held by the CWS SE Archive.

1   See Chapter 7, p.180.
2   Minutes, RACS Central Members' Council, 25 September 1956 and 20 November 1956.
3   See Chapter 5, pp.77-79.
4   See Chapter 6, pp.130-131.
5   Keesings Contemporary Archives, 3-10 November 1951, p11813.
6   Minutes, Political Purposes Committee, 1 May 1959.
7   Ibid.
8   Minutes, Political Purposes Committee, 16 October 1959.
9   Minutes, Political Purposes Committee, 18 September 1960.
10 Ibid.
11 Ibid.
12 Ibid.
13 Ibid.
14 Minutes, RACS Central Members' Council, 27 September 1960.
15 Minutes, Special Meeting, Political Purposes Committee, Scarborough, 3 October 1960.
16 Minutes, Joint Meeting RACS Committees, 22 November 1960.
17 Minutes, Political Purposes Committee, 2 December 1960.
18 Minutes, Political Purposes Committee, 6 January 1961.
19 Minutes, Political Purposes Committee, 3 April 1959.
20 See Chapter 6.
21 Minutes, Political Purposes Committee, 2 May 1959.
22 See Chapter 7, p.173.
23 Co-operative Union Ltd, Report of 1967 Congress, Douglas, pp.191-192.
24 Ibid., p.195.
25 Minutes, Political Purposes Committee, 6 May 1966.
26 Co-operative Union Ltd, op.cit., p.196.
27 Minutes, Political Purposes Committee, 7 June 1963 and 1 November 1963

28 Minutes, Political Purposes Committee, 2 July 1965.

29 CWS SE Archive, Interview with Hilda Smith recorded by Ron Roffey, 10 May 1992.

30 See Chapter 7.

31 Minutes, Meeting of Political Purposes Committee with A L Williams, Secretary, Labour Party, and Sarah Barker, LP National Agent, 7 May 1965.

32 Ibid.

33 Ibid.

34 Ibid.

35 Shrive, Colin, Letter to author, 24 May 1997.

36 Donoughue, Bernard and Jones, G W, *Herbert Morrison - Portrait of a Politician*, Weidenfeld & Nicholson, London, 1973, pp.546-547.

37 Minutes, Political Purposes Committee, 6 September 1968.

38 Minutes, Political Purposes Committee, 14 April 1967.

39 Minutes, Political Purposes Committee, 3 June 1967.

40 Minutes, Political Purposes Committee, 30 September 1966

41 See Chapter 5, p.93 and Chapter 6, p.149.

42 Minutes, Political Purposes Committee, 6 January 1967.

43 Minutes, Political Purposes Committee, 26 January 1967.

44 Minutes, Political Purposes Committee, 7 July 1967.

45 Minutes, Political Purposes Committee, 4 November 1955.

46 Minutes, Political Purposes Committee, 3 February 1967.

47 Minutes, Political Purposes Committee, 19 March 1971.

48 Minutes, Political Purposes Committee, 7 July 1967.

49 Minutes, Political Purposes Committee, 7 June 1968.

50 Minutes, Political Purposes Committee, 5 July 1968.

51 Minutes, Political Purposes Committee, 19 July 1968.

52 Minutes, Political Purposes Committee, 4 July 1969.

53 Minutes, Political Purposes Committee, 7 November 1969.

54 Minutes, Political Purposes Committee, 5 December 1967.

55 Minutes, Political Purposes Committee, 2 January 1970.

56 Minutes, Political Purposes Committee, 7 May 1971.

57 Minutes, Political Purposes Committee, 20 October 1972.

58 Minutes, Political Purposes Committee, 15 December 1972.

59 Shrive, Colin, op.cit.

60 Minutes, Political Purposes Committee, 2 May 1975.

61 Minutes, Political Purposes Committee, 6 June 1976.

62 Minutes, Political Purposes Committee, 19 January 1973.
63 Minutes, Political Purposes Committee, 14 September 1973.
64 Minutes, Political Purposes Committee, 19 October 1973.
65 Minutes, Political Purposes Committee, 6 March 1979.
66 Minutes, Political Purposes Committee, 10 October 1975.
67 Shrive, Colin, op.cit.
68 Minutes, Political Purposes Committee, 5 September 1975.
69 Ibid.

CHAPTER NINE

Shifting Sands

Introduction
The period 1979 to 1996 was one in which the Labour Party was in continuous opposition to government. For the RACS Political Purposes Committee it was a period which could be described as one of shifting sands. During this time the Committee's main bases, the Royal Arsenal Co-operative Society and the Labour Party, both changed fundamentally thus causing the Committee to change also.

This Chapter will broadly divide into two. The first part will examine changes in the Labour Party and how the Committee responded to these. The second will trace the merger of the Royal Arsenal Co-operative Society with the Co-operative Wholesale Society Ltd and follow through its implications for the Committee.

Shifts within the Labour Party
There seems much to commend A J Davies's view, expressed in his book *To Build a New Jerusalem*, that Labour's General Election defeat in 1979 marked the end of the second phase in Labour history. The first had been a pioneering phase concerned to win hearts that had ended with the collapse of the Ramsay MacDonald Government in 1931. The second had been mostly concerned with consolidation and administration and with the creation of a modern social democratic state based on three main principles; government intervention, public ownership and the creation of a welfare state. Davies calls this the 'minds' phase and suggests that it was largely accomplished by 1951.

Thereafter, both Conservative and Labour governments 'basically just administered this machine'.[1] One problem, however, defied solution. It was how to maintain steady economic growth and the quest for this led governments to resort to drastic efforts such as 'Wilson and Castle's *In Place of Strife*, Edward Heath's free market policies of 1970-72 and his Industrial Relations Act, and the Callaghan government's 5 per cent pay policy'. As economic growth faltered and the number of unemployed grew, the relationship between government, employers and the trade unions became ever more strained. It was not surprising, therefore, that in this situation relations worsened within the Labour Party. Some argued that the Party had 'lost its moral dimension'. For his part, Davies believed that it had certainly 'failed to rise to the intellectual challenge of constructing a post-Keynesian order', and that the question facing it after its 1979 General Election defeat was whether it could

> ... move on and create a new programme which built on the best of the two earlier phases - a synthesis of both 'hearts' and 'minds' - and secure its place in a post-industrial Britain unsure of its role or its future.[2]

It was not only the Party's internal divisions which brought an end to the second phase of its history. Margaret Thatcher's 1980's Conservative Governments also marked a new era in British politics, overthrowing the earlier consensus on fundamental issues such as government intervention, public ownership and the welfare state. One effect was an indirect undermining of the Labour Party. For example, the trade unions lost members under industrial relations legislation that went much farther than Labour's proposals in *In Place of Strife*. Linked to this was the freedom of market forces to operate in the manufacturing sector where consequently few attempts were made to save firms from going to the wall. Many of these disappearing firms employed traditional Labour voters.

Local government, in which there had been some Labour strongholds, was weakened through the sale of council houses, often housing Labour supporters, rate capping and reduced powers in health and education. The Greater London Council was abolished. The Labour Party proved to be in little shape to fight back. As Davies observed:

> The Parliamentary Labour Party in the 1970s was on the

221

whole dull, stodgy, middle-aged, male and, of course, white. New ideas whether they were to do with feminism or the environment, workers' co-operatives or libertarian issues, simply passed them by.[3]

In local government, on the other hand, authorities that had traditionally been right-wing now became more left-wing; some, such as Liverpool, Islington and Lambeth notoriously so. Indeed, two main polarising developments occurred. Their effects were to come right into the Political Purposes Committee of the Royal Arsenal Co-operative Society. One was a powerful lurch to the left within the Labour Party. The other resulted from those who felt unable to go along with this and departed to form the break away party, the Social Democratic Party (SDP).

Typical in the move to the left was the Campaign for Labour Party Democracy with which Tony Benn was particularly associated. Benn argued that Party activists should be more involved in Party affairs. At the same time he suggested that a future Labour Prime Minister's powers of patronage should be reduced by the Cabinet being elected by the whole Parliamentary Party whose members should no longer be representative of all their constituents but rather the delegates of their Constituency Labour Parties. In turn, these should have a greater say in shaping Labour Party Conference decisions which should then form the policy of the Party in Parliament.

In the late 1970s and early 1980s, Labour Party Conferences agreed to the broadening of the system for electing the Party's leader and also to the mandatory re-selection of MPs. The former was confirmed by a Special Party Conference at Wembley in 1981 which approved the creation of an Electoral College divided between 40 per cent for the trade unions, 30 per cent for the Parliamentary Labour Party and 30 per cent for Constituency Labour Parties. Before that, however, in November 1980, James Callaghan stood down as Party Leader with the apparent hope that right-winger Denis Healey would succeed him. Instead, it was the left-wing veteran, Michael Foot, who was elected.

Like Benn, Foot was a notable and much respected left-winger and also a supporter of unilateral nuclear disarmament. It is interesting to note that, coinciding with the Labour Party's shift to the left, there was a resurgence in strength of the Campaign for Nuclear Disarmament. Besides being agreed on nuclear disarmament, Foot and Benn were also united in their opposition to the European Economic Community and pressed for British withdrawal.[4] Those who were to form the nucleus of the Social Democratic Party - Dr David Owen, Shirley Williams, Bill Rodgers and Roy Jenkins - were opposed on all these major issues. Shortly after the Labour Party's Special Conference at Wembley in February 1981 which ratified the creation of an electoral college, they resigned from the Labour Party. As Davies observes:

> From this point on - and of crucial importance for the 1980s as a whole - the anti-Conservative opposition was now fragmented between the SDP, the Liberals and Labour.[5]

Impact on the Political Purposes Committee

These events were bound to have an impact on the RACS Political Purposes Committee, tied up as it was with Labour politics. A three-way split appeared but the Committee continued to function as before, saved by its tradition of open membership and the eligibility of any Society member to seek election to Society Committees. It had long got used to working with communists, or communist sympathisers, elected to the Committee. Such experience now stood it in good stead.

Two of the Committee's members, John Cartwright MP and the Committee's Vice-Chairman, and A J Wellbeloved MP, joined the SDP. However, they did not resign from the Committee but stayed on, Wellbeloved until 1984 and Cartwright until 1992. During that time the latter often topped the poll in elections to the Committee. Until 1992 he remained the MP for Woolwich East but as an SDP candidate. Initially, this gave rise to the bizarre situation where he attended meetings of the Political Purposes Committee which set about nominating a successor to him as the RACS candidate to the Woolwich East Constituency Labour Party. However, the practice immediately developed where he and Wellbeloved abstained from voting on Labour Party issues coming before the Committee. The first occasion this happened was when, in the wake of the setting up of the SDP, the Committee's Chairman, Hilda Smith, delivered the following statement at a meeting of the Committee in March, 1981:

> We are living through stirring political times. I hesitate to stir the pot still further, but we cannot ignore the formation of a new Party and that a quarter of that group are Co-operative MPs and a further member is also an elected member of the Political Committee.
>
> We are a Co-operative Society which has been affiliated to the Labour Party for nigh on fifty years. Our links are long and strong at local, regional and national level.
>
> Anyone who is an active Co-operator if they comply with the rules of the Society, and are elected by members, can serve on any Committee. However, our work must be in the mainstream of Labour politics and through the Labour Party which always has been and remains the main vehicle of change within our society. Anyone who doubts this has not read Labour history, nor even Clause IV of the Constitution of the Labour Party to which we all as members subscribe.
>
> The bonds we adhere to have been forged by the work and dedication of many thousands of Co-operators who have also been political activists willing to give time, money and effort to making Clause IV a reality. We cannot let them down.
>
> Socialism will not be achieved without a long hard fight. At times we take a leap forward, sometimes we mark time and consolidate. There is no easy path of opting out for consensus politics, only a step by step progression which is made easier and faster if we know where we are going, and understand the problems this country faces, then use our brains, initiative and the practical experience of our members to find the answers.
>
> I hope that during the coming months the Political Committee can contribute to this and to the strengthening

of our Party - THE LABOUR PARTY - in challenging the policies of this disastrous Tory Government and getting ready to fight and win the next General Election.

Hilda Smith,
Chairman,
Political Purposes Committee[6]

Copies of this statement, endorsed by the Committee, were sent to a number of newspapers including *Labour Weekly* and *The Co-operative News*. In passing we can perhaps note that Hilda Smith's statement touches on the embarrassment felt by the Co-operative Party when four of its fourteen MPs, and one of its seven Lords, crossed to the SDP.[7] Such moves were, perhaps, not all that strange, given that the Co-operative Party traditionally reflected a distinct form of socialism based on co-operative social ownership and democracy, rather than some other forms. However, the Co-operative Party as a whole remained firmly allied to the Labour Party. At the end of 1981, reviewing events of the year, the Co-operative Party acknowledged:

> ... the substantial benefits that had accrued from the partnership between the Labour Party and the Co-operative Union, and again asserted that the formal Agreement that existed between these two organisations provided and remained the most appropriate and advantageous constitutional basis for political action by the British Co-operative Movement.

The statement went on to say that:

> ... the Co-operative Party believes that there is room in the Labour Movement and Party for a wide spread of opinion on detailed aspects of policy provided that all give general support to the principles and practices of democratic socialism.
> Our particular task within the Labour Movement and Party is to advocate policies which, whilst accepting the mixed economy, will lead to a strengthening of

the co-operative sector; which will extend true democracy; which will curb bureaucracy and advance accountability; which will encourage equality yet allow choice; which will lead to a regeneration of our economy and the return of full employment ...

The statement also reaffirmed the Co-operative Party's support for 'democratic socialism by parliamentary means' and stressed its opposition to 'policies and programmes based on confiscation, confrontation with and even opposition to, the rule of law'. It, therefore, went on to support Michael Foot's decision to 'conduct a thorough inquiry into the activities of the Militant Tendency'. The Co-operative Party believed that such an inquiry was 'both necessary and urgent'.[8]

We should, however, return to the reactions of the RACS Political Purposes Committee on the formation of the Social Democratic Party and the defection of two of the Committee's three sponsored MPs. Now that this study has reached the 1980s we can gain insights from oral as well as written accounts. Reactions to John Cartwright's decision to move to the new Party were particularly strong. Even fifteen years after, oral accounts reflect the strong feelings it aroused, ranging from the bitter to the perplexed to admiration for his integrity, while strongly disagreeing with his decision. That caused some loyal Labour Party supporters to think hard. One told the author: 'Cartwright was known for never having put a foot wrong. For him to leave the Labour Party like that made you think that he had very good reasons for doing so, and that there must be something seriously wrong with the Party'.

It has since become clear that Cartwright carried much popular sympathy in the Woolwich area, which suggests how far the political climate of the area had changed from Labour's heyday in the first half of this century. As we have noted, Cartwright went on to retain his Woolwich seat for the SDP until 1992. He was also regularly re-elected by RACS members to the Society's Political Purposes Committee until 1992 when he took up a position with the Police Complaints Authority and no longer sought re-election. Then RACS recorded its appreciation of his service to the Society 'as an official and elected member'.[9] This sentiment seems to have been based on genuine regard; when Cartwright and his wife celebrated their 30th wedding anniversary three years earlier the Committee had taken the unusual step of sending congratulations.[10]

However, in 1981 the Committee was not only embarrassed by two of its members defecting to the SDP but by the later defection of its new Political Secretary, Paul Rossi. Appointed Political Secretary in January 1980, Rossi[11] had succeeded Richard Balfe after his election to the European Parliament. By that time Balfe had also been elected a member of the Political Purposes Committee and was eventually to follow Cartwright as the Committee's Vice Chairman. Later he became its Chairman. Rossi's short tenure of the Political Secretaryship, though, came to an abrupt and dramatic end during the 1981 Labour Party Conference. Eye witness accounts, rather than the Minutes, tell us what occurred. Apparently Rossi revealed his indecision about whether to move to the SDP to an indiscreet confidant. Much to the embarrassment of the members of the Political Purposes Committee attending the Conference, rumours of his possible defection began to circulate around the Conference. During late night meetings pressures were exerted to get him to resign the Political Secretaryship. These succeeded and Paul Rossi wrote to Hilda Smith, the Committee's Chairman:

> Following our conversation yesterday, and mine today with Richard Balfe, I write to confirm that because of serious policy differences between myself and the Committee, I must resign from the position of Political Secretary. I think this course is in the best interests of both the Committee and myself.
>
> I confirm that I agree the terms which have been discussed:-
> 1   That I will leave the Department on Friday, 16 October, 1981
> 2   That I will receive four months salary and Car Allowance in lieu of notice.

227

In her letter of acknowledgment Hilda Smith confirmed these terms and agreed that the reason for Rossi's resignation was indeed 'serious policy differences' between himself and the Committee.[12]

Rossi's sudden departure could have left the Committee without a Secretary had it not been for an earlier and fortuitous development. In November 1979 Hilda Smith had proposed an important expansion of the Committee's staff, which was also an acknowledgement of how its work had grown. Her proposal was to create the position of Political Organiser who would deputise for the Political Secretary when necessary, and liaise 'with Co-operative Groups throughout the Society's area ... and Constituency Labour Parties', as well as 'build up links with sympathetic organisations within the Society in order to build up our membership, eg Trades Councils, Labour Groups in CLPs, SERA, Local CDA groups etc'.[13] In July 1980 a Job Description was drawn up and terms and conditions approved.[14] Four people were short-listed, two women and two men, from whom Glenys Thornton was appointed in January 1981. Although she had been working in the position for only a matter of months she was the natural choice to become the Acting Political Secretary. Within a very short space of time, and from a short-list of three, two woman and one man, Glenys Thornton was appointed Political Secretary in December, 1981,[15] the first woman to hold the position.

In passing we should perhaps note that difficulties over Rossi's departure at the 1981 Labour Party Conference tended to detract from an important event for the Committee at that Conference. To some extent it could almost be described as the Committee's last big grand gesture. Earlier we saw how the Royal Arsenal Co-operative Society showed a great capacity for mounting huge events, whether they be massive exhibitions or celebrations in the Royal Albert or Royal Festival Halls. Its Political Committee was part of that tradition and to celebrate its 60th anniversary in 1981, and the Labour Party's 80th anniversary, it proposed a joint event with the Labour Party. Termed the '60/80 Event' it took the form of a Buffet Supper and was held at the Metropole Hotel, Brighton, during the Labour Party Conference. To enable RACS supporters to be part of the celebrations, coaches were hired to take them to the event.[16]

We should return, however, to the question of how the Political

Purposes Committee was affected by the divisions which occurred in the Labour Party during the late 1970s and the early 1980s.

How the Committee Divided

In addition to the personal upheavals described above, the Labour Party's problems in the 1970s and 1980s had two noticeable effects on the RACS Political Purposes Committee. One was that the Committee became more divided than previously. The other was that, in keeping with much of the Labour Party, it moved to the left. Consequently, the Committee shifted from its earlier mainly right-wing positions, such as its nomination of right-wing candidates for Labour Party positions[17] and support for multilateral disarmament.[18]

Specific issues illustrate this move to the left. One was the Committee's opposition to Britain's membership of the European Economic Community. It, and indeed the Royal Arsenal Society, had long been opposed to the EEC. However, this became more marked in the late 1970s[19] and thus in line with the Benn/Foot position. Another example of the Committee's move to the left was its support for Militant. We have already noted the inquiry that Michael Foot instituted into the activities of Militant Tendency, and the Co-operative Party's statement welcoming this. The RACS Political Purposes Committee largely endorsed that statement but expressed its 'strong opposition' to the paragraph referring to support for Michael Foot's inquiry.[20]

The Committee's support for Militant was shown even more clearly when it moved an amendment to a motion on relations with the Labour Party which was submitted to the 1982 Co-operative Party Conference. The motion read:

> This Conference reaffirms its policy decisions on the Co-operative Commonwealth, parliamentary democracy, and social ownership within a mixed economy and expresses its concern at the ultra left-wing drift within the Labour Party which will eventually challenge and contradict our own policies. Bearing in mind our relationship with the Labour Party, Conference requests the NEC to give consideration to those factors in relation

to the difficulties they are likely to present to the whole
of the Co-operative Movement and to report to the 1983
Conference of this Party whether or not political re-
alignment or no re-alignment at all, has now, or will
become necessary.

Strong words indeed! Moreover, they hinted at a possible shift in
support by the whole Co-operative Movement. Even so, the RACS
Committee's response ignored this, as well as reaffirming support
for a 'mixed economy'. Its amendment graphically illustrated its
support for Militant by proposing the deletion of all the motion
after '... social ownership' in line three.[21] Although the Co-operative
Party motion did not refer directly to Militant, it was undoubtedly
included in the reference to 'the ultra left-wing drift within the
Labour Party'. But the RACS Committee did not hesitate to name
Militant in the resolution that it passed in July 1982:

> This meeting of the RACS Political Purposes Committee
> rejects the attack made by the National Executive
> Committee of the Labour Party on supporters of the
> *Militant* newspaper. In our opinion the proposal to set
> up a Register of Groups within the Party will only lead
> to further divisions and eventually to witch hunts and
> purges against the membership. The proposals coming
> at a time of increased attack by the Tory Government on
> Labour Movement organisations can only cause
> disillusionment amongst the electorate and lose the
> Labour Party votes. We, therefore, call upon the NEC to
> withdraw its proposal and in conjunction with the TUC
> to immediately organise a publicity campaign around
> the manifesto and against unemployment.[22]

Richard Balfe moved an amendment to delete all words after
'proposal' (line 12) so that the resolution could 'be clearly seen
to be directed at the pressing problem of the Register'; this was
accepted by the mover of the motion.

Before noting the outcome of the amended motion we should
recall that, earlier in its history, the Committee recorded voting

figures in its Minutes but not of who voted for what. Indeed, the supposed leaking of the latter had heightened tensions in the debate about possible changes in relations with the Labour and Co-operative Parties during the Skeffington and Furness period. The Secretary of the RACS had written to remind the Political Purposes Committee that 'It is not the practice in the Society for records to be kept of the way in which members of a committee vote at committee meetings ...'[23] During its swing to the left in the late 1970s and early 1980s, the Political Purposes Committee had tended to move away from this practice. The occasion of the resolution opposing a Labour Party Register of Groups provided an example. Then, the Minutes recorded that those voting for the amended motion were:

> Mr R A Balfe MEP
> Mrs V P Balfe
> Mr A Cumner
> Mr A V Henning
> Mr K J Sneddon
> Mr L Stannard
> Mrs A Walker

Those voting against it were listed as:

> Mr B W Coppock JP
> Mr G Hunn
> Mr C S Shrive
> Mrs Hilda Smith

The Minutes added that 'Mr J C Cartwright MP and Mr A J Wellbeloved MP did not participate in this item'.[24]

It would be misleading to suppose that the Committee invariably divided along the above lines. Non-SDP voters tended to shift between the left and the far left as in 1982 when there was a vote to decide whether to nominate Les Huckfield or the Committee's own Chair, Hilda Smith, for election to the Labour Party National Executive Committee. On that occasion Mr and Mrs Balfe joined Coppock, Hunn, Shrive and Mrs Smith in voting for Hilda Smith. Another member to shift her vote on occasions was Alice Walker. Keeping these exceptions in mind it would mean that the Committee's core of the far left comprised Cumner, Henning, Sneddon and Stannard. Apart from its SDP members, however, the Committee, overall, moved to the left in the late 1970s and early 1980s. Besides the question of Militant there was also its practical support for the Campaign for Labour Party Democracy. With Cartwright and Wellbeloved abstaining, the Committee had unanimously agreed to donate £25 to the Campaign and to affiliate to it at an annual rate of £25.[25]

We should, however, return to the question of the Committee's nomination to Section 11 of the Labour Party's National Executive Committee. Quite apart from illustrating the Committee's changed voting patterns, this issue also reflected how changes in the Labour Party were impacting on the standing of the RACS's Political Purposes Committee.

Challenges on Labour Party's National Executive
Established when the Labour Representation Committee was formed in 1900, Section 11, or the Socialist Societies Section of the Labour Party's National Executive Committee, had initially been intended to include representatives of the Independent Labour Party and the Fabian Society. It grew to comprise a variety of small Labour and socialist organisations such as Poale Zion, the Socialist Health Association, the Association of Labour Social Workers and the National Union of Labour and Socialist Clubs. Because the Co-operative Movement preferred to have an electoral alliance with the Labour Party, rather than affiliate to it, few Co-operative Societies had affiliated directly, RACS was the major exception and affiliated in 1927. Four years later it gained a seat on the NEC representing Section 11. Under the Party's 1937 Rules, Section 11 had just one seat on the NEC. From then on, until 1975, this was held continuously by RACS nominees. These were:

T E Williams	until 1935
W A H Green	until 1947
Joe Reeves	until 1953

Arthur Skeffington	until 1958
Tom Agar	until 1959
Arthur Skeffington	until 1971
John Cartwright	until 1975
John Cartwright re-elected	until 1977.[26]

Cartwright failed to hold the seat in 1975 but regained it in 1976 and then held it for two years. During this period the main contender for the Section 11 seat had become the National Union of Labour and Socialist Clubs, its most notable nominee the left-winger Les Huckfield.

After Cartwright joined the SDP, Hilda Smith, Chair of the Political Purposes Committee, became RACS's nominee for the NEC's Section 11. An indication of left-wing pressures in the Committee came in July 1982 when five of its members voted to nominate Les Huckfield rather than their own Chair. But six others voted for Hilda Smith.[27] Although she gained the nomination, however, she failed to regain the seat. From RACS's point of view the issue had become complicated by the fact that the London Co-operative Society had also affiliated to the Labour Party in 1979. That entitled it to nominate also for Section 11; it supported Huckfield. Herbert Morrison had worked so hard to gain the LCS's affiliation but had failed. It had now come about for other reasons.

Important among these was an electoral shift within the London Society. For some years its Political Committee had been notably left-wing. The rest of the Society also began to move in that direction after the 1960 Committee replaced the London Co-operative Members' Organisation as the Society's main electoral organisation. In passing we can perhaps note that there had been occasional attempts to extend the LCMO to RACS. However, that had maintained its democracy through its system of proportional representation which, linked to open membership election to Society committees, stimulated electoral activity through the Labour Party, Co-operative Guilds, communists and Catholics. By contrast the LCMO brought such interests together and put forward the candidates it approved for election to LCS Committees.

During the 1960s, however, the LCMO's hold weakened following the emergence of a new electoral group, the 1960 Committee.[28] That later became part of the Federation of Progressive Co-operators. Both organisations were much farther to the left than the earlier LCMO. As a result the London Society, which had always been a radical body, moved even farther to the left.

Throughout this study we have used terms such as 'communists', 'communist sympathisers' or 'far left', but they are not very precise terms. They became even less so in the late 1980s following the break up of the Communist Party. Although this relaunched itself as the Democratic Left in 1991, a number of far-left groups had previously emerged including the Trotskyist Militant Tendency, the Leninist Socialist Workers' Party, the Workers' Revolutionary Party and the Socialist League. The last of these had previously been the International Marxist Group and, as such, had become active in CND. Like Militant Tendency it also practised some degree of entryism into the Labour Party by backing Benn's Campaign for Labour Party Democracy.[29]

Such splits make it difficult, within the context of the RACS and the LCS, to know which brand of communist or far left supporter we are talking about. The important point is that both co-operative societies offered a point of entry to the Labour Party. Hence the competition for the Section 11 seat and also the loss of RACS's earlier hold on it. It thus became a matter for negotiation between the LCS and RACS Political Committees as to which candidate they should nominate and support. Agreement, however, sometimes proved difficult.

Talks between the two Political Committees had not led to agreement in 1982 and the RACS Committee had proceeded to vote for Hilda Smith's nomination. It seems that it later became necessary to reiterate that decision. A Special Meeting of the Committee was requested and five members tabled the following motion:

> This Political Purposes Committee, recognising that at its meeting on Friday the 2nd of July, had nominated Mrs Hilda Smith for Division 11 of the National Executive

Committee of the Labour Party do recommend the Members' Council (of RACS) that they advise the Political Committee delegates to conference to vote in support of the Chairperson of the Political Committee.

An amendment was moved by Les Stannard which recognised:

> ... the developments that have taken place since that date, particularly the joint meeting with the CRS London Region Political Committee, believes it is in the best interests of the Co-operative Movement that a joint approach be made by both organisations in their attitude to the National Executive Committee Division 11. Accordingly we recommend, on this occasion, we agree to support Les Huckfield, MP and further that a joint meeting take place before December in order to establish an agreed approach in future.[30]

The amendment was defeated by six votes to five, and the motion carried by the same figures. In each case a request was made that a record be taken of the way that members voted. At the Labour Party Conference neither Hilda Smith nor Les Huckfield was elected. The votes were:

J Evans	32,000 votes
Hilda Smith	19,000 votes
L Huckfield	10,000 votes.[31]

Later the Minutes of the RACS Committee record that, in the aftermath, the two Political Secretaries had met and discussed the result:

> Both agreed that a deplorable situation had arisen showing a lack of understanding between Co-operators in which recriminations on either side would not be helpful. We are pleased to report to the Committee that, due to a lot of work by the delegation an understanding attitude was shown by the media, the daily newspapers and the Labour Press.

Nevertheless, internal recriminations continued. At the same meeting of the RACS Committee Vic Henning moved a motion which showed that the Committee's earlier appeal to the RACS Central Members Council had been over-ruled:

> In view of the Central Members' Council recommendation to the Labour Party Conference delegation to cast the RACS vote in Division 11 for Leslie Huckfield we strongly disapprove of the delegates decision to ignore this recommendation.

The Central Members' Council decision in favour of Huckfield had, however, been very narrow; 26 votes to 25. As it had on an earlier occasion, namely nuclear disarmament in 1960, the Political Purposes Committee kept to its agreed course. Now, in the aftermath, five of its members voted for Henning's motion of disapproval while six voted against it, including John Cartwright and A J Wellbeloved. As SDP members, they usually abstained on Labour Party matters but did not do so on this occasion.

The narrowness of these votes, and the way in which they were fought and recorded, point to how evenly the RACS and its Political Purposes Committee were divided during the Labour Party's troubles of the late 1970s and early 1980s. By the mid-1980s, while it was still difficult to reach agreement with the London Political Committee on Section 11 nominations,[32] the RACS Committee was starting to become less left-wing.

Following Labour's defeat in the 1983 General Election, and the subsequent stepping down of Michael Foot, the Committee supported Neil Kinnock rather than Eric Heffer for the Party Leader, and Michael Meacher as Deputy Leader.[33] A year later the Committee again supported Kinnock as leader but Roy Hattersley as Deputy. On this occasion it supported the nomination of Stan Newens MEP, a member of the London CRS Political Committee, for Section 11 of the NEC.[34]

In concluding this section we should recall that one of the two main pillars of the RACS Political Purposes Committee was the Labour Party. The Party's move to the left contributed to RACS's loss of its seat on Section 11 of the Party's NEC. It also made it difficult to regain it but the issue was complicated by the fact that the London Co-operative Society had also affiliated to the national Labour Party and also had a right of nomination.

Just as RACS was about to move out of its left-wing phase, another of the main-stays of the RACS Political Purposes Committee was also about to change. Early in 1985 the Royal Arsenal Co-operative Society merged with the Co-operative Wholesale Society.

RACS Merges with Co-operative Wholesale Society

At the same time that the RACS Political Purposes Committee was affected by divisions in the Labour Party it also faced threats to its main base, the Royal Arsenal Co-operative Society. It was not likely that the Society would cease to exist. Rather there were pressures for it to join a larger co-operative grouping which could then affect the way that its Political Purposes Committee operated. The reasons for the Society to become part of a larger retail operation can be roughly divided into two. The first was internal and arose from RACS's difficulties in adapting to modern retailing requirements. The other was external and included changes in retailing and attempts within the wider Co-operative Movement to rationalise so as to be better able to respond to them.

At this point we should remind ourselves how far the RACS had travelled. When the Political Purposes Committee was established in 1922 the Society had been a growing but relatively uncomplicated business. It had been based on a reasonably homogeneous and settled geographical area with a strong identification with Woolwich. Although the Society had a number of trading departments and productive units, as well as housing estates, it had a clear democratic structure. Members' meetings elected a Management Committee as well as Education and Political Purposes Committees and these came together to discuss matters of mutual concern in Quarterly Joint Meetings. Any member had the right to seek election to these committees and there was strong competition to do so. This democratic structure was encouraged in a number of ways. Member loyalty was closely linked to the payment of a half-yearly dividend which was used either to buy more goods from the Society or placed in members' savings accounts held with the Society so contributing to its capital base. Other member benefits included educational classes and social events and the Society's support for a strong network of Co-operative Guilds - Women's, Men's and Mixed - within its area. Members' identification with the Society was further assisted by its monthly journal *Comradeship*, whose circulation had been as high as 20,000.

Like other consumer co-operatives of the period, the Royal Arsenal Co-operative Society contributed a clear system that worked and provided benefits for its members. Each of the system's parts was inter-related. If one changed, the others became less effective. However, as early co-operators had found with Owenite co-operative communities, consumer co-operatives could not function in isolation. They had to be part of the economic and social life surrounding them. Whereas the nature of the British economy, society and culture in the late 19th century and the first half of the 20th century had been conducive to the development of consumer co-operatives, they became far less so in the second half of the century.

Co-operatives had not been blind to the need to restructure. The problem was how to adapt. We have noted the unsuccessful attempts in the 1930s to create a Greater London Co-operative Society based on the main London co-operatives of Royal Arsenal, South Suburban, Enfield and the London Society.[35] In the 1930s also Joe Reeves had recognised the need to introduce new methods of Co-operative democracy. His pamphlet *New Forms of Government in the Co-operative Movement* had included proposals for Members' Councils. However, even in his own society of RACS, only a limited version had been put into operation.[36]

Recognition that continued co-operative expansion was not inevitable was instanced by the warning of the RACS Secretary, W J Morton, in 1955 that the Society's 'rate (of expansion) must to some extent decelerate'.[37] Among other things, this appears to recognise the post-war changes in retailing and also the way that the Society was being affected by population shifts and the threatened decline of local industries. Handling change can be that much more difficult when much of your previous experience has been in handling success. The dilemma was well summed up by the RACS's last Secretary, Ron Roffey:

The RACS had always been successful especially since the turn of the century. The Committee and management seemed to adopt the attitude that a corrective measure here and there would suffice. This attitude could be partly explained by the Society's strong capital base - which allowed the odd mistake to be swallowed.[38]

Roffey also noted that the Society's traditional dividend had continued to be paid 'for some time after it was not being earned' in the hope that business would be recovered. The Royal Arsenal Society was not alone in this. Other retail co-operatives in the 1970s did likewise, leading to the sale of co-operative property to sustain continued dividend payments. However, in the case of RACS, Roffey illustrates a point made earlier. If one part of the co-operative system changes, the rest becomes affected. Roffey noted that the discontinuation of the traditional dividend led to a 'decline in member loyalty, coupled with failure to attract younger customers who were car-borne and could shop at out of town superstores'. Failure to streamline earlier, and to take action on the proposals of the 1958 Independent Commission and the Co-operative Union's 1968 and 1974 Regional Plans, had taken a heavy toll on co-operative societies generally. As far as Royal Arsenal was concerned, Ron Roffey adds that its position was made worse by its failure to react quickly enough to major multiples such as Tesco and Sainsbury which first developed their large stores in London.

The Society's ability to respond was 'frustrated in part by little co-operation from local authorities' in granting planning permission. This was significant in the context of the Society suffering from a preponderance of small food shops of typically less than 3,000 sq.ft. which needed to be replaced by larger stores. Moreover, escalating land prices meant that the replacements would necessarily be more costly. Added to this was the cost of the Society's failure to rationalise supporting services including administration.

Besides having too many small food stores the Society also had the problem of almost 20 small department stores. These had become uneconomic as competitors developed one-floor, free car parking units. Touching again on the earlier point of how to handle change when you have previously been used to success, Ron Roffey suggests that the necessary closure of the Society's food shops and department stores 'created the impression of an organisation that was going downhill'.[39]

The situation was not helped by competitors' increased use of effective advertising and promotion. Believing that the Co-operative Movement should have responded nationally, but failed to do so, Roffey added that there had even been 'great difficulty to secure agreement between metropolitan Societies let alone nationally'. This highlights the difficulty that independent and autonomous consumer co-operatives had in working together. Put into a historical context, though, it makes it all the more remarkable that they had come together in the late 19th century to form the main national federations, the two Co-operative Wholesale Societies and the Co-operative Union. By the third quarter of the 20th century, and in vastly changed conditions, there seemed little will or capacity to work together. Just as it had proved impossible to form a Greater London Society in the 1930s, the London societies failed in the 1970s and 1980s to even agree a joint approach on advertising and promotion.

In 1978, nevertheless, a further attempt was made to merge the two South London societies, Royal Arsenal and South Suburban. It failed and Ron Roffey observed:

> It could be argued that such a course of action would not have helped in the 1980s - but it could have helped in the '60s. Although the computer services were merged in the early stages, other fusions of departments came too late. All this in spite of a call from the Co-operative Union to come together under its two Regional Plans.[40]

Although Roffey points to some rationalisation of their functions the two societies did not amalgamate. This was despite the fact that at one point during the negotiations, the Royal Arsenal Society indicated its readiness to come into line with South Suburban by having a part-time rather than a full-time Board and being prepared to change its name.[41]

After the failure to achieve a merger with South Suburban, the Royal Arsenal began talks with the Co-operative Wholesale Society. This time the talks succeeded and an amalgamation was confirmed by RACS members' meetings in January 1985.

The Political Purposes Committee's Response to Merger

Before looking at the Political Purposes Committee's response to the RACS merger with the CWS we should note some of its reactions to events leading up to it. We have previously seen[42] that the Committee's concern about the Society's move away from its traditional dividend had been mainly about its possible effect on the Committee's grant. New ways were found to compute this but the change also affected the Society's Rules. These laid down candidates' qualifications when seeking election to Society Committees and included requirements on length of membership, shares subscribed and level of purchases. It became difficult to determine the last of these after the abandonment of dividend because it was no longer necessary to keep a record of members' purchases. Dividend, although essentially a reward for loyalty, had been a deferred benefit. It had now been replaced by the immediate benefit of deep price cuts. To make a success of its new policy, however, the Society needed to attract increased numbers of customers who did not necessarily have to be members.

The ramifications of the change on RACS's traditional democracy were highlighted in a letter from Ron Roffey, the Society's Secretary, to the Political Purposes Committee in March 1980:

> The General Committee recently considered a letter from the Education Committee concerning the problem that candidates for the Society's Standing Committees will encounter in the future when endeavouring to meet the purchasing qualifications required under rule. This has been brought about by a gradual policy of reducing the issue of Dividend Stamps on purchases and substituting deeper cut prices.[43]

The General Committee was seeking the views of the Political

Purposes Committee on 'this growing problem'. In its reply the Committee urged that some purchasing qualification be retained 'if possible', but that other methods should also be considered, including attendance at Quarterly Meetings, and service on the Society's Members' Councils. Later, in respect of nomination to the Parliamentary and Local Government Panels, the Committee proposed that the qualifications should be:

1   Membership for at least two years immediately preceding the date of nomination.
2   Holding of at least five paid-up shares.[44]

The Society's Rules could be changed to include amended qualifications, but other underlying trends could not be tackled so easily. One was that the move from dividend came at a time when member involvement in RACS was declining. A number of factors were undoubtedly at play. For example, in an earlier submission to the RACS General Committee the Political Purposes Committee had noted that 'Activists in politics do not seem to be joining the Society as they formerly did before the introduction of Stamps'. It also observed that the Society's Members' Councils were, 'in some areas, collapsing'.[45] The Committee became even more concerned when even the Society's Annual Meetings sometimes failed to achieve a quorum.[46]

One reason for reduced member involvement was that RACS membership was falling as is illustrated by the figures below:

1978	428,883
1980	416,283
1984	306,503.[47]

The longer-term movements in RACS membership can be found in the Table at the end of this study.

Most co-operative societies periodically cleaned up their membership lists and RACS was no exception. But the decline it was now experiencing was likely to have been due to a combination of factors. One was that the move from dividend, and the sale of smaller food shops and uneconomic small department stores, had given the impression that the Society 'was going downhill'. Another reason was a weakening of the co-operative auxiliaries, particularly the Women's, Men's and Mixed Guilds. They had been an important voluntary element within the Society both in providing candidates, helping to run Society elections and in pressure group activity within the Society. On occasion the Women's Guild had been a channel through which the Co-operative Party could bring pressure to bear on the Political Purposes Committee. For a number of reasons, therefore, not least because the Guilds provided a ready source of RACS nominees to Constituency Labour Parties, the Political Purposes Committee sought good relations with the Guilds. It regularly accepted invitations to Guild birthdays, although by the 1970s this practice was declining and by the 1980s had ended. Thus, when the Motspur Park Co-operative Women's Guild invited the Committee to its 50th Birthday celebrations in March 1985, no one from the Committee went.[48]

Whether due to the decline of member involvement in the Society, or in the Guilds, by the 1980s the Political Purposes Committee had increasing difficulty in maintaining the Society's full quota of delegates to Constituency Labour Parties. The position fluctuated but gradually worsened during the 1970s and early 1980s. By 1985, although the Society could have appointed delegates to 51 Constituency Labour Parties, it made no nominations to 21 of these. Of the remainder it appointed its full entitlement in only three, Deptford, Gravesham and Vauxhall. Even in RACS's old heartlands of Greenwich, Lewisham, West Woolwich and Eltham, it failed to appoint its full complement of delegates.[49] Three years later the position had worsened still further. Of the 59 Constituency Labour Parties to which the Society was affiliated, as many as 36 received no nominations. Out of the remainder only four received full delegations.[50]

Against this changing background there was almost a sense of inevitability that the RACS would change and, with it, the base of the Political Purposes Committee. We should now turn to examine the Committee's response to the RACS merger with the CWS. For some years the possibility of RACS merging with another co-operative society had been known and had allowed the Political Purposes Committee to come to a considered response. During the negotiations with the South Suburban Society it had sought the following 'safeguards':

> 1 The RACS affiliation to the Labour Party at local, regional and national level should remain to be determined according to the present rules of the Royal Arsenal Co-operative Society.
> 2 There should continue to be a high level of political activity and any new responsibilities should be reflected in the grant.
> 3 The electoral system for the new Political Committee should be based on the same principle as at present used by the Royal Arsenal Co-operative Society. Proportional Representation, and voting, not to be placed under the control of Branch Managers.[51]

As we noted, the RACS/South Suburban merger failed to take place. When the possibility of one between RACS and the CWS became an active issue in the autumn of 1984, the Political Purposes Committee took a similar position. Namely:

> 1 That the democratic structures of Society and, therefore, of the Political Committee should be safeguarded;
> 2 That affiliation to Labour Parties at local level and the Committee's power of appointment to General Management Committees should continue:
> 3 That a grant and staff resources should be available to the Department which will allow the Department to continue both its work on behalf of the Society and its affiliation to the Labour Party at national and regional level.[52]

In November 1984 a Special Meeting of the Political Purposes Committee was held to discuss the merger then under active consideration by the RACS and the Co-operative Wholesale Society. In passing we should note that, although the CWS had been formed as a wholesaling and productive federal of primary retailing co-operatives, it had developed a limited retailing arm in the 1930s. As the momentum gathered, from the 1960s onwards, for rationalisation in the Co-operative Movement, the CWS became increasingly engaged in retailing. Under the same push the London Co-operative Society merged with the Co-operative Retail Services in January 1981.

With the prospect of a merger proceeding between RACS and the CWS, the Political Purposes Committee called a Special Meeting in November 1984 to consider the draft Regulations of the new 'Society'. Under these the Committee would become a 'Branch Political Committee', and would comprise thirteen members, eight elected by members, with two appointed each by the Member Relations Committee, (previously the Education Committee) and the Branch Committee, plus the Chairman of the Branch Committee.[53] Its proposed functions were:

(a)   to arrange for the Branch to be affiliated to:
1   Constituency Labour Parties in the area of the operations of the Branch;
2   the National Labour Party and Regional Labour Parties, the Co-operative Party;
(b)   to arrange maximum practicable Branch representation on all bodies to which the Branch is affiliated or where there is an association;
(c)   to seek to secure the election of Branch members to local governing bodies and other governmental and public organisations;
(d)   to draw up a budget and administer a fund for the promotion of the Society and the Co-operative Movement through political and other appropriate channels, to assist in the development of co-operation and in all ways to further the interests of the Society;
(e)   to ensure the optimum use of resources and report to Branch general meetings, its stewardship of the political function and fund;
(f)   to be consulted by the Society on the appointment of a Political Officer who shall be appointed by the Society;
(g)   to meet as and when required and to appoint a

Chairperson and Vice-Chairperson from amongst themselves.[54]

A Political Fund of an unspecified amount or formula was to be provided which would be 'of sufficient resource to ensure the promotion of the Society's political aims and interests' and in accordance with the functions outlined above. Funds would also be provided for the payment of affiliation fees paid to each Constituency Labour Party within the area of the operations of the Branch but these would be 'reduced by an amount which is in the same proportion to the original total as is the number of members who have notified the Branch Secretary in writing of their objection to such a payment to the total membership'.

During a meeting the previous September with RACS officials, including Glenys Thornton, the Political Secretary, the CWS Secretary, Graham Melmoth, was reported to have said in respect of the political grant that it was 'not possible to put down "in tablets of stone" that the grant shall be escalated for all time in the future, as it could place burdens on the Society ... and be impossible to meet in the light of future trading conditions'. Assurances were, however, given that:

> The CWS recognises the historic association of the RACS with its local constituency Labour Parties and would intend that the level of payment in real terms by way of affiliation fees would continue ...[55]

While affiliations to the Labour Party were set to continue under the new Society, the financial arrangements seemed less secure. Before RACS members could confirm the merger, the CWS Board expressed concern 'about the implications of the costs of the RACS Political and Education activity in the context of what is likely to be a protracted difficult trading performance in the South East'.[56] Nevertheless the merger went ahead and was approved by the CWS and RACS, the latter in January 1985.

What the Merger Meant to the Political Committee
Through the various stages of the merger the Political Committee

had continued its customary political work, but its capacity in terms of personnel was soon to be reduced. Ron Roffey, who had been the Secretary of the Royal Arsenal Co-operative Society, and had now become the Branch Secretary, wrote to the Branch Political Committee in February 1985:

> You will all know that the main objective of our merger with the CWS was to obtain their stronger resources in order to improve our trading profile and competitive trading edge with the ultimate objective of moving towards a South Eastern Regional operation. In addition it was envisaged that savings could be achieved by a reduction in the cost of administration, accounting, and other services by better utilisation of resources and increased productivity.
>
> … During the merger talks it became clear that the integration of the three administrations (General, Education and Political) would have to be effected in order to achieve a more efficient bridge between management and members. As a result a distinct change in the style and responsibility of the Secretariat has come about.
>
> I have always been proud that my appointment as Secretary (RACS) was one that was approved by members of the Society. This gave me an independence which I jealously guarded and I am in a way sorry to have lost. In my new role I am responsible to the Chief Officer of the branch whilst maintaining a close functional link with the Secretary of the CWS whose remit is oversight generally of the Society's relations with its members.

Ron Roffey continued that:

> We, and I refer to Roy Martin (Member Relations), Glenys Thornton, myself and all our respective staff, are now part of the management team and we shall follow the policy laid down by management. In practice this means

that we have the functional task of administering the policy decisions that you take within the confines of the Branch Regulations and advising you, where necessary, of management's view when this has a bearing upon these. In turn, Roy Martin, Glenys Thornton and their staff are responsible to me, and all matters relating to them, their staff, discipline, salaries, welfare and the conduct of their administrative function are my direct responsibility ...

Moving on to the question of cuts in administration Ron Roffey stated:

> ... it seemed to me right and proper that we should take on board the same level of cuts as was being taken by the general administration of the branch. The Chief Officer informed me that the administration and accounting services of the branch would be cut by between thirty and thirty-five per cent, and in view of this I decided that this should apply to us as well.

In this light Ron Roffey had decided that:

> The casualty in the Political Office is the Organiser. I have looked carefully at this position and it is my judgement that in spite of the removal of this appointment, the Secretariat will be able to maintain the organisational programme.[57]

It will be recalled that the position of Political Organiser had been created in 1980.[58] Glenys Thornton had first held it but after she had moved into the position of Political Secretary following Paul Rossi's departure in 1981, Mary Honeyball had been appointed. She was now redundant. Despite protests[59] the Political Committee was unable to prevent this. Ron Roffey's letter, and Mary Honeyball's redundancy, provided pointers to the Political Committee's future. Although it had been preserved and affiliations to the Labour Party maintained, ultimate control had been removed from Woolwich to Manchester.

With the benefit of hindsight we can see that the merger between the RACS and the CWS marked the beginning of the end of RACS's distinct political tradition. The stepping stones along that path should now be followed.

The End of a Political Tradition

Following the merger of the RACS and CWS the name of the Committee changed to the CWS Ltd Royal Arsenal Branch Political Committee[60] but the Committee's structure was little changed. Instead of the earlier twelve members there were now thirteen with the Branch Chairman joining the customary eight elected members and two each from the Member Relations and Branch Committee. The Committee retained its previous right to elect its own Chairperson and Vice-Chair.

It had, however, lost some control over staff. As we have seen, the Political Organiser had become redundant, and the Political Secretary part of the Society's Management Team. In 1986 Glenys Thornton took maternity leave during which the Committee was 'serviced by the Branch'.[61] This arrangement continued when, shortly afterwards, the CWS released Glenys Thornton 'to work until a General Election assisting the Labour Party in London'.[62] During this time she became the full time Chair of the Greater London Labour Party.[63] From August 1986 to May 1987 Tony Crowter acted as Political Secretary doubling up on his position as the Society's Member Relations Officer. Kathryn Smith, Richard Balfe's Personal Assistant, then followed him.[64] When it seemed unlikely that Glenys Thornton would return the Committee requested the CWS to make a new appointment. The Branch Management team, with Richard Balfe, representing the Branch Political Committee, appointed Shaun Spiers in October 1987.[65]

The Committee's activities were relatively unchanged. It continued its affiliation and nominations to Constituency Labour Parties, Southern Regional Council and Greater London Labour Parties, and to the national Labour Party. Similarly, it remained affiliated to and active within the Co-operative Party. The Committee also maintained its Local Government and

Parliamentary Panels. However, with the reduction in co-operative members' qualifications, and changes in selection criteria, the Committee was now contributing to election expenses rather than sponsoring candidates as it had previously.

The Committee's other activities also remained relatively unchanged. This is illustrated if we make a comparison between those for 1988 and the list we compiled in Chapter Eight for 1977;[66] 1987 would not have been a good year because of its General Election and the fact that the Committee lacked a full time Political Secretary during much of it. From the Committee's 1988 Minutes we find that it became involved in some way with the following: EEC Food Surpluses, Housing Co-operatives, Municipal Funerals, various protests against the Poll Tax, Medical and Scientific Aid for Vietnam, Laos and Kampuchea, Salvadorean Refugees Appeal, Surcharged Lambeth Councillors, local Co-operative Development Agencies, the London Marathon, Lewisham Council for Community Relations, various Pensioners' activities, Institute for African Alternatives, Industrial Common Ownership Movement, the Free Nelson Mandela Campaign, United Campaign Against Strip Searching, P & O Strikers, Occupied West Bank and Gaza Appeal, Socialist Health Organisation, Liberation, Sandinista Six, National Health Service 40th Birthday Celebration, London Labour Party Blood Donors Campaign, War Toys, Fabian Society Conference, Socialist Societies and Black Sections, Co-operation in the Curriculum, Sexism in Co-op Literature, and Lambeth Community Radio. From these it would appear that, while items changed, the tone and thrust of the Committee's work had remained much as it had been eleven years earlier.

What did change was the Committee's relations with the Co-operative Party. These became more strained, although those with the Political Committee of London CRS became closer. Despite continuing difficulties in agreeing who should be nominated for Section 11 of the Labour Party's NEC,[67] the post-merger period saw the two Committees introducing a joint periodical *Commonweal* and holding regular conferences on major issues. But relations deteriorated with what had been the Political Committee of the South Suburban Co-operative Society, and the national Co-operative Party. Those with the South Suburban Political Committee became complicated by attempts to merge the two Committees. Such moves seemed reasonable given that the Committees were adjacent, and that the South Suburban Society had also merged with the CWS. These attempts, however, were made difficult by the two Committees having different traditions. Thus, when talks began in the spring of 1985 the RACS Branch Committee laid down two 'principles' with which it bound the Political Committee's representatives. These were that any future structures should be 'based on members, ie Members' Councils', and an 'adherence to a proportional system of voting'.[68]

The issue of the merger of the two Committees was further complicated by a Co-operative Party proposal to create a Regional Co-operative Party Council. The RACS Political Committee rejected this on the grounds that it 'would be at variance with the principle of open membership and detrimental to the future interests of the Political Committee'.[69] Similarly, a Co-operative Party Interim Report on Local Party Constitutions, published in August 1985, also complicated relations. What becomes interesting during this period is that the RACS Political Committee was not acting alone but had the support of the Branch Committee and members' meetings. For example, the CWS Royal Arsenal Branch Half-Yearly Meeting in October 1985 passed the following resolution in connection with the Co-operative Party's Report:

> This meeting of members notes with alarm that the Co-operative Party's NEC proposals on re-organisation would, if implemented, abolish the Political Committee and replace it with a Co-operative Party Council. This would mean that Co-operative Party members only would be eligible to play a full part in the political life of the Branch, and it would prevent the full representation and participation by all members of the Branch in promoting events and campaigns on issues which affect the membership.
>
> This meeting of members of the CWS Royal Arsenal Branch supports the continuation of the Political Committee as a directly elected Committee of the Branch,

where all the members are entitled to stand for election and to vote.

This meeting calls upon the Branch Committee, acting on behalf of the membership, to use every means at its disposal to ensure that the CWS keep to the agreement reached upon the transfer of engagements from the RACS to the CWS, embodied within the Rules of the Branch, which state that the Political Committee should continue to exist on the basis of open membership.[70]

This resolution is significant for four reasons. The first is that it is a resolution of a Members' Half-Yearly Meeting. Second, it reflects a continuing strength of feeling about maintaining the principle of open membership; the Political Committee still remained a broad church ranging from far-left members to one from the SDP. Third, the Co-operative Party's proposals ran concurrently with the talks with the South Suburban Political Committee and those, if acted upon, would bring the RACS Committee into line with that Committee's existing practices. Fourth, only nine months after the merger with the CWS fears appear to emerge that the CWS might not keep to the agreements reached during the transfer.

Talks with the South Suburban Committee remained protracted and difficult. On its side the RACS Political Committee again reaffirmed its opposition to a Regional Co-operative Party Council.[71] On its side the South Suburban Committee rejected even the idea of an exchange of observers between the two Committees: '... our Committee's membership is restricted to members of the Co-operative Party, therefore as not all members of your Committee are members of the Co-operative Party, I regret that we are unable to agree to the proposition'.[72]

Then, in an attempt to have some kind of dialogue, each Committee agreed to produce a position paper. That of the RACS Committee argued that there should be a single Committee covering the whole of the Branch, including the original RACS and South Suburban areas. In line with this the membership of the Committee should be increased with ten directly elected

252

members rather than the present eight. The RACS Committee believed that this would be appropriate given that:

> Of the present directly elected Committee (RACS) two members are from the area of the former Woking Society, one is from the area of the former Gravesend Society and one from the former Faversham Society. We are sure that if elections were held over the whole area we would similarly have representatives from the South Suburban area. Incidentally, as far as we know, at least four of the present South Suburban Political Committee members live within the Royal Arsenal area, in either Lambeth or Lewisham.

But it was the second RACS point that was always going to be more difficult for the South Suburban Committee to accept, namely that the new,

> Political Committee must be truly representative of the total membership and not just representative of the handful of people who are in the Co-op Party. The Committee believes that it would be totally wrong for a sum of over £50,000 a year to be disposed of by a Committee drawn from only 500 of the membership. We also believe that it would be wrong to disenfranchise our Communist and SDP Members.
>
> Finally, there are many members of the Labour Party who have not joined the Co-operative Party and would not be eligible, and amongst this number is the present Chair of the Branch.

By contrast the South Suburban paper proposed a new Political Organisation based on four geographical areas. Each of these would become 'a district Co-operative Party Committee/ Council with functions according to Co-operative Party Rules. They would include affiliation to local Labour Parties, affiliation to the national Co-operative Party and affiliation to the relevant Regional Labour Party'.[73]

253

When, by April 1987, the two Committees had failed to agree, their memberships were frozen, while the whole question was passed to the Regional Committee, namely the combined RACS and South Suburban Branch Committees.

> During the interim period May 1987 to September 1988 it is agreed that the Regional Committee should consider and make proposals that shall apply to the political structure after September 1988.[74]

In other words, the question was being taken out of the hands of the two Political Committees, although their Chairmen were allowed to sit on the Regional Committee during the interim period as ex officio members. It is perhaps as well to keep in mind that it was during this period that the CWS allowed the appointment of Shaun Spiers to proceed, thus reflecting its commitment to political development in the area.

In late December 1987 a Draft Agreement had been provisionally reached for a new Political Structure for CWS South East and was put to the Political Committee in January 1988. The Regional Committee seemed to have fared no better in settling the question than the two Political Committees, reflecting how deeply still lay the loyalties to the two traditions.

The main point of the Regional Committee's proposals was that there would be two political bodies. One would be a Regional Political Committee with thirteen members, eight directly elected by proportional representation across the whole region plus three appointed from the Regional Committee, including its Chair, and two appointed from the Co-operative Party Council. The second body would be that Co-operative Party Council just mentioned. This would have nineteen members, eight directly elected across the whole region, six from existing Co-operative Party Branches, three appointed from the Regional Committee, including the Chair, and two appointed from the Regional Political Committee. All the members of the Co-operative Party Council had to be members of the Co-operative Party.

The proposals were introduced to the RACS Committee by their Chair, Richard Balfe, who had been an ex officio member of the Regional Council. He admitted that the proposals 'fell short of an ideal position which would be one Committee for the Region'. But he went on:

> ... CWS South East Co-op Party Committee were unwilling to accept a single committee unless it was composed solely of Co-op Party members. The Political Committee were unwilling to give this concession as it believed strongly that political activity should be open to all co-operators.

At the end of its discussion of the proposals the Committee was evenly divided; four for acceptance and four for rejection. Not wishing to use a casting vote, Richard Balfe re-opened the discussions at the end of which a second vote was taken. This time there were three in favour and four against. The Committee, therefore, resolved that it could not accept the proposals.[75] Notwithstanding this rejection the Regional Committee went ahead and 'agreed a new structure broadly in line with the proposal rejected by the Political Committee'.[76]

Besides the Political Committee, the Co-operative Party also expressed its unease with the solution.[77] Nevertheless, the new set up came into being and the CWS South East Co-op Regional Political Committee held its first meeting in October 1988. Its membership was largely unchanged from the earlier Committee and Richard Balfe remained Chair and Jim Little the Vice-Chair.[78] Essentially, the new arrangement was an uneasy one. In late 1989 the two Committees agreed to try a more evolutionary approach by setting up a South East Co-op Political Standing Review Body; subsequently known as the Review Body. With two representatives from each Committee, its remit was to develop joint areas of work. Shaun Spiers became its Secretary.[79] However, little progress was made.

Now that the old RACS and South Suburban Societies were part of a nationwide trading group, there was always the possibility that events elsewhere could trigger a change. As a result local difficulties might then be resolved in unexpected ways. In 1993 Co-operative Retail Services Ltd decided to transfer its political staff and political budgets to the Co-operative Party. This meant that co-operative societies that had joined CRS, including London Co-operative Society, and had had political departments, would now find them coming under the direction of the Co-operative Party.[80] In late 1994 the CWS decided to follow CRS's example and this, of course, affected the SE CWS Regional Political Committee. Under an Agreement in January 1996 it transferred:

> the management of its Political Officers and their support staff to the Party with the Society's political budgets and consequent affiliations, with a view to achieving better co-ordination of CWS political activity, more cost effectiveness and enhanced value for money from the Society's political expenditure.

As far as the old RACS area was concerned the Agreement included the assurance that:

> ... the CWS will support the Co-operative Party in its employment at its Headquarters of a Political Officer and an Administrative Assistant to fill the two such vacancies in CWS South East which arose as a result of the election of Shaun Spiers as an MEP ...

Shaun Spiers had been elected to the European Parliament in 1994 for the London South East Constituency. Pamela Sheppard, his Personal Assistant, who had been Secretary to RACS Political Secretaries from Edwin Furness onwards, had left to become his Constituency Office Manager. Under the Agreement between the Co-operative Wholesale Society and the Co-operative Party these two positions would now be filled by Co-operative Party Headquarters staff.[81]

Such changes meant that the SE CWS Regional Political Committee would become fully part of the Co-operative Party. At long last the political tradition begun in 1921 with the setting up of the Political Purposes Committee had come to an end. The Committee was due to close in September 1997 and to be replaced by Co-operative Party structures. So strong remained the loyalty to the earlier tradition that all but two of the Committee's members had resigned before its end.

Conclusion

This Chapter has traced the troublous final stages of the RACS Political Purposes Committee. The period covered, 1979 to 1996, could rightly be called one of shifting sands. Both the Labour Party and the Royal Arsenal Co-operative Society, the two pillars on which the Committee was based, changed fundamentally during the period. For over seventy years the RACS Political Committee had enshrined distinct political tradition. In this Chapter we have seen that, even when the RACS became part of the Co-operative Wholesale Society, that tradition could not be easily melded into the new regional set up. Moreover that it was not only defended by the Political Committee but also by the RACS Branch Committee and members.

The RACS political tradition was, therefore, one that was forcefully articulated and staunchly defended until wider developments eclipsed it. It has now passed into history but it raises some interesting questions which will be addressed in our final Chapter.

Notes

References to Minutes are to RACS Minutes held by the CWS SE Archive.

1 Davies, A J, *To Build a New Jerusalem*, Abacus, London, 1992, p.366.

2 Ibid., pp.367-368.

3 Ibid., p.382.

4 Coxall, Bill and Robins, Lynton, *British Politics since the War*, MacMillan Press Ltd, London, 1998, p.184.

5 Davies, A J, op. cit., p.385.

6 Minutes, Political Purposes Committee, 6 March 1981.

7 Co-operative Union Ltd, *Report of 1981 Congress, Edinburgh*, p.27 and *Report of 1982 Congress, Brighton*, p.25.

8 Co-operative Union Ltd, *Report of 1982 Congress, Brighton*, p.24.

9 Minutes, Political Purposes Committee, 30 October 1992.

10 Minutes, Political Purposes Committee, 3 March 1989.

11 Minutes, Political Purposes Committee, 4 January 1980.

12 Minutes, Political Purposes Committee, 9 October 1981.

13 Minutes, Political Purposes Committee, 2 November 1979.

14 Minutes, Political Purposes Committee, 4 July 1980.

15 Minutes, Political Purposes Committee, 4 December 1981.

16 Minutes, Political Purposes Committee, 6 November 1981.

17 See Chapter 7, p.180.

18 See Chapter 8, pp.195-197.

19 Minutes, Political Purposes Committee, 2 May 1980.

20 Minutes, Political Purposes Committee, 8 January 1982.

21 Minutes, Political Purposes Committee, 5 February 1982.

22 Minutes, Political Purposes Committee, 2 July 1982.

23 See Chapter 6, p.160.

24 Minutes, Political Purposes Committee, 2 July 1982.

25 Ibid.

26 CWS SE Archive, Paper entitled *Socialist Societies Section of the NEC - The Case for Separate Co-operative Representation*, by Mary Honeyball, 1983.

27 Minutes, Political Purposes Committee, July 1982.

28 Newens, Stan, *Working Together - a Short History of the London Co-op Society Political Committee*, pp.31-36.

29 Coxall and Robins, op. cit., pp.192-193.

30 Minutes, Special Meeting, Political Purposes Committee, 20 September 1982.

31 Minutes, Political Purposes Committee, October 1982.

32 Minutes, Political Purposes Committee, 4 July 1986 and 5 September 1986.

33 Minutes, Political Purposes Committee, 1 July 1983.

34 Minutes, Political Purposes Committee, 14 September 1984.

35 See Chapter 5, pp.107-111.

36 See Chapter 5, pp.106-107.

37 See Chapter 7, p.184.

38 Roffey, Ron, letter to author, 24 July 1997.

39 Ibid.

40 Ibid.

41 Roffey, Ron, taped interview, 10 July 1997.

42 See Chapter 8, p.214.

43 Minutes, Political Purposes Committee, 7 March 1980.

44 Minutes, Political Purposes Committee, 5 December 1980.

45 Minutes, Political Purposes Committee, 7 April 1978.

46 Minutes, Political Purposes Committee, 1 May 1981.

47 CWS SE Archive, Returning Officer's Report on the Election of the General Committee, Education Committee and Political Purposes Committee, 1984.

48 Minutes, Political Purposes Committee, 29 March 1985.

49 Minutes, Political Purposes Committee, 1 March 1985.

50 Minutes, South East Co-op Political Committee, 25 March 1988.

51 Minutes, Political Purposes Committee, 31 August 1979.

52 Minutes, Political Purposes Committee, 7 September 1984.

53 Minutes, Special Meeting, Political Purposes Committee, 21 November 1984.

54 Ibid.

55 Ibid.

56 Ibid.

57 Minutes, Branch Political Committee, 1 March 1985.

58 See this Chapter, p.228.

59 Minutes, Branch Political Committee, 1 March 1985 and Special Meeting of Branch Political Committee, 29 March 1985.

60 Minutes, Branch Political Committee, 1 March 1985.

61 Minutes, Branch Political Committee, 2 May 1985.

62 Minutes, Branch Political Committee, 6 June 1985.

63 Minutes, Branch Political Committee, 5 December 1986.

64 Minutes, Branch Political Committee, 3 July 1987.

65 Minutes, Branch Political Committee, 4 September 1987 and 6 November 1987.

66 See Chapter 8, p.213.

67 Minutes, Branch Political Committee, 4 July 1986.

68 Minutes, Branch Political Committee, 3 May 1985.

69 Minutes, Branch Political Committee, 7 June 1985.

70 Minutes, Branch Political Committee, 4 October 1985.

71 Minutes, Branch Political Committee, 4 July 1986.

72 Minutes, Branch Political Committee, 5 September 1986.

73 Minutes, Branch Political Committee, 7 November 1986.

74 Minutes, Branch Political Committee, 3 April 1987.

75 Minutes, Branch Political Committee, 8 January 1988.

76 Minutes, Branch Political Committee, 5 February 1988.

77 Minutes, Branch Political Committee, 25 March 1988 and 3 June 1988.

78 Minutes, Branch Political Committee, 4 November 1988.

79 Minutes, Branch Political Committee, 5 January 1990.

80 Co-operative Union Ltd, *Report of 1994 Congress, Rochdale*, p.20.

81 CWS SE Archive, CWS Agreement with the Co-operative Party, 15 January 1995.

CHAPTER TEN

Review of a Political Tradition

Introduction

In this final Chapter we will review the distinct political tradition embodied in the political activities of the Royal Arsenal Co-operative Society and, in particular, those of its Political Purposes Committee. When deciding its political course the RACS had a number of options. One was to have maintained the Rochdale Co-operative Principle of political neutrality and abstained from political activity. A second was to have followed the course set by the wider Co-operative Movement in setting up its own Co-operative Party. A third option was to have subscribed to the view that there could be only one main party of the left in Britain and that that should be the Labour Party. The RACS chose the third option. It embraced it wholeheartedly and held to it consistently over a period of 70 years.

This final Chapter will divide broadly into two parts. The first will examine the options before RACS in a little more depth so as to help us better understand the nature of the Society's choice. The second will examine the consequences of that choice, not only as far as relations with the Labour Party were concerned, but also those with other co-operative societies and the wider Co-operative Movement. Through this two-stage process we hope to recall the main points of this study and suggest conclusions.

Option of Political Neutrality

The Royal Arsenal Co-operative Society was founded in 1868, its beginnings very modest. Although the Society was firmly in the Rochdale tradition, it kept to the Principle of political neutrality for only a very few years. One reason was that the Society soon became a significant rate-payer which meant that it had an interest in the Woolwich Borough Council, as well as other local bodies such as the Boards of Guardians.

The second reason was the nature of the area in which the Society grew. It was essentially a working class area. Initially the Society attracted members who were working class Liberals. In the last years of the 19th century they may also have been possibly members of the ILP or SDF. From the early years of this century, however, the Woolwich area became a Labour stronghold.

A third reason why the young Royal Arsenal Co-operative Society kept so briefly to the Principle of political neutrality was that the Principle itself came to mean different things at different times. For the Rochdale Pioneers it, and religious neutrality, became a defensive mechanism by which they could distance themselves from the secular 'rational religion' of Robert Owen and the 'militant atheism' of George Jacob Holyoake; in politics the Pioneers could be 'neutral between Socialists, various brands of Chartists, and adherents of the Anti-Corn Law League'.[1] In his book *A Century of Co-operation*, G D H Cole suggests that the Co-operative Movement's ideas of political neutrality shifted as political parties developed and politics changed.

Certainly, we noted in Chapter Two that by the end of the 19th century British consumer co-operatives were discussing whether they, themselves, needed to take some kind of political action over and above the representational and lobbying work of the Joint Parliamentary Committee. Support for co-operative political action grew after societies' experiences during the first world war.

Political neutrality, therefore, soon lost its force as a defensive mechanism. It then became difficult to sustain as the Co-operative Movement found itself against what it believed to be the political actions of its private enterprise competitors, and it was tempted to counter these by direct political activity.

Option of Affiliating to the Co-operative Party

Moving now to the option of joining with the rest of the Co-operative Movement in setting up and supporting its own political party, we have seen that although the Royal Arsenal Co-operative Society eventually affiliated to the Co-operative Party, it did so half-heartedly. The Co-operative Party was formed in 1917. The RACS did not affiliate to it until 1930.

Much of this reluctance appears to be explained by its prior loyalty to the Labour Party. The Society, through its Political Purposes Committee, had begun affiliating to Divisional Labour Parties in 1922. Thereafter it affiliated to the London Labour Party and in 1927 to the National Labour Party. Subsequent relations with the Co-operative Party seem to have been influenced by the RACS's wish not to jeopardise the arrangements it had developed with Divisional Labour Parties. In effect these had become the Society's local political organisation and Co-operative Party branches might have detracted from these.

The Society's links with local Labour Parties had quickly become sophisticated and involved. It needed to determine how many of its members lived within each constituency. These then became the basis of the RACS's affiliation to the Divisional Labour Party. Over the years the number of Divisional or Constituency Labour Parties with which the RACS Political Purposes Committee dealt varied. Earliest Minutes refer to 14. Later Minutes to 59. It, therefore, becomes apparent that nominating and appointing delegates to local Labour Parties required considerable effort and formed a large part of the work of the Political Purposes Committee.

Under the original procedure the Committee made nominations to the Quarterly Joint Meetings of Society Committees which then confirmed and appointed delegates. Subsequently, delegates were kept in line through 'whips', but were able to report back, and to be kept informed, through Quarterly Political Conferences organised by the Political Purposes Committee. By the 1960s this procedure began to be modified. However, at the time that affiliation to the Co-operative Party became an active issue, it was already extensive and complicated. Unscrambling it, and replacing it with local Co-operative Parties, would have been troublesome.

Besides such practical reasons the Society also hesitated to support the Co-operative Party because it believed that there could only by one workers' party, and that it should be the Labour Party. This view was expressed by a number of RACS leaders but was summed up by Joe Reeves's view that, 'Ultimately there can be only one party for the workers ...'

Option of Affiliating to the Labour Party

Some of the above point to why the RACS chose the option of affiliating to the Labour Party. Particularly important seems to have been the assessment that there could only be one party for the workers. Davies and Carbery in their respective books[2] refer to doubts that there was room for a second and smaller left-wing Party in British Politics.

Such views tend to overlook the idiosyncratic nature of the British consumer Co-operative Movement, however. Membership of retail societies was open to all which meant that their members came from all kinds of political persuasion. Some members might be offended by too close a relationship with the Labour Party and create an adverse effect on co-operative trade. Supporters of the view that there was room for only one left-wing Party also tended to overlook the fact that the decision to set up a separate Co-operative Party was taken at a time when the Labour Party was still immature and had not even achieved its 1918 Constitution. In such circumstances it is not surprising that the Co-operative Movement, believing that it needed political protection, thought that it had better supply it itself.

The expectation of adverse reactions certainly shaped the Co-operative Movement's decision in 1927 to have an electoral alliance with the Labour Party rather than full affiliation. Thereafter, arguments in favour of retaining a separate Co-operative Party have included an important one; namely that it represented the consumers' rather than the producers' point of view in British politics.

From the above it would appear that the RACS was less open to the kind of arguments that shaped Co-operative political attitudes elsewhere. One reason is likely to have been the distinctive political climate in Woolwich. For example, we noted in Chapter Four that for 'years the polls at Woolwich were the highest in London. Voting, and voting for Labour, was a declaration of membership of the Woolwich community'. Such an ambience shaped not only political life in Woolwich but also that in RACS. It became reflected in the attitudes of RACS leaders, the articles they wrote, the speeches they gave, and in their relations with Labour Leaders, including Herbert Morrison.

Such local circumstances help to explain RACS's loyalty to the Labour Party. Less easy to explain is why RACS never really sought to persuade other co-operative societies to follow this example. An obvious occasion was the lengthy debate about an electoral alliance with the Labour Party at the 1927 Cheltenham Congress. However, in Chapter Five, we noted that of the 39 delegates to speak during this debate, not one came from the RACS. The Society, having taken its own course, seemed content to remain the odd one out.

Having examined the factors that shaped RACS's opting for affiliation to the Labour Party, we should now turn to consider the consequences of that decision.

Consequences of RACS's Affiliation to the Labour Party

These were not necessarily clear cut or independent of each other. They are, therefore, not in any particular order.

A good starting point is, however, the setting up of the Political Purposes Committee. This had been one of the main recommendations of the RACS's Special Political Committee which reported in May 1921. Another of its recommendations had been to affiliate to local Labour Parties 'in preference to co-operation with the separate and distinct co-operative machinery, viz the Co-operative Party'. Further recommendations included the allocation from each half-year's surplus of 3d. per member. This was to go to a political fund from which one penny was to be set aside for affiliation fees, another penny for funding RACS Parliamentary Candidates, while the third penny was to go towards a general political purposes fund to cover administrative expenses and financial support for candidates to local governing bodies.

The Committee's Minority Report related only to RACS Parliamentary Candidates. Whereas the Majority Report recommended that there should be just one RACS candidate, the Minority Report proposed that 'proportional aid should be given to all constituencies within our area with a view to making the best possible fight for a Labour candidate within each'. This second view was endorsed by RACS members, and had considerable ramifications for relations with the Co-operative Party.

Regarding the full report of the Special Political Committee, two important points should be noted. One was that the Report's Recommendations would be reflected in, and subsequently protected by, the Society's Rules. Thus, 'the Political Purposes Committee ... would derive its authority under a new Rule in the Society's Rules'. Moreover, a new Standing Order was to be introduced 'to ensure that all Society nominees were "bona-fide Co-operators" by requiring that they observe the same qualifications as those seeking election in the Society in terms of membership and purchases'.

The other point to note was that the Report reflected the Rochdale Principle of 'open membership' in proposing that the larger part of the Political Purposes Committee should comprise the directly elected representatives of Society members. This proposal also brought it into line with the Society's General and Education Committees. The only caveat was that the directly elected members should be 'bona-fide Co-operators', confirmed by the length of their membership and extent of their purchases.

In this study we have seen that the later phasing out of dividend made it more difficult to establish whether someone was a 'bona-fide Co-operator'. However, the principle of 'open membership', in the sense that any member of the Society could seek election to the Political Purposes Committee, remained to the end and thus proved more durable and workable than the Principle of 'religious and political neutrality'.

Now that we have reached the end of this study we can see that the Political Purposes Committee's relations with the Co-operative Party and the Political Committee of the South Suburban Co-operative Society were complicated by the practice of open membership. The same could be said for the Committee's work and this stemmed from an apparent contradiction in the Special Political Committee's Report. On the one hand it obliged the subsequent Political Purposes Committee to observe the principle of open membership. On the other it laid down that one third of the Committee's budget should be used to 'pay affiliation fees to local Labour Parties pro rata to the Society's membership in the area of each'. This was a fudged situation which it was difficult to believe could work; but it did, and did so for over seventy years.

The decision had also taken the RACS beyond the position taken by the wider Co-operative Movement which had been hesitant about setting up its own Party and then having an electoral alliance with the Labour Party. Other co-operative societies feared antagonising their Conservative and Liberal members, yet here was the RACS affiliating to local Labour Parties while making it possible for Liberals and Conservatives and members of any other parties, to seek election to their Political Purposes Committee.

This could have been a recipe for confusion had it not been for Labour's strength in the Woolwich area. From the beginning there was an assumption that if the representatives of other political parties sought election to the Committee, they could be contained. Yet, as we noticed in the period leading up to the Cheltenham Congress, and the Co-operative Congress's decision to have an electoral alliance with the Labour Party, there were strong opposing voices, even in RACS, and these were allowed space in the columns of the RACS journal, *Comradeship*. Among RACS members there were eminent Co-operators such as Mary Lawrenson, a prime mover in the founding of the Co-operative Women's Guild, and Edward Owen Greening, a pioneer in establishing the International Co-operative Alliance, who were opposed to co-operative political action. While Greening did not speak in the 1927 Cheltenham Congress debate, he had been a strong and vocal opponent of the setting up of the Co-operative Party in earlier Congress debates. We can, therefore, deduce that RACS leaders had rightly calculated that Labour was sufficiently strong in the Society's area to ensure that there could be both open membership in elections to its Political Purposes Committee and affiliation to the Labour Party.

Subsequent events proved that this confidence was justified. Even if non-Labour members gained election to the Political Purposes Committee they would be contained. Until 1996 Labour, of varying shades, maintained its majority on the Committee. One reason was that RACS gave lively expression to another Rochdale Principle of member democracy through 'one member one vote'. It is difficult to say whether the Society's system of proportional representation, set up at about the same time as the

Political Purposes Committee, stimulated electoral interest, or whether this arose from the competition between various members' constituencies, ie Labour, Communist, Co-operative Guilds, Trade Union, Catholic, etc. For whatever reason, RACS remained in better democratic shape than many other co-operative societies. For example, in elections to the CWS South East Political Committee in 1991, 5,380 members voted for 13 candidates seeking election to eight places. John Cartwright topped the poll with 771 votes, followed by Richard Balfe at 736. By contrast, and about the same time, an election for the London CRS Regional Political Committee was not held because there were fewer candidates than vacancies.[3]

Apart from Labour the most consistent element in the Political Purposes Committee was the communists. Although small in number and usually contained, they sometimes impacted on the Committee's relations with the Labour Party. The first occurred during the 1920s when communists attempted to remain within the Labour Party. The next came during the second world war when communists campaigned for a Peace Conference and a Second Front in the West. The third came during the struggles between unilateral and multilateral nuclear disarmers in the late 1950s and early 1960s; in particular we noted the difficulties experienced by the Committee at the 1960 Labour Party Conference. The fourth example of communist pressure came during Labour's problems in the 1970s.

In addition to the directly elected members of the Committee who were communist, there was always the possibility that their numbers could be increased by the appointment of communist representatives from the General and Education Committees. The prime example, mentioned in Chapter Eight, was that of Charlie Job who was delegated to the Committee from the General Committee. However, representatives appointed from these Committees could only ever account for one third of the Political Purposes Committee. While the communist vote on it could thus be augmented it never became the majority. The balance must have shifted though, when the Labour majority was weakened after John Cartwright and James Wellbeloved moved to the SDP.

Moving on to the financial consequences of the RACS

affiliation to the Labour Party we should note that over the years quite considerable amounts were paid. In addition to affiliation fees at local, regional and national levels, additional grants were made during elections. Both fees and grants are listed in the Table at the end of this study. The Society was always proud of its financial support for the Labour Party. Such support appeared to bring two benefits to RACS. One was that for many years a Society representative held a seat on Labour's National Executive. The second was that the Society enjoyed good access to the Party's highest officials. On a number of occasions we have seen that the Party's General Secretary, and other high level officials, readily attended meetings to try to iron out difficulties.

RACS's prior loyalty to the Labour Party caused two main problems for the Co-operative Party. The first concerned its Parliamentary Panel. For long periods RACS also had its own Parliamentary Panel. Whereas RACS operated a system of open membership, the Party required that all those seeking local and Parliamentary nominations under its auspices were members of the Co-operative Party. Moreover, those nominating and selecting them must also be members of the Co-operative Party. We have thus seen repeated difficulties in bringing the Party and RACS Parliamentary Panels together because of this difference.

The second main difficulty for the Co-operative Party was that RACS relations with the Labour Party potentially complicated renegotiation of the Co-operative Movement's Agreements with the Labour Party. Two examples were quoted in this study. The first, in Chapter Six, were the events leading up to the first post-war Agreement in 1946. The other, in Chapter Seven, was the sudden decision by the Labour Party to seek renegotiation of that Agreement in 1957 following the Wilson Report. A common element in both was that RACS offered a ready example of the financial benefits that could accrue to the Labour Party if more co-operative societies could be persuaded to affiliate directly. As the Wilson Report stated: 'It would be to the benefit both of the Labour Party and of the Co-operative Movement if more societies were to affiliate direct to the Party'. Had more co-operatives done so, however, the future of the Co-operative Party would have been prejudiced and the nature of future agreements between the Co-operative Movement and the Labour Party quite changed.

Conclusion

We can, perhaps, end by noting that despite such difficulties, and despite the apparent fudge of maintaining open membership while affiliating to the Labour Party, the RACS developed a successful political tradition. It survived for over 70 years and owed much to the members of the Society's Political Purposes Committee. Their names appear in the Table at the end of this study. Their distinct tradition was based on co-operative trade, however. When the pattern of that was forced to change, RACS's political organisation also had to change.

Notes

1   Cole, G D H, *A Century of Co-operation*, Co-operative Union Ltd, Manchester, 1944, pp.72-73.

2   Davies, A J, *To Build a New Jerusalem*, Abacus, 1996, and Carbery, Thomas F, *Consumers in Politics*, Manchester University Press, Manchester, 1969.

3   *Commonweal*, Issue 3/91.

RACS FINANCIAL TABLE 1923-1984

Year ending Jan	Members (7)(20)(21)	Sales (5)	Pol com grant (11)	CLP	National	London (2)
1923	95818	2864526	2273	716		50
1924	100565	2999503	2365	830		150
1925	109535	3327762	2504	835		200
1926	120979	3792689	2745	915		200
1927	140988	4313982	3063	974		
1928	201204	6156745	4062	1402	50	316
1929	217671	6546925	5060	1687	250	400
1930	233955	6785164	5556	1852	400	400
1931 (8)	240005	6758512	2895	1933	400	400
1932	247249	6746830	5874	1993	400	400
1933	278446	6860348	6071	2169	534	400
1934	286602	6916521	6899	2313	534	400
1935	317624	7553329	7041	2489	534	400
1936	318960	8045906	7857	2635	600	400
1937	361614	8817900	7924	2818	600	400
1938	362110	9344429	8990	2977	700	400
1939	381309	9817926	9006 (10)	3104	700	400
1940	381737	9511113	9485	3163	700	400
1941	332567	9100724	9495	3144	700	400
1942	307110	8006227	7509	2713	525	300
1943	318003	8662626	5214	2572	525	300
1944	326186	9139735	5237	2665	525	300
1945	330235	9394937	5398	2723	525	300
1946	335208	9746704	6852	2756	700	400
1947	336285	11588072	8330	2741	700	400
1948	336750	12569032	8236	2794	770	420
1949 (14)	338255	14370831	8389	2798	840	440
1950	341579	16157665	8413	2817	840	440
1951	342489	17761728	8492	2839	770	440
1952	345687	19311339	8528	2849	700	440
1953	348029	21123666	8590	2880	460	240
1954	356416	22533599	8670	2900	810	520
1955	366142	22660418	8805	2987	810	526
1956	369261	24005905	9079	3054	910	527
1957	370219	24616423	9588	3073	817	545
1958	370935	25018387	10000	3080	817	525
1959	378057	27663185	10021	3141	819	411
1960	370593	26590207	10304	3129	810	525
1961	367546	26916276	10068	3105	885	530
1962	365682	25738696	10050	3066	735	530
1963	374860	26251343	9939	3030	810	530
1964	383153	27713837	9974	3144	825	520
1965 (19)	388285	29040421	10330	3198	830	520
1966	398213	30634116	11272	3238	830	520
1967	401683	31778967	12467	3322	833	520
1968	404377	31014554	12514	3347	835	520
1969	492192	36138627	12595	3509	837	895
1970 (18)	515305	41740931	14174	4102	837	953
1971	521691	44457476	15426	4203	1208	960
1972	509751	52487125	16488 (16)	4370	1207	960
1973	466023	58981196	19221	4675	1727	960
1974	448339 (17)	63120338 (6)	17949	4599	2081	1100
1975	446446	78979658	17756	4451	2954	1350
1976	435583	96934356	22309	4464	3150	1550
1977	431523	109022403	26121	4353	3780	1650
1978	428883	119912523	30196	4300	4200	2260
1979	422187	134982214	33006	4330	5220	2460
1980	416283	145227383	56000	7190	3280	1820
1981	402850	152083376	63976	8034	10400	4062
1982	365529	146631186	63976	8261	7040	3688
1983	327684	146207357	78895	9871	8700	3842
1984 (22)	306503	152535350	81814 (15)	10213	8500	3832
			921336	208835	92479	50647

270

(See Notes on pp.272-274)

Labour P Grants (1)	Co-op P Affiliation (4)	TOTAL (3)(13)	E (9)	Cost of Living Index (23)	Adjusted Total (24)	Year ending Jan
1239		2005	E	100.0	29506	1923
949		1929	E	92.7	30623	1924
1834		2869	E	92.2	45792	1925
1287		2404		93.8	37716	1926
1407		2381		91.6	38252	1927
1464		3232		88.5	53742	1928
850		3187		88.2	53174	1929
1586	50	4288	E	87.2	72365	1930
1425	180	4338		84.8	75281	1931
2005	350	5148	E	81.1	93413	1932
1388	425	4915		79.2	91325	1933
1393	400	5039		77.5	95682	1934
1871	400	5694		77.3	108400	1935
1887	400	5922		78.0	111728	1936
1580	400	5798		78.8	108278	1937
2613	400	7090		80.4	129771	1938
2401	400	7005		82.6	124800	1939
1719	400	6382		84.8	110751	1940
1620	400	6264		99.3	92831	1941
783	300	4621		109.7	61990	1942
738 (12)	300	4435		117.0	55782	1943
618	300	4408		121.1	53566	1944
838	300	4686		123.6	55792	1945
3924	400	8180	E	127.0	94785	1946
1476	400	5717		131.6	63930	1947
1771	400	6155		141.1	64193	1948
1678	400	6156		151.9	59639	1949
2623	405	7125		157.7	66488	1950
2051	424	6524	E	160.2	59930	1951
1417	429	5835		175.2	49011	1952
1021	429	5030	E	184.5	40120	1953
313	479	5022		188.7	39165	1954
168	529	5020		192.3	38416	1955
1533	649	6673	E	199.1	49322	1956
576	797	5808		208.0	41092	1957
492	1209	6123		215.0	41910	1958
1033	1207	6611		222.6	43705	1959
1248	1235	6947	E	223.9	45660	1960
172	1185	5877		226.3	38217	1961
617	1179	6127		233.0	38697	1962
330	1165	5865		241.7	35709	1963
339	1218	6046		245.8	36197	1964
1164	1316	7028	E	254.7	40606	1965
42	1220	5850		267.2	32219	1966
784	1555	7014	E	277.8	37156	1967
462	1678	6842		285.1	35316	1968
222	1680	7143		293.0	35876	1969
25	1680	7597		315.3	35457	1970
1248	1730	9349	E	333.7	41229	1971
228	1685	8450		362.4	34313	1972
773	1718	9853		386.1	37554	1973
962	1820	10562		417.9	37193	1974
1896	1815	12466	E	488.8	37531	1975
	900	10064		605.0	24480	1976
89	450	10322		699.6	21712	1977
1279	550	12589		804.0	23042	1978
1927	1000	14937		877.7	25044	1979
2265	4606	19161	E	997.1	28279	1980
110	5250	27856		1158.7	35378	1981
729	4450	24168		1290.2	27566	1982
1415	6808	30636		1403.5	32123	1983
1310	7060	30915		1471.6	30915	1984
73207	68515	493683			3329735	

Notes to Table on pp.270-271

1   The category 'Labour Party grants' includes election grants at all levels, and also grants for general purposes. These are here all aggregated into the single total, for the reason that their identification over the years in the Annual Reports is not without ambiguity.

2   Included with the London Labour Party affiliation is the Southern Region Labour party fee.

3   Certain contributions, mostly very small, have been ignored. These include:

> Fabian Society
> Hansard
> UNA
> National Film Association
> Standing Joint Committee on Women's Organisations.

4   The Co-operative Party affiliation figure is an aggregate of one major fee and one or two other small fees. No further Co-operative Party grants are listed.

5   The sales figure is not taken from the verbal report but from the accounts tables, and the latter is slightly less than the former in the early years.

6   In the years since 1974, turnover includes VAT, and 'Sales' is the figure with VAT deducted.

7   After the first years, the membership is usually given in the Annual Report. For the year ending Jan 1962 no membership figure is given. Where it has not been given, I take the membership figure from the overall tables regularly given in the later Annual Reports.

8   1931 is the first year in which the report for the period ending Jan 19— is for 12 months, not 6 months. The July 1930 report has no statement from the Political Purposes Committee (PPC), which is unusual.

9   Column 'E' marks years in which general elections were held.

10   During the war years the full grant was reduced by a 'refund' from the PPC. I have given the reduced amount.

11   The PPC grant was from the start calculated as 3d. per member per half year, but went up to 3¼d. in 1956; it was possible for a member to object and then it would not be paid in that instance.

12   From this date, for some years, affiliation fees to Labour Parties by Guilds are listed and I have included them.

13 The rest of the political grant has generally gone on:
>Committee fees and expenses
>Printing, postage and stationery
>Salaries and secretarial
>Conferences, etc
>Office
>*Home* magazine
>Representatives' fees and expenses

14 In the late 1940s a new paper called *Citizen* came into existence which consumed over £2,000 pa, but I have disregarded this item.

>It is noteworthy that the proportion of the PPC grant going to political parties declined over the years. At the same time, the PPC developed its own campaigning role as the references to 'conferences' in note 13, and the case of the *Citizen* here illustrates.

15 The source in the later years for the PPC grant is a different account, 'Consolidated Revenue Account'. Initially this grant was given in the 'Final Revenue Account'.

16 In this year the PPC grant was not stated in the Report as usual and I infer that the term 'proposed grant' here, exceptionally, covers it.

17 In the year ending Jan 1975, the verbal report states that there were 446,446 members out of 700,000 households in RACS shop areas, a remarkably high level of membership.

18 This is the last year of the old style of detailed reports. Thereafter they are much less substantial.

19 In 1965 and 1962, the verbal report contains a 'grossing up' of sums spent in the long term on all forms of membership benefits. It is used to show that £35-40 million in sum over the years has been redistributed in member benefits. It should be noted however that fluctuations in the cost of living may invalidate this calculation. However the highest rate of inflation occurred later, as the RACS came to an end, and therefore will affect the annual accounts much less than it affects the modern reader's perception of monetary values.

20 In 1920 when the possibility of the PPC was first discussed, a member nominally was expected to buy 2 x £1 shares, though in practice only the first 1/- was called upon.

21 The report setting up the PPC was issued in March 1921, and an SGM held in May 1921 to implement it. (I believe the Board became

full time in the same set of rule changes.) Therefore the first grant to the PPC is proposed in the report of the half year to January 1922, and is recorded with a PPC statement in the report of the Half Year to July 1922. I have aggregated this into the line of the tables for the full year ending January 1923.

22 The last Annual Report under the RACS title is for the year ending January 1984, and thereafter the transfer of engagements to the CWS became effective.

23 The Cost of Living index is constructed from tables in Pratten, C: *The Stock Exchange*, and HMSO: *Retail Prices 1914-1990*.

24 The adjusted total is the real total for the year, indexed according to the increase in cost of living between 1922 and 1983.

List of Members of the
Royal Arsenal Co-operative Society
Political Purposes Committee 1922-1996

Name	Service
Mrs Jennie Laurel Adamson MP	1934-1947
Mr Thomas W Agar	1953-1963
G J Ainsley	1924-1926
Mr David Lionel Allonby	1995-1996
Mr John William Andrews	1946-1966; 1969-1971
Mrs Margaret A Arran	1926-1928; 1932-1933
Mr John Eric Austin-Walker MP	1988-1993
Mr Edward James Bale	1931-1933
Mr Richard Andrew Balfe MEP	1991; 1994-1997
J M Barker	1926-1928
Mr Nicolas Guy Barnett	1984-1986
Mr Michael Allen Barrett	1980-1984
Mr Christopher Nigel Beard	1984-1997
Mr George Norman Bennett	1951-1952
Mrs Wilhelmina Bilney	1940-1957
Mr William Alfred George Brooks	1957-1960; 1961-1964
Mrs Rosa Alice Brown	1942-1943
Mrs Jessie Burgess	1946-1947; 1951-1957; 1960-1961
Mr George Burgneay	1924-1928
E G Burns	1922-1924
J A S Butts	1922-1924
W O Carr	1934-1940
Mr John Cameron Cartwright MP	1976-1992
Mr Raymond Chant	1990
Mrs Elizabeth Chapman	1936-1946
Mr Vincent Cheek	1940-1946
Miriam Edith Clark	1953-1955
Mr David Richard Coates	1962-1969; 1971-1976
Mr John Churchill Coleman	1946-1947
Mrs J Coleman	1946
Mr James Patrick Connor	1949-1951
Mr Barry William Coppock	1980-1984
Miss Angela Cornforth	1994-1996
Mrs Mary Elizabeth Corrigan	1934-1935
Mr John Alfred Cox	1947-1949
Mrs Evelyn Victoria Coyle	1943-1955
Mrs Amy Crossman	1946

Mr Alan Cumner	1980-1984; 1985
S Curtis	1929-1930; 1932-1936
Mrs Matilda L H Dadson	1940-1945
A T Dashwood	1922-1934; 1934-1935; 1936-1938
Mr J Dickinson	1930-1933
Mr Jeremiah Peter Thomas Duggan	1946-1949
Mr Henry Charles Ellis	1939-1946
A G Evans	1940-1943
Mr Robert John Emlyn Evans	1994
Mr Will Fancy	1969-1972
J Farrell	1922-1925
Mr Sidney Ernest French	1966-1976
W M J Friend	1938-1940
Mr Thomas Richard Goy	1928-1936
Mrs A E Gray	1930-1934
C H Grinling	1922-1926
Mr Dennis Grover	1984-1997
Mr Bernard Denis Hammill	1952-1977
Mr Robin P Harling	1995-1996
Mrs Susan Hayward	1978-1980
Mr G J Henderson	1927-1939
Miss Catherine Letitia Hoey MP	1984-1996
Miss Mary H R Honeyball	1991-1994
Mrs L James	1936-1937; 1940-1941
Miss (Mrs Balfe) Vivienne Patricia Job	1980-1984; 1988-
Mr Charles Job	1959-1960; 1975-1976
Mrs Kate Amelia Kempton	1938-1946
Mr Sidney Harling Kennard OBE	1957-1962; 1976
Mrs Marie Iris Kingwell	1965-1966; 1967-1972
Mr Henry George Lamborn MP	1963-1965; 1976-1980
Mrs Helen Tulloch Leighton	1928-1940
Mr James Frederick Little	1984-1994
F Lockyear	1925-1928
Mr Terence Arthur John Malone	1968-1969
Mrs Elizabeth Munson	1922-1927
Lady Anne Murray	1994-1996
Mr Barrie Edward Murray	1984-1985
Mr Charles Henry New	1926-1932
Mr James Newman	1922-1946
Mrs Francis Alice Powell	1938-1939
Mrs Emily Real	1922-1924; 1930-1931
Mr Joseph Reeves MP	1946-1953
Mrs E Reid	1926-1927
C H Reynolds	1922-1924

F J Reynolds	1922-1926
Mrs Frances Albina Rittman	1935-1936
Mr James Augustine Roche	1949-1951
Miss Elizabeth G Rogers	1996
Mr Ernest Ed Salmons	1922-1925
Mrs L Scarlett	1924-1928
Mrs Katie Maude Shade	1946-1949
Mr John Thomas Sheppard	1938-1940
Mr Colin Stanley Shrive	1972-1976
Mr Arthur Massey Skeffington MP	1949-1969
Mrs Hilda Smith	1966-1984
Miss Kathryn Ann Smith	1994-1996
Mr Keith John Sneddon	1969-1984
Mr Walter Stanley Spencer	1946-1968
Mr Leslie Francis Stannard	1980-1986
Mr Frederick William Styles	1960-1968
Mr Harry Sykes	1926-1930
Mr John Thomson	1995-1996
Mrs Rona Ann Thomson	1990
Mrs Evelyn Todd	1940-1941
Mr William Arthur Trott	1936-1946
Mrs Ada Ann Truman	1928-1946
Mrs Mary Ann Tucker	1928-1929; 1935-1946
Mr Martin David Walker	1994-1996
Mr William Thomas Wall	1926
Mr Reginald George Ward	1990
Mr James Wellbeloved MP	1972-1984
Mrs Edith Emma Williams	1934-1935
Mr Thomas E Williams	1930-1936
Mr Peter Willsman	1988-1996
Mrs Eliza Jane Wood JP	1928-1929; 1938-1939; 1944-1945; 1948
Mrs Miriam M Yates	1942-1943
W C Young	1924-1930

BIBLIOGRAPHY

Attfield, John, *With Light of Knowledge - A Hundred Years of Education in the Royal Arsenal Co-operative Society, 1877-1977*, RACS/Journeyman Press, 1981.

Bailey, Jack, *The British Co-operative Movement*, Hutchinson University Library, London, 1960.

Birchall, Johnston, *Co-op: the people's business*, Manchester University Press, 1994.

Bonner, Arnold, *British Co-operation*, Co-operative Union Ltd, Manchester, 1961.

Carbery, Thomas F, *Consumers in Politics - A History and General Review of the Co-operative Party*, Manchester University Press, 1969.

Carr-Saunders, A M, Florence, P Sargent & Peers, Robert, *Consumers' Co-operation in Great Britain*, Allen and Unwin, 1942.

Cole, G D H, *A Century of Co-operation*, Co-operative Union Ltd, Manchester, 1944.

Co-operative Union Ltd, *Co-operative Congress Reports 1896-1996*.

Coxall, Bill & Robins, Lynton, *British Politics Since the War*, Macmillan Press Ltd, 1998.

Davies, A J, *To Build a New Jerusalem*, Abacus, 1996.

Davis, T Walter, *The History of the Royal Arsenal Co-operative Society Ltd, 1868-1918*, RACS Ltd, 1920.

Donoughue, Bernard & Jones, G W, *Herbert Morrison, A Portrait of a Politician*, Weidenfeld & Nicholson, 1973.

Garnett, Mark, *Principles and Politics in Contemporary Britain*, Longman, 1996.

Harris, Kenneth, *Attlee*, Weidenfeld & Nicholson, 1995.

International Co-operative Alliance, *Results of State Trading*, International Co-operative Alliance, 1933.

Longden, Fred, *Co-operative Politics Inside Capitalist Society*, Cornish Brothers Ltd, Birmingham, 1941.

McLeod, Alex & Arnold, T Geo, *Royal Arsenal Co-operative Society, Origin and Progress*, Royal Arsenal Co-operative Society, London, 1896.

Newens, Stan, *Working Together - a Short History of the London Co-op Society Political Committee*, CRS (London) Political Committee, 1988.

Phillips, Gordon, *The Rise of the Labour Party 1893-1931*, Lancaster Pamphlets, 1992.

Pimlott, Ben, *Harold Wilson*, Harper Collins, 1993.

Rhodes, G W, *Co-operative-Labour Relations 1900-1962*, Co-operative College Papers, Co-operative College, Loughborough, 1962.

Rhodes, Rita, *The International Co-operative Alliance During War and Peace 1910-1950*, International Co-operative Alliance, Geneva, 1995.

Shaw, Alex, *The Labour Party Since 1945*, Blackwell, Oxford, 1996.

Snell, Lord, *Men, Movements and Myself*, J M Dent and Sons Ltd, London, 1936.

Shea, Peter, *Times Past: Paragraphs on the History of the Co-operative Party*, Co-operative Party, London, 1955.

Society for Co-operative Studies, *Journal of Co-operative Studies*, Number 82, December 1994.

Tilley, John, *Churchill's Favourite Socialist*, Holyoake Books, Manchester, 1996.

Youngjohns, R J, *Co-operation and the State 1814-1914*, Co-operative College Papers, Co-operative College, Loughborough, 1954.

Index

The abbreviation RACS is used throughout for Royal Arsenal Co-operative Society

Cartwright, John
    Labour Party RACS representative, 233
    parliamentary candidate, 210-211, 212
    Political Secretary, 205-207, 208, 209
    Social Democratic Party, 223, 226-227
    voting in committee, 231, 232, 236
Chapman, Mrs E, 145
Cheek, Vincent, 130, 131, 150
Cheltenham Agreement, 76, 81-91, 94, 95, 140
chief executives of co-operative societies, 42-43
Chrisp, Arthur, 160
Christian Socialists, 5, 7
Citizen, 157-158, 159, 174
Clancy, J G, 80
Coldrick, Will, 155
Cole, G D H, 3, 82
Coles, T, 5
Comerton, F J, 125-126
Commonweal, 250
Communist Party
    links with Labour party, 77-81, 132, 193, 234
    RACS membership, 77-81, 130-132, 150, 194-197
Comradeship
    contributors, 5, 8
    publication threatened, 44-45
    RACS publication, 8, 58, 59, 238
Conservative Party, 83
Cooper, F R, 62, 92-93, 147, 150
co-operation as alternative to nationalisation, 181-182
Co-operative and Labour Weeks (RACS), 46, 58
Co-operative Congress
    Cheltenham Agreement, 82-83, 85-86, 90
    Co-operative Party and Labour Party, 35-36, 139, 143, 188
    mergers and regional plans, 186-187
    National Council of Labour, 134
    parliamentary representation, 22-25, 27-28, 31-34
Co-operative Development Agency, 214
Co-operative Insurance Society, 155, 182
Co-operative News, 3, 24
Co-operative Party
    branches, 133, 135, 139-140, 141-142
    Cheltenham Agreement, 76, 81-91, 94, 95, 140
    conference debates on Labour Party, 82-83, 142
    conference debates on nationalisation, 181
    conference RACS representatives, 97, 98, 131, 134, 138
    conferences, 134
    constitution, 134-135, 140
    CWS and CRS transfer of political work, 255-256
    formation, 25-34
    General Elections, 74, 99, 103-104, 147-148, 197-198
    individual membership within RACS, 135, 136, 140, 141-142, 156, 157, 180
    links with Labour Party early period, 33, 34-36, 46, 75-76
    links with Labour Party later period, 81-91, 138-144, 187-189, 229-230
    local organisation, 45-46
    nationalisation, 181
    parliamentary candidates, 33, 90-91
    reaction to Social Democratic Party, 222, 223, 224-226
    RACS affiliation fees, 162, 174, 179, 212, 270-271